Ofer Arazy

Artificial Semantics in Text Retrieval

Ofer Arazy

Artificial Semantics in Text Retrieval

VDM Verlag Dr. Müller

Imprint

Bibliographic information by the German National Library: The German National Library lists this publication at the German National Bibliography; detailed bibliographic information is available on the Internet at http://dnb.d-nb.de.

Cover image: www.purestockx.com

Publisher:
VDM Verlag Dr. Müller Aktiengesellschaft & Co. KG, Dudweiler Landstr. 125 a, 66123 Saarbrücken, Germany,
Phone +49 681 9100-698, Fax +49 681 9100-988,
Email: info@vdm-verlag.de

Produced in USA and UK by:
Lightning Source Inc., La Vergne, Tennessee, USA
Lightning Source UK Ltd., Milton Keynes, UK
BookSurge LLC, 5341 Dorchester Road, Suite 16, North Charleston, SC 29418, USA

ISBN: 978-3-639-02613-9

Abstract

The increase in the amounts of available information, coupled with the rising importance of information for planning and decision making purposes, stress the need for effective information retrieval (IR) techniques. Specifically, we are interested in the retrieval of textual information from general – i.e. large and heterogeneous - collections. One of the most critical problems impeding the performance of retrieval systems is the gap between the way in which people think about information (though semantic representations) and the natural language form of textual documents.

Bridging this gap requires that documents be translated to semantic representations. For general document collections, the extraction of semantic representation has to be automated, as manual effort and the use of domain-specific resources are inappropriate. We have identified four types of artificial (i.e. automatically extracted) semantic units that are the building blocks of IR representation: 'Tokens', 'Composite Concepts', 'Synonym Concepts', and 'Topics'. These artificial semantic units have been employed in a variety of retrieval system; however, the isolated effect of semantic units on retrieval performance has not been studies previously.

This dissertation investigates the effect of semantic units on retrieval performance. Our findings suggest that (a) there are significant differences in performance between semantic units, and (b) our proposed combinations of semantic units into a coherent retrieval model result is performance gains. In addition to the academic contribution in this dissertation, our findings are of importance to practitioners interested in the design of retrieval systems.

Contents

List of Tables

List of Figures

Acknowledgements

I am very grateful to Dr. Carson Woo, my research supervisor, for his support and guidance throughout the course of my work. I am indebted to Dr. Woo for his patience and kindness.

Sincere thanks to members of my Supervisory Committee: to Dr. Yair Wand for his advice on Conceptual Modeling, to Dr. Raymond Ng for his help with computational aspects, and to Dr. Rick Kopak for introducing me to the field of Information Science.

Many thanks to Edmund Szeto, Andy Leung, and Richard Sze, for their help in software development.

Thanks to David Patient for his assistance in English writing, to Aviad Pe'er for critical feedback, and to Jacob Steif for hours of brainstorming.

Thanks to Richard Sze and Nawei Yin for extending my ideas through their Master of Science degrees.

Lastly, many thanks to my wife, Naama, and my two daughters – Addi and Talya - for their support and encouragement throughout this long journey.

Ofer Arazy

The University of British Columbia
August 2004

To my wife, Naama

Part I - Setting the Stage

In the first part of this dissertation we lay the ground for the entire research. In Chapter 1 we introduce the problem of text retrieval, discuss the unique requirements for accessing information from large and heterogeneous collections (namely the reliance of completely automatic techniques), and review prior work in the areas of retrieval systems design, by focusing on the research outputs: Constructs, Models, Methods, and Instantiations. In Chapter 2 we describe our approach – focusing on the Constructs (i.e., semantic units) at the core of retrieval models – studying the effect of semantic units on retrieval performance. In Chapter 3 we propose a categorization of automatically extracted (i.e., artificial) semantic units, which includes 'Tokens', Composite Concepts', 'Synonym Concepts', and 'Topics'. This framework serves to guide the proceeding chapters. In Chapter 4 we pose the two main research questions of this study: the first concerning typical performance levels of semantic units, and the second concerning the combination of distinct semantic units into one coherent retrieval model. Finally, in Chapter 5 we discuss our research method for addressing the two research questions.

The dissertation will continue beyond Part I as follows. In Part II we will address the first research question and establish typical performance levels for each semantic unit category (in 4 distinct chapters, correlating to the four categories of semantic units). In Part 3 we will address the second research question and propose five different retrieval models that combine semantic units from distinct categories. Finally, we will conclude the dissertation in Part IV, where we will summarize the findings, discuss their implications, and point to future directions that could extend this research.

Chapter 1: Introduction

1.1 Motivation

Throughout history, knowledge has been viewed as a critical asset, and institutions and societies have jealously guarded and restricted access to their knowledge. In today's economy, the importance of knowledge and information is greater than ever before, and increasingly knowledge is viewed as a critical organizational asset and an essential component of any competitive strategy.

'Knowledge' is defined as the awareness and understanding of facts that can be obtained through cognitive processing of information. With the advent of the information revolution, we are experiencing an explosion in the amount of available information. This rapid growth in the availability of information, coupled with the strategic importance of knowledge raises the need for effective techniques for accessing & sharing information. *Knowledge Management* (Davenport & Prusak 1998, Nonaka & Takeuchi 1995, Alavi & Leidner 2001) is the name given to a set of systematic procedures an organization can take in order to obtain the greatest value from its information and knowledge assets (Marwick 2001). Nonaka & Takeuchi (1995) provide a framework of knowledge management procedures, based on the distinction between tacit and explicit knowledge[1]. *Tacit knowledge* is captured in people's minds, while *explicit knowledge* (or information) is represented by some artifact, such as a document or a database.

While both types of knowledge are important for organizational effectiveness (Nonaka & Takeuchi 1994), this dissertation is restricted to studying the use of explicit knowledge. Specifically, we focus on access to *unstructured[2] text documents*. Textual information assets are of key importance and are estimated to make up 80% of organizations' explicit knowledge assets (Chen 2001). Gartner Group, one of the leading analysts of information technology, suggests that a firm's knowledge management architecture centers on text retrieval techniques (Gartner Group 1999). *Text Retrieval* enables access to textual information, and is the focus of this dissertation. Text retrieval is

---

[1] This distinction was introduced first by Polanyi in the 1950's (Polanyi 1962, 1996)
[2] We make the distinction between unstructured textual information that is in the form of free text, and structured information (referred to by Van Rijsbergen (1979) as 'data') that is traditionally captured in databases.

18

the most popular *Information Retrieval (IR)* technique (other IR techniques are video, audio, and image retrieval), thus we will use the terms 'Information Retrieval' and 'Text Retrieval' interchangeably throughout this thesis. Text Retrieval systems are a core component of an organization's technological infrastructure, and are employed to access information from a variety of applications, for example in Business Intelligence (BI) systems, Supply Chain Management (SCM) and Customers Relations Management (CRM) applications, the organization's information portal, and its web site.

In order to transform unstructured textual information into meaningful knowledge for decision-making and planning purposes, effective information retrieval and text processing techniques are required (Chen 2001). Despite significant efforts and capital invested in recent years by both governments and the private sector to develop effective IR techniques, the performance of current IR systems is often unsatisfactory, as large amounts of irrelevant information are retrieved by the systems (Baeza-Yates & Ribiero-Neto 1999).

This dissertation is interested in the design of text retrieval systems that will deliver relevant documents to users, and more specifically - in the identification of design principles for developing effective retrieval systems. Retrieval systems that are more effective will enable organizations to exploit their textual information better to attain a competitive advantage.

1.2 Information Retrieval

In information retrieval, static document collections and incoming stream of information requests are assumed. Documents are processed in advance to generate indexes representing their meanings, and at run-time - when a user submits a request, usually in the form of query keywords - the request, too, is indexed. Commonly, the meaning of queries and documents is represented through a weighted vector of terms. Matching of query to documents is performed by measuring the similarity between their representations, to return to the user a ranked list of documents predicted to be of relevance to the query. The information retrieval process is depicted below.

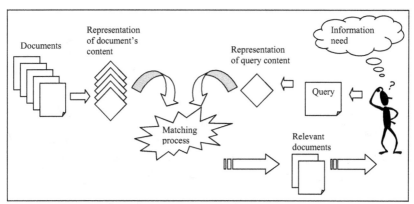

Diagram 1-1: the information retrieval process

The main challenge inhibiting the performance of current retrieval systems is the gap between the way in which people think about information, and the way in which the information is represented in IR systems (Landauer et al. 1998, Deerwester et al. 1990, Baeza-Yates & Ribiero-Neto 1999). While people understand the world through semantic representations and would like to retrieve information based on conceptual content, text retrieval systems require that both documents and the requests of users be formulated in words. Words are inherently ambiguous, most words refer to more than one semantic element (Megerdoomian 2003), and one semantic element could be described with several words, thus the relations between words and semantic units are Many:Many. Two distinct phenomena are associated with word ambiguity: Synonymy and Polysemy.

- *Synonymy* refers to the fact that there are many ways to describe the same semantic unit. For example, the two words "manufacture" and "produce" carry similar meaning.
- *Polysemy* refers to the fact that most words relate to more than one semantic unit (i.e. may carry different meanings), depending on the context. For example the word "virus" may be interpreted as a computer virus or as a biological virus. A related issue is that some semantic units could only be described by a combination of words, for instance phrases (e.g. "business intelligence").

Both synonymy and polysemy impede retrieval effectiveness, though in different ways, as discussed below.

The effectiveness of retrieval systems is evaluated by the extent to which they are able to deliver relevant information to users. Effectiveness of IR systems has traditionally been measured using Recall and Precision, where

- *Precision* = number of retrieved relevant documents / total number of retrieved documents, and

- *Recall* = number of retrieved relevant documents / total number of relevant documents.

Synonymy leads users to miss relevant information (resulting in low Recall), since many relevant documents may not be identified (e.g. a query "car producer" will judge a document describing "automobile manufacturer" as irrelevant). Polysemy, on the other hand, leads to a different problem: irrelevant documents are likely to be retrieved, resulting in low Precision (e.g. a person interested in computer viruses submitting the query "virus" may be presented with documents describing biological viruses).

For some retrieval tasks, such as retrieval of medical information, Recall is of critical importance, as the user may be interested in retrieving every possible piece of information regarding a specific medicine. However, in most other cases, retrieving only a few relevant documents is sufficient, the user is interested in exploring only the documents at the top of the results list, and Precision is most important. In this dissertation, we study both Recall and Precision measures in order to evaluate IR effectiveness.

There are two approaches for addressing the problem of word ambiguity: the first focuses on disambiguating the user's information request through query refinement techniques, while the second is centered on the document corpus, and exploits the patterns of words' usage in the document collection to generate representations of documents' and queries' meanings. The two approaches are complementary and are essential for the design of effective retrieval systems. In order to restrict the scope of this dissertation, we take the latter approach and explore IR design principles by focusing solely on the document corpus.

1.3 General Document Collections

This thesis focuses of retrieval of textual information from large and heterogeneous document collections, also referred to as '*general collections*'. With the rapid explosion in the amounts and coverage of available information, both internally in organizations and in public domain, effective retrieval techniques that can scale up to these settings are essential. The growth in amounts of information used by organizations is to a large extent a result of the increased sharing of information with business partners, and the emergence of network organizations[3] (Van Alstyne 1997). These types of inter-organizational collaborations result in document collections of enormous sizes that cross domains and organizational boundaries. In addition, external resources of gigantic size and heterogeneous content, most notably the World Wide Web, are becoming an essential source of knowledge for organizational purposes (UCLA 2002). We situate our study in these unique settings, and explore retrieval techniques that are appropriate for large and heterogeneous collections. We make a distinction between these collections - referred to as 'general collections' – and specific collections that are used in restricted organizational settings. Specific collections are usually focused on a relatively small set of documents, employing a restricted subset of the language, adhering to particular structures, and covering few topics. The distinction between general and specific collections is of importance, as the IR techniques available for specific collections are often inappropriate for general collections (see discussion in the section below).

---

[3] Network organizations have permeable boundaries and are formed through the collaboration of several business entities. They are also referred to as 'virtual organizations', 'adhocracy', 'cluster organization', 'value adding partnership', or 'modular cooperation'. Driven by efforts to achieve greater structural effectiveness and responsiveness, and enabled by digital networking technology, more and more network organizations have emerged in recent years (Ching 1997). Network organizations are heavily dependent on fast flowing information to enable them to adjust to competitive pressures, and access to information is critical for prompt decision making (Favela 1997).

1.4 Designing Text Retrieval Systems for General Collections

This dissertation in interested in studying design principles for effective general-collections IR systems, and we try to address the problem of word ambiguity by analyzing the patterns of words usage in the document collection. The approach we take is *Design Research* (Simon 1996, Owen 1997, Takeda et al. 1990, March & Smith 1995), which involves the study of designed artifacts (in this case – a retrieval system) to understand, and often to improve, the usability of the artifact. March and Smith (1995) describe four classes of outputs for design research: Constructs, Models, Methods, and Instantiations. *Constructs* arise during the conceptualization process, and are the building blocks of the models. A *model* is a "set of propositions or statements expressing relationships among constructs". *Methods* are goal-directed plans or procedures for manipulating constructs. An *instantiation* is the operationalization of constructs, models, and methods, and the realization of the artifact in a specific environment.

The problem we are trying to address – word ambiguity – is at the core of the Information Retrieval field, and has been studied extensively. Some of the classic manuscripts in the field of IR include: Salton 1968, van Rijsbergen 1979, Salton & McGill 1983, and Baeza-Yates & Ribiero-Neto 1999. When mapping previous works in IR to the classes of Design Research outputs, we realize that a vast majority of the works in the field are concerned with 'Methods' (i.e., algorithms in the case of IR) and 'Instantiations' (i.e., retrieval systems), with relatively little discussion on 'Models'. 'Constructs', the last of these Design Research outputs, is rarely explored in IR literature.

The sciences of the artificial investigation process (Simon 1996) involves moving from construct definition and model development, to 'methods' and 'instantiations' (i.e. operationalizing the models), and then back to theory building and construct refinement (based on the lessons learned from the empirical evaluation of the systems). Hence, investigations at all four levels of the Design Research outputs are valuable. Since the introduction of the prominent IR models in the 1970s (see discussion later), IR research has focused primarily on method development and system construction. 'Constructs', and to a lesser extent 'Models', have not been explored extensively. We believe that a sufficient knowledge has been obtained through experimentation with IR systems in the past 40 years to inform retrieval models and refine constructs. Furthermore, we believe that advancing the elementary units of retrieval models – the constructs – could lead to the development of more effective information retrieval systems. Thus, this dissertation will focus on the role of 'Constructs' in the design of retrieval systems.

In order to position our study in the broad context of IR and distinguish it from previous works, we will describe in the following sections how IR literature corresponds to each of the four Design Research outputs. We will review only briefly 'Instantiations' and 'Methods', and will expand on 'Models' (which are necessary for discussing 'Constructs') and 'Constructs'.

1.4.1 Instantiations in Text Retrieval

'Instantiation', i.e. deriving knowledge through the post-hoc observation of successful constructions, is not a unique approach to IR research, and has been the general practice of obtaining knowledge for many Design Research fields [for example, Architecture (Alexander 1964) and Aeronautical Engineering (March & Smith (1995)]. In Information Retrieval, this approach dominates the research in industry labs, and the development of retrieval systems is carried out in numerous academic institutions. IR research on 'Instantiations' is interested in developing the most effective and efficient system. In recent years, the Text Retrieval Conference (TREC; http://trec.nist.gov/), co-sponsored by the National Institute of Standards and Technology (NIST) and U.S. Department of Defense, has become the primary meeting place for researchers involved in the design of retrieval systems, where each year systems compete on a common benchmark. This annual meeting is the primary venue for testing new ideas in IR and plays a major role in the development of the Information Retrieval field. The major challenges for the IR "Instantiations' research is to identify the contribution of specific methods (since many different features are combined into one system) and to enable knowledge transfer (since many of the system developers are commercial entities, unwilling to share proprietary information).

1.4.2 Methods in Text Retrieval

The development of '**methods**' is the other popular approach in IR research, as evident from a reading of the classic IR manuscripts listed above and a survey of the main IR journals: Information Processing and Management[4] (IP&M by Elsevier), Journal of the American Society for Information Science[5] (JASIS by ASIS), Information Retrieval[6] (by Kluwer), Transactions on Information Systems[7] (TOIS by ACM), and Transactions on Knowledge and Data Engineering[8] (TKDE by IEEE). By 'Methods' in IR we refer to algorithms and procedures for converting text documents to document indexes (performed as a pre-process), and for generating a query index and matching that index against document indexes (performed at run-time). IR research on 'Methods' is mainly concerned with the conservation of computational resources (i.e., efficiency of algorithms) and human effort. The main contribution of IR 'Methods' research is in the development of efficient algorithms that allow automatic retrieval systems to scale-up to very large collections (e.g., Web search engines).

The methods in IR could involve manual or automatic processing, which may be based on linguistic or statistical techniques, and may rely on external – semantic or linguistic – resources. The choice of methods is determined by the specific settings where the retrieval system is to operate. The types of methods used are directly related to the type of representations generated. We will provide more details on the methods in the section describing models and representations in Text Retrieval below.

1.4.3 Models in Text Retrieval

Modeling in IR involves the development of representation schemes to index documents and queries, and the introduction of operations for measuring the similarity (or distance) between these representations. Since the matching of query to documents should be based on similarity of meaning, the challenge for IR models is in offering representations that capture the semantics of information elements (i.e., documents and

---

[4] http://www.elsevier.com/wps/find/journaldescription.cws_home/244/description#description
[5] http://www.asis.org/Publications/JASIS/jasis.html
[6] http://www.kluweronline.com/issn/1386-4564
[7] http://www.acm.org/tois/
[8] http://www.computer.org/tkde/

queries). The process of designing the semantic representation schemes is referred to as *Conceptual Modeling* (Brodie et al. 1984). While conceptual modeling is at the core of database design and has been explored extensively for modeling structured data [e.g. Entity-Relationship diagrams (Chen 1976)], this approach has *not* featured prominently in IR research. The reason is that text documents are unstructured, and Conceptual Modeling in IR requires a mapping from unstructured text to structured semantic representations. Hence, the models and representations used in IR are restricted by the effort involved in the mapping process. The specific setting where the system is to be deployed and the nature of the document collection determine to a large extent the methods for extracting semantic representations, and thus the type of models that could be used.

Designing retrieval systems for very small text collections may allow for manual mapping (i.e. annotating the documents manually with semantic representations), thus enabling the use of expressive representations. Examples for the use of such representations in IR include Conceptual Graphs (Ounis & Pasca 1997, Crye 1997, Martin & Alplay 1996), Index Expressions (Wondergem et al. 2000), Frame-CG (Martin 2000), and Semantic Networks (Asnicar et al. 1997).

For large collections, manual indexing is not feasible as it is effort intensive, requiring automatic processing. When the document collection is homogeneous in terms of format and topics, linguistic analysis and semantic resources could be employed to convert text documents automatically to semantic representations. Users of linguistic techniques argue for the use of Natural Language Processing (NLP) methods for identifying concepts in the text, and understanding the meaning of the text as a whole. The use of NLP for the mapping from text to semantic units requires that the techniques be tailored for the specific collection, due to the great variability in language forms used by people (McDonald 2000)[9]. Semantic resources, such as lexicons and ontologies, could be used to disambiguate words and map textual elements to semantic representations, and

---

[9] Liddy (1998) identifies several levels of NLP techniques – Phonological, Morphological, Lexical, Syntactic, Semantic, Discourse, and Pragmatic, and discusses their potential use in IR. According to Liddy (1998), these levels of linguistic processing reflect an increasing size of the unit of analysis, as well increasing complexity in processing. At the lower levels, variability in the possible linguistic forms remains relatively small, and processing is simple. As we move up the levels, the language phenomenon is less precise and the variability in possible forms is greater.

this approach has been explored extensively for domain-specific collection (for instance see Mayfield 2002).

However, for heterogeneous collections, which is the focus of this dissertation, most NLP techniques are not appropriate as they cannot easily port across domains, and they rely on semantic resources. Reliance on these resources (e.g., ontologies) is often not appropriate, for several reasons. First, semantic resources exist for only a few domains, and for many topics there are no available resources. Several high-level resources exist, but these are too general and do not contain domain-specific terms[10]. Developing ontologies is a effort-intense task, and clearly is not possible for all knowledge domains. Furthermore, ontology development is not a one-time effort, as the ontology needs to be continuously updated as the domain evolves. Second, even if ontologies existed to cover the variety of topics in an heterogeneous collection, how would we know which ontology to use? Mapping a document (or a set of documents) and a query to a specific ontology is challenging, and we are not aware on any existing solution to the problem. Third, even if we were able to associate documents and queries with the appropriate ontology, semantic inter-operability is still required, and bridging across ontologies is a very difficult problem. Whether ontological-based approaches will be able to scale-up to general collection remains to be seen in the future. What is clear is that currently semantic-resources are not employed in general collections, due to the limitation highlighted above.

Thus, for general collections, the mapping from text to semantic representations should be fully automatic and relies almost exclusively on statistical techniques, without using external resources. Statistical techniques assume that the occurrence of words in a text is not random (i.e., that patterns of words' usage in the text convey meaning), and that statistical and mathematical methods could be used to extract these meaningful patterns. We refer to the semantic units that are generated through a fully automatic process as "*Artificial Semantic Units*", and to the schemes arranging these units as "*Artificial Semantic Representations*".

The automatic mapping process from text to artificial semantic representations in general-collections IR puts severe restrictions on the type of representations and models

---

[10] For example WordNet (Miller 1995), a Terminological Ontology based on psycho-linguistics principles, which covers a wide array of domains, but includes only general terms for each domain.

that could be employed. In Text Retrieval models employed for these settings, a (artificial) semantic space is defined by a set of (artificial) semantic elements, documents and queries that are mapped onto that semantic space; the similarity of a query to documents is measured in that space. The diagram below illustrates a simple semantic space that is defined by two semantic units.

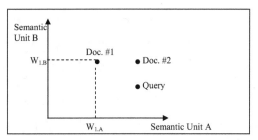

Diagram 1-2: IR models for general collections, illustrated through a simple semantic space (defined by two terms: A and B), where query and documents are mapped onto that space.

In these IR models, documents and queries are represented through a vector of weighted units (Salton & Lesk 1971), where the weight of the unit defines the positioning of an information element in the semantic space (in the diagram above we depict the weights for Document #1).

The modeling literature in IR focuses on the schemes for assigning weights to semantic units in the vector representations, with two general approaches - Deterministic, namely the Vector-Space Model (Salton et al. 1975), and Probabilistic (Robertson & Spark-Jones 1976) - and numerous extensions to these models (Baeza-Yates & Ribiero-Neto 1999). The two fundamental models introduced in the 1970s comprise the most important developments in the IR field; current retrieval systems are still based on these models. The Vector-Space model is the de-facto standard for general-collections IR, due to its simplicity, and is heavily used in current commercial retrieval systems. A formal definition of the Vector-Space model is given as follows:

Let t be the number of index terms in the system and k_i be a generic index term.

$K = \{k_1, \cdots, k_t\}$ is the set of all index terms. A non-binary weight $w_{i,j} > 0$ is associated with each index term k_i of a document d_j. For an index term which does not appear in the document, $w_{i,j} = 0$. The document d_j is associated an index term vector $\vec{d}_j$ represented by $\vec{d}_j = \left(w_{1,j}, w_{2,j}, \cdots, w_{t,j}\right)$. Further, let g_i be a function that returns the weight associated with the index term k_i in any t-dimensional vector (i.e., $g_i\left(\vec{d}_j\right) = w_{i,j}$). The index terms in the query are also weighted. Let $w_{i,q}$ be the weight associated with the pair $\left[k_i, q\right]$, where $w_{i,q} \geq 0$. Then, the query vector $\vec{q}$ is defined as $\vec{q} = \left(w_{1,q}, w_{2,q}, \cdots, w_{t,q}\right)$ where t is the total number of index terms in the system.

Therefore, a document d_j and a query q are represented as t-dimensional vectors. The semantic space for the vector model is defined by the total number of unique semantic units, and each document or query could be represented as a point in this space.

Weights assigned to semantic units in the vector representations reflect the units' resolving power, or the extent to which terms are significant for indexing a document. Methods of calculating tokens' resolving power through weighting have been an area of extensive study in IR since the 1960s. There are two important factors determining the effectiveness of retrieval: *exhaustivity* and *specificity*. Indexing exhaustivity is defined as the number of different subjects indexed, and is usually associated with Recall. Indexing specificity is defined as the ability of the index to describe subjects precisely, and is associated with Precision. Weighting schemes try to balance these two factors by including (1) local, document-specific factors, such as token frequency in the document (often normalized, to counter the variations in document length), and (2) global, corpus-level, factors, such as the number of documents and the frequency of the token in the entire collection. The resolving power is correlated positively with local factors in the document, and negatively with the token global factors.

Different weighting schemes could be used with the Vector-Space model, and the de-facto standard is Term Frequency – Inverse Document Frequency (TF-IDF), defined formally below.

Let N be the total number of documents in the collection and n_i be the number of documents in which the index term k_i appears. Let $freq_{i,j}$ be the raw frequency of term k_i in the document d_j (i.e., the number of times the term k_i is mentioned in the text of the document d_j). Then, the normalized frequency $f_{i,j}$ of term k_i in the document d_j is given by $f_{i,j} = \dfrac{freq_{i,j}}{\max_l freq_{i,j}}$, and is referred to as the *Term Frequency*, *TF*, factor. The maximum, $\max_l freq_{i,j}$, is computed over all terms which are mentioned in the text of the document d_j. If the term k_i does not appear in the document d_j then $f_{i,j} = 0$.

The *Inverse Document Frequency* factor, *IDF*, for k_i is given by $IDF_i = \log \dfrac{N}{n_i}$. The best known term-weighting scheme use weights which are given by

$$w_{i,j} = TF \times IDF = f_{i,j} \times \log \frac{N}{n_i}.$$

The TF component is associated with exhaustivity - it describes the relative frequency of the specific token in the document, and is positively correlated with the weight. The second component, IDF, is associated with specificity - it describes the relative frequency of the token in the entire collection, and is negatively correlated with the weight.

While TF-IDF weighting of documents' indexes is very popular, there is less agreement on the weighting of query indexes, and many TF-IDF variations have been proposed (Baeza-Yates & Ribiero-Neto 1999).

For matching query to document indexes, the Vector-Space model employs an inverted matrix (of tokens to documents; van Rijsbergen 1979), where query is matched with only documents containing at least one query term. Thus, the complexity of the matching process is linear with H (H<<N), the number of documents that contain query terms. The similarity of a query to a document is commonly calculated through the Cosine function, i.e. the cosine of the angle between the two index vectors (or by the dot product of the two normalized vectors).

To summarize, classic IR models, and specifically the Vector-Space model, have had a tremendous impact on IR; nevertheless, these models are rather simplistic and offers inexpressive representations. Research on weighting schemes has been able to enhance models' effectiveness, and is still an active area of research. The major challenge for the development of IR models is in designing representations of documents and queries contents that (a) can be automatically generated from text, even for large and heterogeneous collections, and (b) can capture the meaning of the information element.

1.4.4 Constructs in Text Retrieval

Constructs, the building blocks of the semantic representations, are rarely discussed explicitly in IR. The constructs in information retrieval are the semantic units used to define the semantic space. While a substantial portion of the IR literature is devoted to weighting schemes for reflecting the resolving power of semantic units in document and query representations, very little attention is devoted to defining the nature of the (artificial) semantic units (i.e. the constructs of Text Retrieval models). Retrieval from large collections requires that the units of meaning used in the representations be automatically extracted from text, and relies mostly on statistical techniques. While in conceptual modeling for structured data the basic semantic units are usually concepts, in large-collections Text Retrieval, due to the limitation of the automatic extraction process, the predominant semantic unit used in representations is a *basic meaning-carrying unit*, also referred to as '*token*'. Thus, the major problem for IR research on 'Constructs' is in proposing semantic units that are meaningful, yet could be efficiently extracted from text (through automatic techniques). Statistical token extraction is based largely on the early works of Luhn (1958), who laid the foundations for many of the approaches still employed today. Tokens are extracted from text through the removal of words that seem not to carry meaning when used distinctively, and the stemming of words to their root form. The token extraction process will be discussed in more detail in Chapter 6.

There are some exceptions, however, where other types of semantic units are used in general-collections Text Retrieval representation, either implicitly or explicitly. For example, phrases (now used by many retrieval systems in addition to tokens) and other compositions of tokens [such as lexical-affinities (Maarek et al. 1991)] describe higher-level semantic units, or concepts. While the composition of terms into higher-order semantic elements (through co-occurrence statistics) has been explored quite extensively in recent years, the focus of these works, in-line with the tradition of IR, is on the extraction methods rather than the semantic of the extracted elements, and rarely are the constructs in the representations discussed explicitly. There is, however, one notable example where semantic units are discussed explicitly – Latent Semantic Indexing (Deerwester et al. 1990). Latent Semantic Indexing (LSI) is the Text Retrieval application of Latent Semantic Analysis (Landauer et al. 1998), a model for automatic concept extraction that is based on mathematical factor-analytic techniques. LSI proposes that the semantic space be defined in terms of automatically-extracted (i.e., latent or artificial) concepts, documents and queries be mapped onto the semantic space, and the distance between a query to documents be measured in that space. LSI and related techniques will be discussed in more detail in Chapter 8.

To summarize, IR literature does not discuss the semantic units employed in the representations, and it is widely accepted that basic meaning-carrying units (i.e., tokens) serve as indexing units. The LSI exception, where semantic units are discussed explicitly, serves only to illustrate the general rule. In addition, there is a significant body of works where the use of alternative semantic units is implicit, such as the studies where co-occurrence statistics is used to group tokens.

1.5 Summary

The management of organizational knowledge, and specifically textual information, is essential for firms' survival in the new knowledge economy. Current information retrieval techniques fail to cope with the amounts and heterogeneity of information, and often deliver irrelevant information to users. Irrelevant information overwhelms the users and impedes effective planning and decision making. The main challenge inhibiting the performance of retrieval systems is the gap between the way in which people think about information (i.e., through conceptual representations) and the way in which the information is captured in retrieval systems (i.e., in textual form). This dissertation investigates design principles for developing text retrieval systems by exploring the extent to which fully automatic techniques could create conceptual representations. Specifically, we explore how the artificial semantic units at the center of retrieval models affect the performance of retrieval systems. A better understanding of the factors affecting the performance of retrieval systems, will lead to the design of more effective systems, thus enable organization to exploit their textual information better in order to attain a competitive advantage.

Chapter 2: The Proposed Approach

This dissertation is interested in the design of IR systems with the aim of addressing one of the most challenging problems of Text Retrieval – word ambiguity. The key to resolving this problem is by representing accurately the meaning of documents and queries, and matching them based on these meaningful representations. We restrict the scope of this dissertation to studying the document corpus as a source for generating representation, thus do not investigate issues related to user-machine interactions and query refinement techniques. We also focus on Text Retrieval from general (i.e., large and heterogeneous) collections, and will restrict our investigations to retrieval methods that are scalable to these environments.

The purpose of this thesis is to identify design principles that are essential for the design of effective retrieval systems in the specific settings described above. We take a Conceptual Modeling approach, and focus on the constructs in IR representations – i.e. the semantic units. Since our focus is on automatically-extracted semantic units and representations, our interest is in artificial semantic units. The broad question this dissertation tries to address concerns the effect of the artificial semantic units in representations on the performance of retrieval systems. We hope to learn the appropriateness and effectiveness of alternative semantic units. For instance, we hope to find that one semantic unit leads to high Precision, making it very suitable for some retrieval tasks, while an alternative semantic unit may be mostly appropriate for enhancing Recall, and thus be suitable for other retrieval tasks. Hence, the findings from this research should have direct implications for the design of retrieval systems. We expect that industrial retrieval systems - either systems that are part of an organization's knowledge management infrastructure, IR applications that serve other organizational systems (e.g., Customer Relationship Management), or systems that enable access to public information (e.g., Web search engines) – will incorporate the findings from this dissertation to enhance their performance.

Our approach to researching the design of retrieval systems is unique in that, by and large, the IR literature is concerned with alternative outputs of Design Research:

34

mainly 'Instantiations' and 'Methods', while we focus on 'Constructs'. The key to resolving IR's main limitation (i.e., resolving word ambiguity) is bridging the gap between conceptual representations and text through artificial semantics. Hence, an understanding of the semantic units (i.e., 'Constructs') that are at the core of the semantic representations is essential. Constructs, as mentioned above, have been discussed in previous studies, either implicitly or explicitly; however, these discussions are usually very restricted in that they proposed one alternative semantic unit. Our approach is comprehensive and aims to study the broad field of IR[11] through the unique perspective of 'Constructs'. Previous comprehensive surveys of IR focus mostly on 'Methods' [see the classical works of Salton (1968), van Rijsbergen (1979), and Salton & McGill (1983)], and to a lesser extent on 'Models' [for instance in (Baeza-Yates & Ribiero-Neto 1999)].

Investigating the effect of artificial semantic units is challenging for a number of reasons. First, token-based models dominate IR literature, and seldom are alternative semantic units employed. Second, in most cases where semantic units other than tokens are employed this is not made explicit, and revealing the semantic elements at the core of the models requires careful reading and thorough examination of the details for each of the studies. Furthermore, often semantic units of different nature, such as tokens and concepts, are mixed in the same representation, making it impossible to distinguish the effect of each semantic element. Third, different semantic elements may be used in alternative retrieval models, making it difficult to distinguish the effect of the semantic unit from the effect of the model. For instance, one study may employ the Probabilistic model using tokens, while another will use the Vector-Space model with phrases as indexing units, making the studies incomparable. Fourth, studies involving alternative semantic units may employ different methods for generating the representations or matching them. For instance, in one study, tokens may be employed and the extraction process will involve word stemming, while the other study will employ concepts and will not stem words in the process of extracting concepts from text, making it impossible to compare the models. Fifth, for studies that focus on the development of systems (i.e. the 'Instantiations' output of Design Research), the semantic element chosen is only one of

---

[11] With the restrictions mentioned above – focus on the document corpus, as a source for generating the representations, and on methods scalable to general collections.

many design consideration for constructing the system. Other considerations may involve the specific retrieval model, the type of methods used, query refinement techniques, and the user interface. Isolating the effect of the semantic unit employed is thus impossible. Lastly, assessing the effect of the semantic units employed in representations requires that we compare the performance of systems that are based on alternative semantic units, and therefore it is necessary that the performance of the competing systems be evaluated in the exact same settings. IR systems are tested on a variety of document collections, and at times even alternative measures of performance are used. Hence, even if the effect of the semantic units is isolated and similar models, methods, and instantiations are used in competing systems, it might be impossible to compare their performance due to differences in the settings where they were tested.

We try to circumvent these limitations, isolate the effect of the semantic units, and compare the performance of systems employing alternative units. Before we proceed to elaborate on our methodology, we need first to define more clearly what artificial semantic units are.

Chapter 3: Introducing the "Semantic Units Categorization" Framework

Below we will develop a categorization of semantic units for IR, based on Knowledge Representation literature and a review of existing IR techniques. An explicit categorization of semantic units for IR does not exist; Knowledge Representation literature includes extensive investigations of semantic elements, but that discussion is very general and not constrained by the need to extract the semantic units automatically from text. IR literature, on the other hand, has been traditionally concerned with methods, and pays little attention to the semantics of the units employed for indexing.

The study of semantics belongs to the field of Knowledge Representation, which has its roots in the disciplines of Philosophy, Logic, Psychology, and Linguistics. Clearly, a review of these scientific fields is well beyond the scope of this work. Our interest is in addressing a specific applied problem, rather than making a theoretical contribution to the study of semantics. Hence, we wish to draw some insights from the large body of works on Knowledge Representation (for instance see Brodie et al. 1984, Sowa 2000). We will *not* restrict ourselves to any specific theory or model; rather, we will identify some general and well-accepted principles of representations, which will guide us in categorizing semantic units.

The Oxford dictionary defines 'Semantics' as "the study of the relationships between linguistic symbols and their meanings". A semantic element, then, is a unit of meaning, described through words. This definition is wide-ranging and includes broad themes (a type or class) as well as very specific concepts. Our most fundamental observation from the Knowledge Representation literature (see a broad review of Knowledge Representation formalisms in Sowa 2000) is that semantic units could be categorized and organized in a hierarchy of increasing specificity, as follows:

- At the top category of the hierarchy are general **topics** or categories which describe themes of knowledge (e.g., 'animals')
- At the lowest category of the hierarchy are **basic meaning-carrying units**. These basic meaning-carrying units are usually described through single words (mostly nouns). It is important to notice that not every word carries meaning – some words,

such as 'the' or 'at', are used to compose linguistic structures out of the basic elements of meaning, but do *not* carry meaning on their own. An additional observation is that basic meaning-carrying units are often ambiguous (e.g., the word 'virus' is a meaning-carrying unit; however, its meaning depends on the context in which it is used).

- At the intermediate level category are **concepts**, which are more specific than the general themes (i.e., 'topics'), yet are more precise than 'tokens' and lack ambiguity.

Although the IR literature, in general, is focused on methods and algorithms rather than semantic elements, we find correspondence between IR methods used to generate representations and the (artificial) semantic units employed in the resulting representations. Chen (2001), in a survey of text processing techniques for Knowledge Management, provides a classification of methods that corroborates the hierarchy described above. Chen's classification focuses on the processes, and lists the following classes of techniques. At the lowest level Chen describes techniques for "identifying key concept descriptors" (p. 23) through statistical and linguistic techniques, and these 'concept descriptors' correspond to the 'Basic Meaning-Carrying Units' category in the hierarchy described above. These basic units are referred to in IR literature as 'tokens' (van Rijsbergen 1979), and throughout this work we will use the terms "Basic Meaning-Carrying Units" and "tokens" interchangeably. Chen's intermediate text mining class includes statistical and co-occurrence techniques for extracting concepts and generating conceptual structures (such as thesauri), and corresponds to the 'Concepts' category above. Concept extraction techniques form concepts through the grouping of tokens, in two alternative forms:

- Tokens of *similar* meaning constituting a concept (e.g., 'make', 'produce', and 'manufacture'). We refer to these concepts as *synonym concepts*. Synonym concepts are extracted by identifying tokens which appear in the same context (i.e., surrounded by the same terms) in the text, and this set of tokens is often referred to as a '*Synonym Set*' (Miller 1995). Throughout this thesis the terms "synonym concepts", "synonym sets", and even simply "synonyms" will be used interchangeably.

- Tokens of *distinct* meaning constituting a concept that when joined together form a new meaning (e.g. 'business' and 'intelligence' forming 'business intelligence'). We refer to these concepts as *composite concepts* (the term is borrowed from (Brodie et al. 1984), who used it in the context of database design). Composite concepts are extracted by identifying tokens in direct proximity in the text, and this set of tokens is referred to as a 'Co-occurrence Set'. Throughout this work the terms "co-occurrence set", "composite concepts", and even simply "composites" will be used interchangeably.

To illustrate the difference between these two types of artificial concepts, consider the following example of a short text:

> *"AAA BBB CCC DDD.*
> *AAA EEE CCC DDD.*
> *CCC FFF DDD."*

Automatic concept extraction techniques will group the words '*CCC*' and '*DDD*' into a co-occurrence set to form a composite concept (the two words appear consecutively in the first two sentences and with one separating word in the third sentence). The words '*BBB*' and '*EEE*', on the other hand, will be grouped into a synonym set, since they appear in similar contexts (in the first two sentences).

Chen's third class of technique includes clustering and classification of documents, which are used to create subject hierarchies, corresponding to the top category of the hierarchy mentioned above - 'Topics'[12]. Topical organization of a document collection has been explored for a variety of applications (e.g., supporting category-driven browsing, such as in Yahoo![13]), amongst them IR[14]. The direct correspondence between Chen's classes of methods and the semantic unit categories validates our proposed categorization of semantic units.

---

[12] Chen (2001) mentions one additional class of techniques – Information Visualization. This technique focuses on the user interface, and has no direct correspondence to the hierarchy of representation we described.
[13] www.yahoo.com
[14] For a survey of classification methods in IR see (Yang 1998); for a survey of clustering methods see (Willett 1988).

We label the proposed classification of artificial semantic units for IR as "The Semantic Units Categorization framework" and employ that framework to guide our investigations in the following chapters. The framework, as depicted below, organizes semantic unit categories in a hierarchy of increasing specificity: in the top category are very broad semantic units, i.e. **topics**; in the intermediate category are **concepts** (of the two types described above – synonyms and composites); and in the bottom category are semantic elements of fine granularity, i.e. **basic meaning-carrying units** or **tokens**.

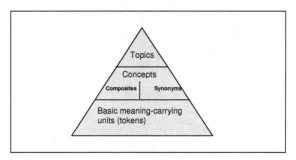

Diagram 2-1: the proposed "Semantic Units Categorization" framework

To better illustrate the types of semantic units, we will provide below some examples:

- Tokens – a token is the root form of a word, e.g. the token 'republ' represents the words 'republic', 'republics', 'republican', etc..
- Composite Concept – phrasal expression are one form of Composites, e.g. 'Artificial Intelligence'
- Synonym Concept – is defined by a group of words carrying similar meaning, e.g. ['create', 'manufacture', 'produce', 'generate']
- Topic – is not defined explicitly, but rather by a set of documents describing similar a theme.

Chapter 4: Research Questions

The broad objective of this research is to assess the extent to which semantic units employed in information retrieval representations impact retrieval performance. Our study will focus on large and heterogeneous text collections, thus we will restrict our investigation to automatic techniques for extracting artificial semantic units. We will employ the "Semantic Units Categorization" framework to assess the performance of artificial semantic units from different categories.

In order to attain our research objective we investigate two research questions. The first concerns the performance of retrieval models, each based on distinct semantic units (from the proposed framework), and the comparison of these retrieval models. The second research questions concerns the interplay between semantic units from distinct levels, and the design of research models that combine different semantic units. We will introduce each question, and its sub-questions, in turn.

Research Question 1: How does the performance of retrieval models that are based on alternative artificial semantic units compare? To address this research question, we propose the following set of more detailed questions:

- RQ 1.1: What is the typical performance level for retrieval models that are based on *basic meaning-carrying units (i.e., tokens)?*

- RQ 1.2: What is the typical performance level for retrieval models that are based on *composite concepts*?

- RQ 1.3: What is the typical performance level for retrieval models that are based on *synonym concepts*?

- RQ 1.4: What is the typical performance level for retrieval models that are based on *topics*?

- RQ 1.5: How does the performance of these *different semantic units compare*?

Once we establish performance levels for each distinct artificial semantic unit, we intend to explore whether combining different semantic units in one coherent retrieval model could enhance performance. To illustrate this idea we will use the analogy of cooking, or more specifically - barbequing a chicken, which is in many ways similar to the process of designing a retrieval system. In the first part, we focus on one aspect of the system's design – the semantic units – and explore typical performance levels for each category of artificial semantic units. In the barbeque analogy, we focus on the effect of spices on the taste, by studying four different categories of spices (say, garlic, honey, salt, and pepper) and fixing the rest of the ingredients chicken type and the cooking process. For the second part, we would like to investigate whether mixing the spices would result in a better product. Mixing the spices is challenging for two reasons. First, it is hard to predict which spices will go well together (e.g., honey and garlic) and what won't (e.g. salt and honey). Second, determining how to mix the two spices in the cooking process is not straightforward. Similarly, combining different semantic units, which traditionally are treated as substitutes, is challenging because (a) it is hard to predict which combinations will prove effective, and (b) it requires designing a retrieval model that combines the different types of semantic units. Existing IR models employ semantic units from only one category of our proposed framework – Tokens, Concepts, or Topics. *Interactions* between categories, though, are only used when representations of Tokens (i.e. token-based representations) are used as an input in the process of generating higher level representations (what we refer to as a 'bottom-up' approach, as illustrated below). For example, normally token-based representations are used as an input for extracting concepts (both synonyms sets and composite concepts), and these token-based representations are employed in the clustering of documents into topically coherent sets. However, to the best of our knowledge, prior work does not consider 'top-down' integration, where higher-level semantic units are used to re-define lower level units (see diagram below).

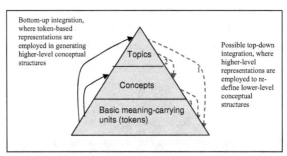

Diagram 4-1: The interplay between conceptual structures from distinct categories of the "Semantic Units Categorization" framework. Solid black lines represent integration between categories, which has been explored in prior work. Dotted blue lines represent potential integration, which has not been explored to date.

We argue that such top-down integration has the potential to enhance retrieval performance beyond the levels obtained for each semantic unit separately. To demonstrate the logic in this argument, assume that semantic units in the top category of the framework proposed in Chapter 3 - 'topics' - are extracted and the collection is decomposed into topically coherent sets, where each document is associated with a topic. This organization provides semantic context and could now be used to better extract artificial semantic units at lower categories, for instance in the extraction of synonym concepts. Traditionally (i.e, with no combinations of semantic units), when a semantic space is generated for a heterogeneous collection and synonyms sets are extracted, tokens that have several meanings may confound the automatic extraction process. For instance, the token 'state' may be associated into the same synonym set as tokens describing a *country* (e.g., 'federation', 'kingdom', 'nation'), as well as tokens describing a *condition* (e.g., 'situation', 'position', 'status'), forming the ambiguous synonyms set {state, federation, situation, kingdom, position, nation, status}. Now assume that we combine different semantic units in one coherent retrieval model, and prior to generating the semantic space we organize the collection into topically-coherent set. This organization is likely to group documents describing *a country* into one set, and documents describing *a condition* into another document set. Now, if we were to produce a distinct semantic space for each topically-coherent set, the generated synonym sets will not be ambiguous

– in the set describing *a country* we will extract the synonym set {state, federation, kingdom, nation}, while in the set describing *a condition* we will extract the synonym set {state, situation, position, status}.

Combining distinct semantic units has not been discussed in the literature, and integrating units of different categories in one retrieval model is not straightforward. Hence, exploring the effect of such combinations would require (a) designing novel retrieval models, and (b) testing these models empirically.

Our second research question is, then, Research Question 2: Does the combination of two distinct artificial semantic units in one coherent retrieval model enable performance gains beyond the levels obtained for each semantic unit separately? Numerous combinations of semantic units are possible, and we will explore the following:

- RQ 2.1: *Could 'Topics' and 'Tokens' be integrated into one coherent retrieval model?* And if yes – how will the performance of the combined model compare to the performance of 'Topics" and 'Tokens'-based models (see Research Questions 1.4 and 1.1)?

- RQ 2.2: *Could 'Topics' and 'Composite Concepts' be integrated into one coherent retrieval model?* And, if yes, how will the performance of the combined model compare to the performance of 'Topics" and 'Composite Concepts'-based models (see Research Questions 1.4 and 1.2)?

- RQ 2.3: *How Could 'Topics' and 'Synonym Concepts' be integrated into one coherent retrieval model?* And if yes – how will the performance of the combined model compare to the performance of 'Topics" and 'Synonym concepts'-based models (see Research Questions 1.4 and 1.3)?

- RQ 2.4: *Could 'Tokens' and 'Composite Concepts' be integrated into one coherent retrieval model?* And if yes – how will the performance of the combined model compare to the performance of 'Tokens" and 'Composite Concepts'-based models (see Research Questions 1.1 and 1.2)?

- RQ 2.5: *Could 'Tokens' and 'Synonym Concepts' be integrated into one coherent retrieval model?* And if yes – how will the performance of the combined model compare to the performance of 'Tokens" and 'Synonym Concepts'-based models (see Research Questions 1.1 and 1.3)?

By addressing the two research questions (and the five sub-questions for each) described above, we hope to attain a better understanding of the effect of artificial semantic units on the performance of retrieval systems. In the following section, we will describe the proposed method for addressing those questions.

Chapter 5: Research Method

The investigation of the impact of artificial semantic units on the performance of general-collections IR will be guided by the framework of semantic units categories, proposed in Chapter 2.

Retrieval performance could be evaluated through effectiveness and efficiency. The primary focus of this study is on enhancing retrieval effectiveness (measured through Precision and Recall, as described in Section 1.2); however, we will also discuss the effect of semantic units on retrieval efficiency, as inefficient techniques will not scale up to large and heterogeneous collections. Retrieval efficiency will be estimated by the computational complexity of algorithms used to generate and match the representations. It is worth making the distinction between the complexity of pre-processing calculations and run-time complexity. In pre-processing, we are mainly concerned with scalability to large volumes of documents, but we are less concerned with the exact timing of these processes, as most of them are only performed once (or at relatively long intervals). However, in interaction time, when a user submits his query, computation has to be performed extremely efficiently, so as not to keep the user waiting for the system's response.

Above we described two research questions, each with its unique challenges. The challenge in addressing the first research question, concerning the typical performance levels of retrieval models that are based on distinct semantic units, is in isolating the effect of the semantic units from other factors. The main challenge in addressing the second research question, concerning the interactions between semantic units, is in designing novel retrieval models. Below we describe the method for addressing each research question.

5.1 Methods for Addressing Research Question 1

To address Research Question 1 we will take the following steps:

1. Studying previous works - investigate the performance levels for each category of semantic elements by surveying the field of IR, mapping previous studies to the different categories, and examining the performance levels obtained in these studies. Mapping previous studies onto the semantic unit categories framework is not simple, since IR literature focuses on methods, algorithms, and the development of systems, rather than the semantic unit at the core of the representations. Thus, a careful and thorough investigation of prior works is required for the very large field of Information Retrieval.

   Mapping prior works in the field to the semantic units categories may help us to get a general idea for the performance levels for each category of semantic elements; however, comparing the performance of different semantic elements will still be difficult due to the problems mentioned earlier – differences in models, methods, instantiations, and experimental setting used in these different studies.

   To circumvent these difficulties, we will take the second step, of empirically testing the impact of semantic units in a controlled laboratory setting. An empirical test requires that we choose a representative technique for extracting semantic units for each of the categories. It is possible that for one category of semantic elements we may find several extraction techniques [for example, composite concepts could be based on phrase extraction, grouping two consecutive words, or on lexical affinities (Maarek et al. 1991), grouping separated terms based on linguistic techniques]. We require that the technique chosen will represent common-practice in the field. Specifically, the technique as to: (a) be completely automatic and domain-independent, (b) prove to be effective, (c) be supported in academic literature, and (d) be used in current retrieval systems. Thus, to estimate the performance of each semantic unit category, we will choose one characteristic technique for each category, justify our choice, and use the technique as a representative of that category. The performance of the common-practice technique will be referred to as the "typical performance" of the specific category.

2. Empirical evaluation - study empirically the performance for each semantic unit category by testing the representative extraction method. We will implement different retrieval systems that are similar in all aspects, except the semantic units employed in the representations. Hence, for the different semantic elements, we will use the same retrieval model, set of methods, and instantiations, arriving at systems that are identical, with the exception of the semantic unit, allowing use to isolate the effect of the semantic unit. We will test these different systems on the exact same benchmark, and using the same performance measures. Through the empirical studies of the representative techniques, we hope to gain an in-depth understanding of their efficiency, as well as the techniques' effectiveness.

Below we will provide more details on the empirical studies.

In order to isolate the effect of the semantic units, we need to choose one retrieval model, set of methods, and instantiations, and use those with all semantic units. We present our choices and justifications below:

- Retrieval model: in our discussion of Information Retrieval in Chapter 1 we've mentioned two retrieval models that dominate in IR: the Vector-Space (Salton et al. 1975) and Probabilistic (Robertson & Spark-Jones 1976) models. For our experimental studies we will employ the Vector-Space model due to its simplicity and popularity. In that model a semantic space is constructed based on the semantic units, and documents and queries are mapped onto that space (see Diagram 1-2). For weighting terms, we will use Term-Frequency-Inverse-Document-Frequency (TF-IDF) weighting scheme, described in Section 1.4.3. We will employ the Vector-Space model with TF-IDF weighting using alternative semantic units to define the space (e.g., to test the performance of 'Tokens' we will implement the Vector-Space model with token-based representations, and to test 'Composite Concepts' we will implement the same model with composite-based representations). Since weighting schemes in general, and specifically TF-IDF, have been associated with Tokens in IR literature and the appropriate weighting scheme for alternative semantic units has been seldom discussed, we will study the impact of weighting through the comparison of TF-IDF to un-weighted (i.e. based on the 'raw' frequency of semantic units) indexes.

- Methods: we will employ the same methods for all semantic units to the extent possible. The extraction process of alternative semantic units is bound to be different, for example, synonym concepts are extracted differently from composite concepts. However, pre-processing in all cases will be identical, and the tokens extracted to test token-based representations will serve as the starting point for extracting higher-order semantic units. Furthermore, we will employ the exact same matching procedures for all semantic units, and in all cases query-document representations similarity will be calculated with the Cosine function.

- Instantiations: for all semantic units the retrieval processes for developing the system will include only the processes for extracting the semantic units and matching them. We will not employ any additional processes, such as interaction with users or query refinement techniques, for any of the cases.

Even after we choose one representative technique for the extraction of each semantic unit and we isolate its effect by fixing the models, methods, and instantiations, establishing typical performance levels may be challenging. Typical performance levels are often hard to establish as performance may depend on various parameters of the extraction technique (for instance, the number of synonym concepts set for LSI can affect the technique's performance dramatically, as we will see in Chapter 8). To address this issue, we conduct an in-depth investigation of each technique, identify the key parameters affecting the technique's performance, and study the parameters effect by testing performance for alternative values of the parameters.

The effectiveness of each retrieval model will be measured through both Precision and Recall measures. Specifically we will employ the following relevance measures: Precision[10] (precision for the top 10 ranked documents), Precision[20], Precision[30], and Recall[1000] (recall for the 1000 top ranked documents). Efficiency will be evaluated through the computational complexity of the algorithms used to create and match the representations.

5.1.1 The TREC Test-Bed

The testing of the retrieval models has to be conducted in a specific setting, thus the results will depend, at least to some extent, on the exact evaluation settings. In order to address this concern we chose to evaluate the retrieval models on a very large and heterogeneous collection, which simulate real-life setting. The retrieval systems, based on the different semantic units, will be tested on the exact same test bed - the Text Retrieval Conference (TREC) database. The goal of the TREC database is to "encourage research in IR from large text applications by providing a large test collection, uniform scoring procedures, and a forum for organizations interested in comparing their results"[15]. The TREC collection is becoming a standard for comparing IR models (Baeza-Yates & Ribiero-Neto 1999). Specifically, we used disks 4 and 5 of that collection, which include 528,030 documents[16], 100 information need descriptions (or queries; referred to in TREC as *topics*), and manually constructed relevance judgments for all documents on each of the topics[17]. TREC topics include three fields: title, description, and narrative. Since user queries in practice are usually short, we used only the topic title and description to generate the query statement (the 100 queries used are listed in Appendix 1). The advantages of the TREC corpus include its status as a benchmark for text retrieval systems, and inclusion of human relevance evaluations (the collection was pre-analyzed manually, to establish which documents are relevant and which aren't for each of the queries). In addition, TREC is particularly suited to emulating general collections, due to the size of the collection (probably larger than any other test database) and the variety of topics (which are not domain specific).

The TREC collection, however, has a limitation that needs to be recognized. Due to the size of the TREC database, it is impossible to manually review the relevance of each document for all queries. Instead, the "Pooling" technique is employed, where only

---

[15] http://trec.nist.gov/overview.html
[16] Documents from The Los Angeles Times (1989-1990), Financial Times (1991-1994), Federal Register (1994), and the Foreign Broadcast Information Service (1996). An example of a document is given in Appendix 4.
[17] Relevance evaluations in the TREC DBs are binary, i.e., the documents are assumed to be either relevant or non-relevant to the query.

documents that are initially ranked at the top relevance list by automated techniques are subject to manual assessment, and all other documents are assumed irrelevant. A study reported by Harman (1994) found that the Pooling technique missed on average 16% of the relevant documents. Another problem with the TREC relevancy judgments is that they are binary, and therefore not detailed enough. Despite these limitations, the TREC database is probably the best available benchmark for testing IR systems, and hence was adopted for this study.

5.2 Methods for Addressing Research Question 2

While the steps listed above are intended to obtain typical performance levels for each **distinct** category of semantic units, we've argued that the **combination** of semantic elements from different categories has the potential to further enhance retrieval performance. In order to evaluate the potential of these combinations, we will (a) attempt to design novel retrieval models that are built on the interplay between semantic unit categories, (b) realize these models by building on the same methods and instantiations described in Section 5.1, and (c) compare the performance of the combined model to the performance of the models employing semantic units from distinct categories, on the same test bed.

The Vector-Space model, with TF-IDF weighting, will serve as the general framework, and the models we'll introduce could be seen as extensions to the Vector-Space model. The TREC database, described above, will serve as the benchmark for testing the combined models. The design of novel retrieval models - the most challenging aspect of this part - will be guided by our findings on Research Question 1 (regarding what are the advantages and disadvantages of each semantic unit) and to a large extent by our intuition. Similar to the approach taken for addressing Research Question 1, we will conduct an in-depth investigation on each of the proposed retrieval models, by exploring its sensitivity to various parameters.

5.2.1 Software Testing

The empirical evaluations of retrieval models (for both research questions) require that a prototype retrieval system be developed. To ensure reliability of the results, it is essential that the correctness of all software algorithms be validated. We performed a comprehensive set of tests for all the software components that were developed in the course of this dissertation, in order to validate the correctness of the software. These test procedures included: black-box tests (testing the correctness of the output, by manually performing the algorithm), white-box test (validating the correctness of the software's internal structure), and intuitive tests (e.g., ensuring that terms grouped into synonym sets are indeed synonymous).

Part I Summary

One of the most critical problem impeding the performance of Text Retrieval systems is the gap between the way in which users think about information (through semantic representations) and the form of text documents (natural language). Bridging that gap requires that users' information needs, as well as the documents, be represented through semantic units. The goal of this dissertation is to explore the extent to which semantic units employed in retrieval models affect the performance of retrieval systems. We focus on large and heterogeneous collections, thus we restrict our investigations to semantic units that could be extracted using completely automatic techniques – i.e., artificial semantic units. Thus, we use the term 'Artificial Semantics' throughout this thesis in a restrictive sense, to refer to patterns that are extracted from text using domain-independent and scalable methods. This view of Artificial Semantics is predominantly statistical, and excludes methods based on linguistic analysis, which are domain specific.

Design Research is interested in studying Constructs, Models, Methods, and Instantiations; however, the field of IR is predominantly concerned with the study of algorithms (i.e., Methods) and the construction of systems (i.e., Instantiations). For studying the semantics of information representations, the conceptual modeling perspective is called for. This approach has been very popular for designing database systems, but is uncommon in IR. Furthermore, a large-scale evaluation of the effect of artificial semantic units on retrieval performance has not been taken in the past. We believe that establishing the effect of automatically-generated semantic units on IR performance is an essential step towards resolving the problem of word ambiguity.

This dissertation is interested in two main research questions: the first concerning the typical performance levels of different semantic units and the comparison of these performance levels, and the second concerns the design of novel retrieval models that integrate distinct semantic units as a way to enhance retrieval performance. To address these research questions we first introduced a categorization of artificial semantic units – 'Tokens', Composite Concepts', Synonym Concepts', and 'Topics' - and will later employ that framework to guide our studies.

Our method for addressing the first research question and establishing typical performance levels for each category of semantic elements will be based on two steps: (1) mapping prior works to the proposed framework categories, then (2) conducting a series of empirical studies to isolate the effect of the semantic units by fixing the Models, Methods, Instantiations, and the test bed. We will test one representative extraction technique for each semantic unit, and conduct an in-depth study of that technique by investigating the key parameters affecting the performance of that technique.

To address the second research question, we will build on the same representative techniques employed for the first research question, will design novel retrieval models that integrate semantic units from distinct categories into a coherent retrieval models, and test these models empirically on the TREC benchmark.

This dissertation combines breadth – in studying a broad area - and depth – in conducting comprehensive studies of several models - with several expected contributions. First, in the methodology: studying the field of IR through a unique perspective – focusing on artificial semantic units – and in the development of the "Semantic Unit Categorization" framework. We believe that the field of IR could benefit by adopting a conceptual modeling approach, and that our proposed framework could be used to map previous research and guide future research. Second, in the performance levels: establishing typical performance levels for representations based on distinct semantic units, and identifying the representation's main advantages and limitations. Knowledge of the performance levels has a direct implication on the design of retrieval systems, and it is expected that IR systems designers will utilize our findings to design systems that are more effective. Third, our in-depth analysis of models that are built on distinct semantic units is expected to provide a deeper understanding of these retrieval models. For example, our analysis of Composite Concepts will be the first large-scale evaluation of that model on a well-accepted benchmark, and our investigation of topic-based models will provide new insights. The in-depth analysis of retrieval models has both theoretic and practical implications: exploring retrieval models' key parameters and revealing the models' limiting factors makes a theoretical contribution, and the knowledge of the optimal parameter settings for each model is essential for practitioners who design systems. Fourth, in addressing the second research question, we will develop novel retrieval models that integrate distinct semantic units, and test these novel models empirically to attain performance gains. For instance, we will show that by combining 'Topics' with 'Synonym'-based representations, retrieval effectiveness could be enhanced. The design of the novel retrieval models makes the greatest theoretical contribution of this dissertation, and we hope it will open the door for more research on the interactions of semantic units.

When addressing such a broad question such as the automatic extraction of meaningful patterns from text, it is obvious that the analysis depth of each method is somewhat restricted. Our approach for studying the extraction techniques for each semantic unit is based on: (a) choosing one representative method, (b) through a review of the literature, identifying the critical parameters of that method and the appropriate value ranges for each parameter, and (c) testing the performance of the method by exploring different values for the critical parameters. We believe that our approach enables to get a good understanding of the effectiveness of each semantic unit, and that we achieve a fine balance between breadth and depth.

We expect to find that retrieval models based on one type of semantic unit (e.g. Composite Concepts) enable high Precision; thus, are appropriate for retrieval tasks where users are interested in few documents that address their needs, while other types of semantic units (e.g., Synonym Concepts) enable Recall gains at the cost of Precision losses and thus are appropriate for retrieval tasks where the users are interested in exploring a large portion of the results lists (for instance in searching for medical information). In addition, we expect to find that the combinations of certain semantic units (e.g., Topics and Synonym Concepts) would enhance performance beyond the levels obtained for Topics and Synonym concepts separately. Other expected findings concern the efficiency of the semantic unit extraction methods and the appropriateness of these methods for large and heterogeneous text collections.

The findings from this research are expected to have both theoretical and practical implications. Through these studies, we hope to enhance our understanding of retrieval systems' design principles, and thus contribute to the design of effective IR systems and enable system designers to choose retrieval models with semantic units that best address their specific requirements. By allowing people access to more relevant information sources, organizations could better exploit their large document repositories to gain a competitive advantage.

It is worth mentioning that the findings from this study are restricted to the specific methods used for extracting the meaningful patterns from text. Although we've argue for our choice of methods and try to choose the most representative technique for each category of semantic units, alternative choices of methods are likely to influence results.

The dissertation will proceed as follows: in Part II we explore typical performance levels for retrieval models that are based on each of the four categories of semantic units – 'Tokens', 'Composite Concepts', 'Synonym Concepts', and 'Topics'. Each chapter in this part will explore one category of semantic units, first by mapping existing works in the field to that category and choosing a representative extraction technique, and then by developing a system based on that extraction technique and testing it empirically. We conclude Part II by comparing the performance of models based on alternative semantic units. In Part III, we try to address the second research question, design five novel retrieval models by integrating semantic units from distinct categories, and then build systems based on these models and test them empirically. Each chapter in Part III will be dedicated to the investigation of one novel retrieval model that combines two different semantic units. Finally, in Part IV we'll summarize the dissertation, discussing its contribution and limitation, and highlighting possible future research directions.

Part II - Typical Performance Levels for Semantic Units

In order to address the first research question, concerning the typical performance levels of alternative artificial semantic units, we will employ the "Semantic Units Categorization" framework introduced in Part I, and evaluate IR models that are based on semantic units at each of the framework's categories. For each category, we will (a) study previous works in the field that employ semantic units at that level and identify a representative technique for extracting that unit, and (b) implement a retrieval system based on that semantic unit and the representative extraction technique, and conduct an empirical study to evaluate the performance of the system.

The representative techniques for extracting semantic units are as follows:

- Tokens: removal of high-frequency words using a stop-word list, stemming words to their root form, and the removal of low-frequency words.
- Composite Concepts: extracting two-token co-occurrence sets using statistical proximity models.
- Synonym Concepts: by using Latent Semantic Indexing (LSI), where factor-analytic techniques are employed to construct a semantic space of lower dimensions.
- Topics: cluster-based retrieval, where topical organization of the collection is employed to restrict the set of documents a query is matched against.

The tokens extracted to test token-based models will also serve as the starting point for extracting higher-order semantic units. Details on the representative techniques, as well as justification for choosing them as representatives, will be provided in the following chapters.

Part II continues as follows: in Chapter 6 we study 'basic meaning-carrying units' (i.e., tokens); in Chapter 7 we survey the use of 'composite concepts' in IR literature, and report the finding of an empirical study of 'composite concepts' extracted with a statistical proximity technique; we study 'synonym concepts' in Chapter 8, and detail the results of a study of Latent Semantic Indexing (LSI); and in Chapter 9 we will survey the use of 'topics' in information retrieval, and describe our experiments with the cluster-based retrieval model. Finally, we will conclude Part II of the dissertation in Chapter 10, and compare the typical performance levels of each semantic unit.

The diagram below illustrates the correspondence between the chapters of Part II and the "Semantic Units Categorization" framework.

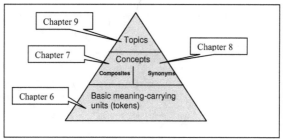

Diagram II-a: the framework of semantic unit categories and the corresponding Part II chapters.

Chapter 6: Basic Meaning-Carrying Units in IR

In this chapter we explore the semantic units at the bottom category of our proposed framework – Basic Meaning-Carrying Units (i.e., Tokens) – as illustrated below.

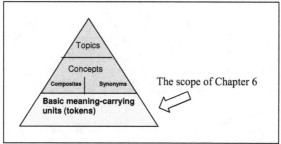

Diagram 6-1: the "Semantic Units Categorization" framework and the scope of this chapter
(highlighted in yellow)

We try to address Research Question #1.1: What is the typical performance level for retrieval models that are based on **basic meaning-carrying units (i.e., tokens)**? To address the question, we will:

- Review prior studies employing token-based representations to gauge a tokens' performance, and identify a representative token extraction technique.
- Conduct an empirical study of tokens, extracted with the representative technique
  - o Study the effectiveness of tokens, by exploring the effect of the techniques' key parameters.
  - o Study the efficiency of token extraction and matching techniques, to assess whether the techniques could scale up to general collections.

This chapter will continue as follows: in section 6.1 we describe the literature survey, in Section 6.2 we report on our empirical study, and we conclude the chapter in Section 6.3.

6.1 Basic Meaning-Carrying Units in IR Literature

The process of converting text into indexes of basic meaning-carrying units (or tokens) is referred to as *tokenizing* (Melnik et al. 2001), and is built on the early work of Luhn (1958). Luhn employed statistical token extraction techniques, and assumed that frequency data could be used to extract significant features to represent a document. Specifically, Luhn analyzed the frequency of words in a document collection, and specified both an upper and a lower cut-off. The *upper cut-off* was used to exclude very common words, such "the" or "'of", and the *lower cut-off* was used to exclude rare words – neither of which were expected to contribute significantly to the representation of the document content (van Rijsbergen 1979). Rather, the *resolving power* of terms (i.e. the extent to which terms are significant for indexing a document), is highest for terms of medium frequency, as shown in Diagram 6-2.

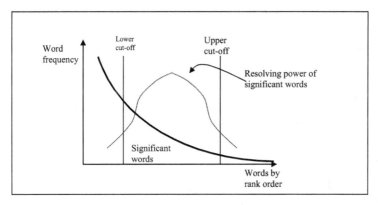

Diagram 6-2: Words' frequencies and their resolving power, based on (van Rijsbergen 1979, p. 11).

It is important to note that these techniques may be useful for eliminating words that do not carry a distinctive meaning, yet the remaining words may still be ambiguous.

Linguistic indexing techniques, on the other hand, rely mostly on simple methods, due to the complexity of more advanced linguistic methods. Specifically, the only linguistic technique that is commonly employed is stemming words through prefixes and suffixes removal. Stemming reduces words' ambiguity by joining words that carry very similar meaning (different stems of the same word, e.g., 'nation', 'national', 'nationality') into one unit. However, synonyms (such as 'car' and 'automobile') are not joined in that process, thus tokens often remain ambiguous.

Traditional IR continues to build on Luhn's early ideas and current systems have converged on the following set of techniques for extracting tokens (Chakrabarti 1998):

- Removal of high-frequency words (Luhn's upper cut-off) which in themselves do not carry meaning (for instance 'the', 'of' and 'at'). The removal of these 'stop-words' is done with the use of a pre-constructed list, such as the one used by the SMART system (Ide & Salton 1971).

- Stemming by removing word prefixes and suffixes. Although this technique is far from full-proof, its pros out-weigh the cons and it is common practice in IR[18]. Porter's stemming algorithm (Porter 1980) is a popular realization of this process.

- Removing infrequent tokens – once an initial token list is constructed, infrequent tokens[19] are pruned (Luhn's lower cut-off). This helps to significantly reduce the complexity of further processing, as usually a relative small number of tokens are retained.

Token-based representations have been invaluable in the development of retrieval systems, and, in fact, to date most of the commercial IR systems are based on these traditional models. The two factors that affect retrieval performance are the selection of the tokens (i.e., the upper and lower cut-off levels) and the weighting scheme used to calculate tokens' resolving power. Techniques for automatically generating token indexes have been studied extensively for the past three decades, and resulted in moderate improvement in relevance. Unfortunately, the results of recent TREC conferences (Voorhees & Harman 1999, 2000) suggest that additional improvements have largely ceased, with the different tokenizing techniques generally producing similar results.

---

[18] However, in some domain specific application stemming is not used, for example in the accounting domain (Gangolly and Wu 2000).
[19] Infrequent tokens are tokens that appear in very few documents or tokens of low total frequency in the entire corpus.

With the advent of the information revolution and the rapid growth of available information, traditional token-based IR techniques are challenged. While these techniques proved efficient enough to handle huge document collections, their effectiveness in these setting is questionable. For general collections, token-based IR models are frequently unable to distinguish relevant documents from irrelevant ones, and the performance of traditional systems is often unsatisfactory (Baeza-Yates & Ribiero-Neto 1999, Chakrabarti et al. 1998).

In the section below we describe an experiment we conducted to test the performance of token-based retrieval. The representative token-extraction technique employed for our experiment is based on the commonly used methods described above – removal of high-frequency words with SMART's stop-word list (Ide & Salton 1971), stemming of words with porter's algorithm (Porter 1980), and the removal of words that appear in very few documents.

6.2 An Experimental Study of the Token-Based Retrieval

In this study we explore the performance of token-based retrieval, with the representative token extraction technique mentioned above, using the TREC database benchmark. The study is designed to measure both the effectiveness and efficiency of tokens. In studying token's effectiveness we will try to identify the critical factors determining retrieval Precision and Recall. Specifically we will explore the affect of (a) the lower cut-off level for removing infrequent tokens, and (b) tf-idf weighting of document indexes. Retrieval efficiency will be measured for both pre-processing (token extraction and indexing) and run-time (matching query to documents).

We used the representative technique to produce the token indexes, and we removed stop-word with SMART's common words list (Ide & Salton 1971), and stemmed words with Porter's algorithm (Porter 1980), leaving 443,826 unique tokens.

In order to explore the effect of the lower cut-off level of tokens, we tested two different lower cut-off thresholds. The first threshold was based on common practice in the field, and removed tokens that appeared in less than 6 documents[20], arriving at 72,354 unique tokens[21]. The alternative lower cut-off level explored left roughly twice as many tokens (143,571 unique tokens)[22].

In both cases of token extraction, the weighting scheme employed for document indexes was TF-IDF.

Retrieval performance when the standard lower cut-off threshold was employed is described below.

Token-based retrieval with standard lower cut-off threshold	Precision[10]	Precision[20]	Precision[30]	Recall[1000]
Average	0.244	0.204	0.177	0.445
Variance	0.060	0.042	0.028	0.058

Table 6-1: effectiveness results token-based retrieval with the standard lower cut-off threshold

The results presented in Table 6-1 represent the average over 100 queries. The findings suggest that, on average, roughly 2.5 of the top ten documents predicted as relevant by the token-based model, and 4 out of the top twenty, were judged as relevant in the manual evaluations. Recall findings suggest that out of the total number of relevant documents, on average 45% are included in the list of documents predicted as relevant by the token-based model (when the list is pruned to the top 1000 documents).

When the alternative lower cut-off threshold was employed, leaving double the number of unique tokens, exact similar results were obtained. This is explained by the fact that none of the queries used in our experiment included any of the additional tokens. These results suggest that using a lower cut-off level indeed removes tokens that are usually unimportant for retrieval purposes. Using such a threshold speeds up processing,

---

[20] The threshold we employed was used in other works, for example see (Deerwester et al. 1990).
[21] With this first threshold, the resulting average document index included 138 tokens.
[22] The new token list threshold pruned every token that appeared in less than 4 documents. This modified tokenizing process resulted in a slightly larger average token index size (139 tokens per document, instead of 138 tokens).

and our findings suggest that it might be possible to use even a stricter threshold, without significant effectiveness losses.

In order to study the effect of token weighting, we measured performance for two cases: in the first, document indexes were weighted; while in the second, the tokens in indexes remained un-weighted and the 'raw' frequency of tokens was used. In both cases we performed the tokenizing process as described above, using the standard lower cut-off threshold (resulting in 72, 354 unique tokens). The results of this experiment are reported below.

Document Weighting	Frequency	TF-IDF
Precision[10]	0.225	0.244
Precision[20]	0.183	0.204
Precision[30]	0.154	0.177
Recall [1000]	0.393	0.445

Table 6-2: effectiveness results for the token-based model for 2 cases of token weighting

The results in the table above suggest that document index weighting has a (statistically insignificant) positive effect, with 8%-14% gains. Recall is affected positively with document weighting, resulting 13% gains. These results suggest that weighting tokens to reflect token's resolving power is useful, which supports prior knowledge in the field.

As for the model's efficiency, the computational complexity of the indexing process in linear with N, the total number of documents in the collection, and the indexing of each document is linear with the number of tokens in the document. For matching query to documents, the token-based model employs an inverted matrix (of tokens to documents; van Rijsbergen 1979), where query is matched with only documents containing at least one query token. Thus, the complexity of the matching process is linear with H (H<<N), the number of documents that contain query tokens.

In this chapter we studied token-based retrieval, and found that the model's effectiveness for a large and heterogeneous collection is rather unsatisfactory – approximately only 20% out of the documents predicted to be most relevant by the model (i.e., the documents at the top of the results list), are actually relevant documents, and 50% of the relevant documents are not included in the result list[23]. The sensitivity of the model to two effects was studied. First, we found that the use of a lower cut-off threshold makes calculation more efficient, with no effectiveness losses. Second, weighting tokens in documents' indexes has a positive effect on performance. The main advantage of the token-based model is its simplicity – the relative low complexity of both indexing and matching processes enable it to scale to very large collections.

In the future we plan to explore the sensitivity of the token-based model to additional parameters not explored here, such as the parameters of the token extraction process (for instance the upper cut-off threshold and stemming).

6.3 Conclusion

Traditional IR models employ token-based representations. Token representation (i.e., the extraction of basic meaning-carrying units from text and the indexing of queries and documents through tokens) is at the core of information retrieval. While token-based indexing is used to date by most retrieval systems, our experiments with the token-based model suggest that it is not very effective. Our experiment was based on one token extraction technique, but we believe that the findings from our study could be generalized to other token extraction methods, as the literature suggests that these extraction methods perform similarly. The major shortcoming of token-based representations is that they do *not* resolve the problem of words' ambiguity. Thus, it is possible that representation of information elements through more concise elements may be required in order to enhance performance. In the following chapters we will investigate retrieval models employing representations of higher-order semantic units.

---

[23] i.e. when the result list is pruned after 1000 documents.

Our contribution here is in establishing typical performance level for token-based models, which could be compared to performance levels of other semantic units.

Chapter 7: Composite Concepts in Information Retrieval

In this chapter, we explore the semantic units at the intermediate category of our proposed framework – Composite Concepts – as illustrated below.

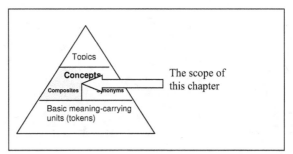

Diagram 7-1: the "Semantic Units Categorization" framework and the scope of this chapter
(highlighted in yellow)

We try to address Research Question #1.2: What is the typical performance level for retrieval models that are based on **composite concepts**? To address the question, we will:

- Review prior studies employing composite-based representations to gauge at composite's performance, and identify a representative composite concept extraction technique.
- Conduct an empirical study of composite concepts, extracted with the representative technique
  - Study the effectiveness of composite concepts, by exploring the effect of the techniques key parameters.
  - Study the efficiency of composite extraction and matching techniques, to assess whether the techniques could scale up to general collections.

This chapter will continue as follows: in section 7.1 we describe the literature survey, in Section 7.2 we report on our empirical study, and we conclude the chapter in Section 7.3.

7.1 Composite Concepts in IR Literature

The use of composite concepts to enhance retrieval performance has been explored extensively in recent years, although composites are hardly discussed in IR literature explicitly, and composite concepts are implicit in the indexing methods. Automatic techniques for extracting composite concepts in order to represent text content rely on the joint occurrence of words in the text (i.e., grouping terms into co-occurrence sets). Word co-occurrence has been explored in a variety of applications, including: Speech Recognition (Jelinek et al. 1992), Language Generation (Smadja & McKeown 1990), Machine Translation (Sadler 1989, Brown et al. 1991), Text Classification (Cohen & Singer 1996, Yang & Chute 1994), Information Filtering (Brouard & Nie 2000), Information Retrieval (Khoo et al. 2001, Keen 1992, Maarek et al. 1991), and text disambiguation tasks (Dagan 1992, Gale et. al. 1992b). Though the results of these studies differ in the importance shown for co-occurrence sets and are in some cases equivocal, a substantial body of evidence suggests that co-occurrence sets are essential for representing the meaning of text documents.

In this study we explore the role of composite concepts for representing textual information in Information Retrieval. Co-occurrence statistics associates terms based on their proximity in the text. This technique usually groups terms that each carry distinct meaning, but which combine to form a new element of meaning – a composite concept [for instance the co-occurrence of '*copy*' and '*file*' described in (Maarek et al. 1991)].

We have identified three classes of techniques for extracting composite concepts: statistical, syntactic, and semantic, as described below.

- Statistic techniques for grouping tokens could either be restricted to sequential patterns, such as phrases, or non-sequential patterns (i.e. non-directional relations between tokens).

o Sequential patterns include both consecutive (i.e. phrases) and non-consecutive (i.e. sparse phrases) patterns. Phrase indexing groups tokens that appear in sequence mostly through the use of statistical techniques, although the use of linguistic methods, as well as pre-processed lists, has been explored. Phrases are the most popular form of composite concepts, and phrase indexing is now used in most commercial systems. The results of TREC7 (Voorhees & Harman 1998, Jones 1998) and TREC8 (Voorhees & Harman 1999, Jones 1999) indicate that the performance gains resulted from this approach is 2%-4%. Non-consecutive phrases, on the other hand, are less popular, due to the complexity of the extraction process.

o Non-sequential patterns group two terms that co-appear within a given distance (or window) in a text, and are symmetric (relation A-B = relation B-A). Non-sequential co-occurrence statistics is restricted to a pre-defined distance, which can be defined at the term level (i.e. number of terms apart), sentence level, or paragraph level. This approach for extracting composite concepts is uncommon in IR from general collections[24].

While general collections techniques automatically extract the composites from documents and queries, the use of a query interface, which enables the user to directly seek co-occurrence sets[25] has been explored in some restricted settings. Although these types of interfaces are outside the scope of this study, we can learn from the experience accumulated with these systems. Early work by Keen (1992) found that restricting the window to 5 terms yields better results than restricting to 10 terms, though both types of co-occurrence sets improve precision. Keen also studied the extraction of co-occurrence sets for different structural elements in the text, and reported that within-sentence co-occurrence is superior to within-paragraph co-occurrence, although both improve precision.

---

[24] However, statistical techniques for extracting non-sequential patterns have been studied in a variety of applications other than IR, including: Language Generation (Smadja & McKeown 1990), Word-Sense Disambiguation (Gale et al. 1992a, 1992b), and Language Modeling in Speech Recognition (Lau at al. 1993).
[25] Baeza-Yates & Ribeiro-Neto (1999) refer to these approaches as "structured IR models".

- Syntactic: relating terms syntactically can provide more direct representation of linguistic information (i.e. subject-verb or verb-object relations), but require part-of-speech analysis that relies on syntactic parsers and is often inaccurate (Dagan et al. 1995). Martin et al's (1983) suggest that 98% of syntactic relations associate terms that are within the same sentence and are separated by 5 or less words.

  The best results obtained by indexing through composites extracted syntactically show effectiveness gains of less than 10% over standard token indexing. In many cases, however, results have actually been worse than token indexing or statistical phrase extraction (Croft 1986, Croft, Turtle & Lewis 1991, Dillon & Gray 1983, Hyoundo, Niimi & Ikeda 1998, Smeaton & van Rijsbergen 1988, Smeaton, O'Donnell & Kelledy 1995). More positive results with this approach have been obtained by Maarek et al. (1991), and recently by IBM's Juru system (Carmel et al. 2001). Maarek et al. (1991) were able to show a 15% effectiveness improvement in comparison to a competing system when employing syntactically-extracted composites[26], and a similar technique was later successfully employed by IBM's Juru system, which ranked first in TREC10. However, IBM's system included enhancements other than the use of composite concepts, and in the experiments with the system the affect of syntactic composites was not tested in isolation.

- Semantic: relating terms based on some meaningful relation is much more expressive than either statistical or syntactic techniques; yet semantic grouping of tokens to composite concepts cannot be easily automated, and the process relies on pre-constructed linguistic and semantic resources. The semantic approach has been explored in the DR-LINK project (Liddy & Myaeng 1993, 1994, Myaeng & Liddy 1993, Myaeng, Khoo & Li 1994)[27], and later by Liu (1997) who obtained positive results for long queries by matching concepts with their semantic role in the sentence. A recent study by Khoo et al. (2001) explored the extraction of composites by identifying cause-effect relations between terms. Khoo et al. employed domain-

---

[26] Maarek et al. (1991) refer to these syntactically-extracted composites as "Lexical Affinities".
[27] The DR-LINK project is perhaps the first large-scale project to investigate general methods for semantically extracting composite concepts for IR. DR-Link employs Natural Language Processing techniques extensively, and uses non-domain-specific resources (dictionary & thesaurus). In DR-Link semantic representations were based on case frames, which were constructed semi-manually.

independent resources, and tested their approach on the TREC1 and TREC2 benchmark[28], but failed to obtain any significant improvements.

The semantic extraction approach relies on some manual processing; thus, is less appropriate for general collections.

Out of these three extraction approaches, only the statistical method has the capability to scale up to large and heterogeneous collections. Syntactic methods are semi-automatic: they are highly structured, require significant effort to tailor rules to a specific domain, and in general not appropriate for heterogeneous collections (Chen 2001). Semantic extraction methods are even more effort intensive and are not easily portable across domains. Hence, from here onward, our discussion of composite concepts will be restricted to statistical extraction techniques.

A key issue in the extraction of composite concepts is maintaining the list of possible unique concepts at a manageable size. Extraction of co-occurrence sets is bound to generate a very large number of composite concepts, as the number of possible sets grows exponentially with the number of unique tokens in the collection. For instance, a collection with 100,000 unique tokens will result in almost ten billion possible unique co-occurrence sets, when considering only two-token sets! A large number of concepts impede both the concept extraction and concepts matching processes, hence there is a need for restricting the number of unique concepts by using thresholds for pruning less important concepts. Our survey of the literature did not yield any prescription for managing this process.

An additional important point for realizing this model is the weighting scheme employed to calculate concepts' resolving power. The literature discusses alternative approaches for extracting composite concepts and employing them in document and query indexes; however, a discussion on weighting these concepts is almost nonexistent. The 'frequency' of a composite could be estimated by the number of times (and the proximity) in which terms co-occur in the text. Weighting of these concept frequencies

---

[28] Which included Wall Street Journal articles from a four-month period.

have been explored by Maarek et al. (1991), which introduce the notion of co-occurrence *affinity* as a measure of the resolving power of co-occurrence sets (where co-occurrence frequencies are weighted, not very differently from the techniques applied to tokens) arriving at a relation affinity index for each document. Composites' resolving power was also employed by (Dagan et al. 1995). The works by Maarek and Dagan point to the importance of composites' weighting, yet an established weighting scheme for composites does not exist.

To summarize the literature review, several approaches for extracting composite concepts have been suggested, and the statistical approach seems most appropriate for general collections. Indexing through composites has not yet proved useful in IR, and the usage of term dependencies to improve retrieval effectiveness continues to be controversial (Baeza-Yates & Ribeiro-Neto 1999). The results from studies matching composite concepts have been weak and inconclusive (Khoo et al. 2001), and to our knowledge no method for employing composites in IR has been tested in isolation on an accepted benchmark for large-scale and domain-independent collections, to yield Precision improvements beyond a few percentage points. However, there is some evidence that recently commercial retrieval systems (specifically, Web search engines) have begun using statistical co-occurrence models in an effort to enhance IR effectiveness (Pedersen 2003), indicating that there is some potential in this approach.

In the section below, we describe an experiment we conducted to test the performance of composite-based retrieval. The representative composite-extraction technique employed for our experiment is based on the statistical techniques, which are scalable to general collections. It is difficult do define a representative technique here as composite concepts have not been explored extensively for large-collections IR, and the only widespread use of this approach is through a simple phrase extraction (often with pre-constructed phrase list). Our choice of extraction method is guided by evidence from other domains. We chose the non-sequential approach as our representative extraction technique, due to the large body of evidence supporting its effectiveness. Statistical non-sequential patterns techniques group two terms that co-appear within a given distance (or window) in a text, and thus are sometimes referred to as 'statistical proximity models'. This approach has proved useful for retrieval in restricted settings, as well as in a variety of other applications, such as Language Generation (Smadja & McKeown 1990), Word-Sense Disambiguation (Gale et al. 1992a, 1992b), and Language Modeling in Speech Recognition (Lau at al. 1993).

7.2 An Experimental Study of the Composite-Based Retrieval

In our experimental study of composite concepts, we employed representative techniques - statistical proximity models - for grouping tokens into co-occurrence sets. In this experiment we used the TREC database benchmark. The study is designed to measure both the effectiveness and efficiency of the model. In studying the model's effectiveness, we will try to identify the critical factors determining retrieval Precision and Recall. Specifically we will explore the effect of (a) restriction of the number of unique concepts through the use of lower cut-off level for removing infrequent concepts, and (b) TF-IDF weighting of document indexes. Retrieval efficiency will be measured for both pre-processing (token extraction and indexing) and run-time (matching query to documents).

7.2.1 Experimental Design

There are many possible variations for extracting non-sequential patterns; below, we describe the design criteria for the method we employed.

- Co-occurrence sets are restricted to two-term sets. Multi-dimensional co-occurrence sets might be more expressive, but are significantly more difficult to extract and manipulate, and thus are limited in their practicality.
- Symmetry – since different ordering of the same terms could be used to express similar concepts (for instance "the child ate the apple" and "the apple was eaten by the child"), we do not consider the ordering of the tokens in the text to be significant. Symmetric extraction methods have been employed by most non-consecutive statistic

extraction technique, as well as by several syntactic extraction approaches (Dagan et al. 1995).

- Intransitivity – it is possible that term A be related to term B, and term B be related to term C, yet term A is not related to term C. For instance "Business" may be related to "Intelligence" (the combination is a new concept, "Business Intelligence"), "Intelligence" may be related to "Emotion" (e.g. "Emotional Intelligence"), yet "Business" and "Emotion" are unrelated. Hence, we do not assume transitive association between terms in our concept extraction process.

- Terms' proximity at different structural levels - we believe that proximate terms forming a composite concept do not have to appear in the same sentence, and may, in fact, appear in sentences further apart. Moreover, we believe that composites can be extracted based on the joint occurrence of terms at the different structural elements of a document (e.g., sentence, paragraph, chapter). The results obtained by Keen (1992) support this and clearly illustrate that within-sentence, within-paragraph, and word-distance relations all carry significant information. Thus, we will extract composite concepts by considering term co-occurrence at these different structural elements.

- Distance between terms – we believe that the affinity between terms forming a composite concepts depends on both the structural element where they co-occur (the tighter the element, the closer the association), and the distance within that structural element (for instance, a distance of two terms within a sentence implies a closer relation than a distance of five terms). Again, this is supported by the early work of Keen (1992), which shows that within-sentence relations are more expressive than within-paragraph relations, and that a five-word distance is more effective than a ten-word distance.

7.2.2 Implementation Procedure

Based on the considerations described above, we extracted composite concepts using the following process:

1. We processed the documents to generate a token index. This tokenizing process was based on well-established techniques, similarly to the techniques we employed in the experiment described in Section 6.2[29].

2. We generated tokenized documents, where tokens replace the text and the original grammatical structure is preserved. We employed the tokenized documents as input for the concept extraction process.

3. We restricted the calculation of co-occurrence to the tokens with the largest resolving power (i.e. weight) in each document, to avoid an exponential increase in the number of co-occurrence sets[30]. For the purpose of concept extraction all other tokens were ignored[31].

4. Co-occurrence set' frequency was based on terms' proximity in the text, by assigning a value to each co-occurrence of the terms (the value depending on the proximity), and then summing-up the values across the entire document. We tried to exploit the structural elements of documents (e.g. sentences, paragraphs) to calculate the frequency, so that co-occurrence within tighter structural elements will carry more importance. However, only sentences were clearly marked in documents in our test collection, so proximity calculations for tokens co-occurring across sentences were based on the number of sentences separating the two tokens. In addition, for tokens co-occurring in the same sentence, we considered the distance between the tokens - the closer the tokens were – the higher the proximity, where the maximum proximity was set to 1. There are numerous possible algorithms for calculating frequencies, and future studies should explore in detail the affect of proximity. In this study, however, we did not explore this aspect thoroughly, and rather chose one specific realization. Below we describe our algorithm for calculating proximity within and across sentences.

---

[29] We used: stop-word removal with SMART's common words list (Ide & Salton 1971), stemming with Porter's algorithm (Porter 1980), removal of tokens that appear in few documents (leaving 72,354 unique tokens, and average document index of 138 tokens), and TFIDF token weighting.

[30] For 72,354 unique tokens there are possibly 5,235,101,316 unique two-token co-occurrence sets

[31] This process alone reduces the number of possible concepts significantly. We employed the top 20 tokens for each document (so the number of unique possible concepts per document was 380, and the total possible number of concepts was approximately 200 million), resulting in 9,831,709 unique co-occurrence sets. Thus, using only the top tokens reduces the possible space by 96% (from 5 billion to 200 million), and in reality reduced the number of concepts by 99.8% (from 5 billion to 9 million).

a) For tokens that co-appear in the same sentence, we assigned a proximity value of 1.00-0.84: from the upper limit to adjacent tokens, down to the lower limit for tokens 14 slots away (tokens within the same sentence, but further apart received a proximity value of the lower limit – 0.84). For the setting of these parameters, we were guided by what works best, as there is no theory to rely on for setting the values.

b) For tokens that were not included in the same sentence, proximity received lower values than those for tokens within the same sentence, based on the number of sentences separating the tokens. Token positioning within sentences was ignored in these cases, and the 'window' was limited to a pre-set value, for computational reasons. For token pairs separated by one sentence, we assigned a proximity value of 0.80, and for tokens separated by more sentences, we assigned a decreasing proximity values, down to a proximity value of 0.10 for a seven-sentence separation. Again, since there is no theory to guide this process, we are guided by our intuition and practical considerations

The accumulated proximity value for a specific co-occurrence set was regarded as the 'frequency' of the composite concept. Examples of the most frequent composite concepts extracted are given in the table below.

Composite Concept	Token 1	Words it represents	Token 2	Words it represents
A	fund	funding, funded, ...	Corp	corporate, corporation, ...
B	grade	grading, grades, ...	math	math, ...
C	gain	gains, gaining, ...	Lab	lab, ...

Table 7-1: Examples of the frequent concepts extracted out of TREC DB disks 4 and 5

5. We pruned infrequent concepts, leaving only a small portion of the several million unique co-occurrence sets produced in step 4. In order to study the effect of restricting of the number of unique concepts through the use of lower cut-off

level for removing infrequent concepts, we explored two different lower cut-off thresholds: (1) pruning every co-occurrence set that appeared in less than 12 documents (this threshold resulted in 551,826 unique concepts, and an average of 19 concepts in a document index), and (2) doubling the number of unique concepts by pruning every co-occurrence set that appeared in less than 6 documents (resulting in 1,046,135 unique concepts and an average of 73 concepts per document index).

6. Queries were processed similarly to produce concept indexes. The different lower cut-off thresholds explored resulted in different query indexes. Since we are interested in estimating the effect of concepts, in our experiments we only employed the queries that contain at least one concept[32]. For the first case (resulting in 551,826 unique concepts), 87 out of the original 100 queries contained concepts, and only these queries were used in this experiment (see the list of queries in Appendix 2). For the second threshold explored (resulting in 1,046,135 unique concepts), 91 out of the original 100 queries contained concepts, and only these queries were used in this experiment (see the list of queries in Appendix 3).

7. Weighting concepts in document indexes. Since the literature provides very little guidance on concept's weighting, and our experiments with token-based representation reveal that weighting of document indexes has an impact on retrieval effectiveness (see Chapter 6), we generated 2 alternative sets of document indexes: the first with weighted indexes, and the other with un-weighted (i.e. using frequency of tokens) indexes. Since the literature provides little guidance on how to calculate concepts' weights, we chose to apply to TF-IDF weighting scheme, to arrive at document indexes (DI) of the following form:

DI_j = [<c1,w1>, <c2,w2>, ... <c_L,w_L>]

J = 1..M; M = number of documents in the corpus

$c_{1..L}$ = concepts; L = number of unique concepts

$w_{1..L}$ = concept weights.

---

[32] We pattern our methodology after Khoo et al. (2001), which also included in their study only queries that contained concepts.

7.2.3 Experiments, Results and Analysis

The first experiment of composite concepts was designed to test the effect of the cut-off threshold for pruning infrequent co-occurrence sets. In this experiment we explored the two thresholds described above (with 0.5 and 1.0 million unique concepts), and document indexes were weighted. The table below describes the results of this experiment.

Case 1 – using 551,826 unique concepts	Precision[10]	Precision[20]	Precision[30]	Recall[1000]
Average	0.234	0.168	0.136	0.180
Variance	0.074	0.044	0.028	0.035
Case 2 - using 1,046,135 unique concepts	Precision[10]	Precision[20]	Precision[30]	Recall[1000]
Average	0.278	0.205	0.180	0.247
Variance	0.085	0.052	0.042	0.046

Table 7-2: the effect of lower cut-off threshold for pruning the concept list on retrieval effectiveness

The results from this first experiment reveal that the lenient cut-off level employed for pruning the list of concepts increased documents indexes lengths considerably (from an average of 19 concepts per index to 73) and enhanced performance by 19-33%, suggesting that possibly using a lower threshold and including additional concepts may yield further gains. Recall, too, is significantly (37%) higher when employing more concepts. It is not possible to estimate the statistical significance of these differences, since the query sets used for the two cases are not identical (in each case we used only the queries that contained relations – 87 queries in the fist case and 91 in the second).

In order to gain a better understanding of this retrieval model, we studied each query independently (rather than looking at the averages for the entire 100 query set). We noticed that queries differ significantly in size (i.e. in both the number of concepts per query index and the concepts' total frequencies), and we suspected that query size affects retrieval performance. In order to test this effect, we employed the document representation from case 2 above (including 1,046,135 unique concepts and document indexes TF-IDF weighted), and analyzed retrieval effectiveness for queries of different sizes.

The table below and the following graph present the results of the analysis on the effect of *the number of concepts* per query on retrieval effectiveness.

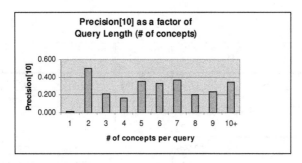

Diagram 7-2: Precision[10] for different queries – based on the number of concepts per query index

Since the graph above does not show direct relation between the number of concept per query and Precision, we divided the set of 91 queries into two groups: one with 1-4 concepts per query, and the other with five or more concepts per query. The table below compares the performance levels for the two groups.

Number of concepts per query	Precision[10]	Precision[20]	Precision[30]	Recall[1000]
1-4 concepts (41 queries)	0.259	0.165	0.139	0.162
5+ concepts (50 queries)	0.294	0.238	0.213	0.317

Table 7-3: the effect of query size (in terms of number of concepts) on retrieval effectiveness

The table and graph above show that there is not a direct link between the number of concepts per query index and retrieval Precision, although, in general, queries with more concepts yield better Precision. Recall is more correlated with the number of relations, and increasing the number of relations has a drastic effect of retrieval Recall.

The following graph and table present the results of the analysis on the effect of *the total frequency of concepts* per query on retrieval effectiveness.

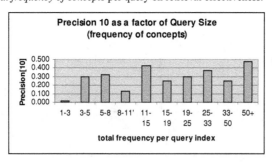

Diagram 7-3: Precision[10] as a factor of the total frequency of concepts in query indexes

Since the graph above does not show direct relation between the total frequency of concepts per query and Precision, we divided the set of 91 queries into two groups: one with a total frequency of 1-15 per query, and the other with a total frequency of fifteen or higher. The table below compares the performance levels for the two groups.

Total concepts' frequencies per query	Precision[10]	Precision[20]	Precision[30]	Recall[1000]
1-15 (46 queries)	0.248	0.154	0.134	0.178
15+ (45 queries)	0.307	0.258	0.227	0.318

Table 7-4: the effect of query size (in terms of total concepts frequency) on retrieval effectiveness

Similarly to the effect of query length, there is not a direct link between the total concepts' frequency per query index and retrieval Precision, although, on average, queries with higher frequencies yield better Precision. Recall, again, is more correlated (positively) with total frequency, and increasing the frequency of query's concepts has a drastic effect of retrieval Recall.

To study the effect of concept weighting we measured performance for 2 cases: the first with weighted indexes, and the other with un-weighted (i.e. using frequency of tokens) indexes. In both cases we performed a similar concept extraction procedure, using the more lenient cut-off threshold in Case 2 (resulting in 1,046,135 unique concepts). The results of this experiment are reported below.

Document Weighting	Frequency	TF-IDF
Precision[10]	0.252	0.278
Precision[20]	0.219	0.205
Precision[30]	0.186	0.180
Recall[1000]	0.243	0.247

Table 7-5: effectiveness results for the for 2 cases of concept weighting

The results obtained above show that documents' weighting have a statistically insignificant effect on retrieval performance. Document weighting has an ambiguous effect on Precision (results in small gains for Precision[10], and minor losses for Precision[20] and Precision[30]), and a similar unclear effect on Recall. Thus, in contrary to token-based representations, where weighting of index terms has been studies extensively to yield some effective weighting schemes, for composite-based representations the TF-IDF weighting scheme (developed originally for tokens) does not yield visible effectiveness gains (and in some cases yield losses).

7.2.4 Efficiency Analysis

As for the model's efficiency – the complexity of the concept extraction process increases in a linear manner according to the number of documents, N[33]. The processing required for each document grows almost linearly with the number of concepts[34]. The complexity of concept matching is similar to that of token matching, since in both cases an inverted matrix of meaning-elements (i.e. tokens or concepts) to documents could be employed, thus matching is linear with the number of documents that contain query terms, H ($H \ll N$). However, the time required for concept matching was much shorter than the

---

[33] $O(N)$; N = # of documents in the corpus

[34] $O(L * \text{Log } L * \text{Log } 2L)$; L = number of co-occurrence sets

time required for token matching, due to the shorter concept index (for both queries and documents).

7.2.5 Discussion

In this study of composite concepts we demonstrated how composites could be extracted using simple statistical techniques that are scalable to large domain-independent systems. Further improvements in efficiency might be achieved by taking steps to reduce computational complexity, an area of potential improvement we did not address in our experiments.

The results of the study reported above reveal that, generally speaking, retrieval based on composite concepts performs similarly to token-based retrieval. Indexing based on composite concepts proved sensitive to the model's parameters. The lower cut-off threshold used for pruning infrequent concepts has a substantial effect on performance, and using a more lenient threshold (i.e. pruning fewer concepts) increases Precision by 20-30% and Recall by 37%. The size of query indexes, in general, affect performance, as long queries yield results that are more effective, yet there is not a direct correlation between query length and Precision or Recall. Finally, TF-IDF weighting scheme, which has proved effective for token-based representations, has nearly no effect on the performance of composite-based retrieval.

When comparing the performance of composite-based retrieval to token-based retrieval (using weighted document indexes) we find that composite-based retrieval is slightly more Precise than token-based retrieval (yielding 4-12% Precision gains), but results in substantial (i.e. over 50%) Recall losses. It is important to note that the comparison described above is not entirely bias-free, as it is based on document indexes of different lengths. For token-based retrieval document indexes included on average 138 terms, while concept indexes included almost half of this number - only 73 items, suggesting that if composite indexes were longer, composite-based retrieval might compare better against token-based retrieval.

In the future, we plan to explore alternative realizations for extracting composite concepts by exploring the effect of:

- Directionality: through comparing the performance of directional composites versus non-directional (i.e. symmetric, as implemented in our study).
- The importance of token proximity at different structural elements of the text – sentences, paragraphs, and entire documents: through studying distinctively the effect of composites calculated at each of these structural elements.
- The effect of token proximity on composites frequency: through exploration of alternative schemes that relate proximity with frequency.
- Lower and upper cut-off thresholds: by testing alternative thresholds.

In addition, we would like to study weighting schemes for composites, as the token-based TF-IDF scheme did not prove effective in our experiments.

7.3 Conclusion

The use of co-occurrence sets has been explored extensively in the past, employing various techniques – statistical, syntactic, and semantic – for concept extraction, and for large and heterogeneous collections, statistical techniques are the most appropriate. The simplest form of composite concepts used in retrieval systems is phrase extraction, resulting in only minor effectiveness improvements (Voorhees & Harman 1999, Jones 1999). In general, purely statistical co-occurrence set extraction techniques, which are scalable and domain independent, have not featured prominently in IR literature, have not been tested on well-accepted benchmarks, and have not been adapted by commercial retrieval systems. However, there are some recent indications that this retrieval model is being adopted by Web search engines (Pedersen 2003).

We studied empirically one representative technique of the statistical co-occurrence set retrieval model (with two-token sets, symmetric, and intransitive token associations) and demonstrated how it could be applied for a large-scale domain-independent collection. Our experiments reveal the model's sensitivity to several parameters, namely the number of unique concepts employed (i.e. the lower cut-off threshold for pruning infrequent concepts), and to a lesser extent – to the size of query indexes. The weighting scheme applied to document indexes, on the other hand, had little effect on performance.

Our results from the study show slight Precision improvements over the token-based model, at the cost of substantial Recall losses. These findings strengthen our argument (presented in Part I) that composite-based retrieval addresses Polysemy, and thus is useful for retrieval Precision. Since our study explored only one extraction technique of composite concepts, the performance levels obtained in this study should be regarded as a lower-boundary for retrieval based on co-occurrence sets, and alternative extraction methods may yield even better performance. Thus, we believe that composite concepts could be utilized for general collections to enhance retrieval Precision.

Our contribution in this chapter is in the empirical study described in Section 7.2. Specifically, in demonstrating how composite-based retrieval could scale to general collections through our representative extraction technique, and in providing the first large-scale empirical test of statistically-extracted co-occurrence sets. The tests of statistical proximity model serve to establish typical performance level for composite-based retrieval.

Chapter 8: Synonym Concepts in Information Retrieval

In this chapter, we explore the semantic units at the intermediate category of our proposed framework – Synonym Concepts (i.e. Synonym Sets) – as illustrated below.

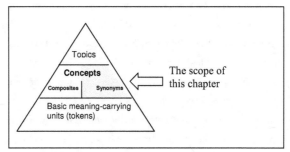

Diagram 8-1: the "Semantic Units Categorization" framework and the scope of this chapter
(highlighted in yellow)

We try to address Research Question #1.3: What is the typical performance level for retrieval models that are based on **synonym concepts**? To address the question, we will:

- Review prior studies employing synonym-based representations to gauge at synonym's performance, and identify a representative synonym concept extraction technique.
- Conduct an empirical study of synonym concepts, extracted with the representative technique – Latent Semantic Indexing (LSI).
  - o Study the effectiveness of synonym concepts, by exploring the effect of the techniques key parameters.
  - o Study the efficiency of synonym extraction and matching techniques, to assess whether the techniques could scale up to general collections.

This chapter will continue as follows: in section 8.1, we describe the literature survey; in Section 8.2 we report on our empirical study, and we conclude the chapter in Section 8.3.

8.1 Synonym Concepts in IR Literature

Synonym sets could be extracted manually, semi-automatically (i.e. by manually tailoring the extraction system for a specific domain), and automatically. As discussed in Section 1.4.3, fully automatic extraction is the only approach that is appropriate for large and heterogeneous collections, thus our discussion below will be restricted to automatic extraction of synonym sets.

The automatic extraction of synonym sets groups tokens that appear in similar contexts in the text, and usually binds synonyms, but may also join together antonyms (opposites) or other related terms that are not strictly synonymous. Automatic extraction of synonyms sets could be based on either (a) clustering of terms, or (b) factor-analytic techniques.

The first technique, clustering of tokens[35], could be used to generate conceptual structures, such as thesauri, lexicon, or ontology. These conceptual structures could be used for two applications: (1) expanding the query to include synonymous terms, or (2) conceptual matching, where both query and document terms are mapped to concepts, and then query and documents are matched based on conceptual similarity. The first application – query expansion to synonym terms (or to more specific terms, referred to as 'term projection') - has been explored extensively in the literature, and have been successful in extending the set of relevant documents retrieved (i.e. improve retrieval Recall). However, improved Recall results are usually at the expense of retrieving many irrelevant documents, resulting in rapid degradation in Precision (Peat & Willett 1991). The alternative application of conceptual structures – term disambiguation through sense narrowing - requires special linguistic resources, such as WordNet (Miller 1995), where each term is associated with multiple concepts, each representing a unique sense of the

---

[35] Clustering of tokens is performed by indexing each token through the documents it appears in (and its frequency or weight, in each document), measuring the similarity between token indexes, and grouping the tokens into clusters based on their similarities.

term. Disambiguating document (or query) terms and associating a term with the correct sense in the lexicon requires linguistic analysis (i.e. identifying the grammatical role of the term) or statistical analysis (i.e. exploring neighboring terms to deduce the terms' context). Disambiguating terms through this approach has been explored in the past [for instance see (Kominek & Kazman 1997, Moldovan & Mihalcea 1999)], usually with domain-specific collections, as it is difficult to port the technique across domains. Notwithstanding these recent studies, unequivocal evidence for the value of automatic term disambiguation is yet to be provided.

A second approach for utilizing artificial synonym concepts in IR is the construction of an artificial (or latent) semantic space using factor-analytic methods. With this approach, the semantic space is defined by a series of orthogonal factors, each representing a unique concept. Terms, documents and queries are then mapped onto that space, and the proximity between any two items (terms, documents, or queries) could be calculated based on their positioning in the conceptual space. The appropriateness of the technique for IR largely depends on the extent to which the artificial concepts resemble human concepts, and its usefulness for IR has been reasonably well established (Transley et al. 2000). Several factor-analytic models have been proposed for IR, amongst them Koll's model (Koll 1979), Latent Semantic Indexing (LSI) (Deerwester et al. 1990, Landauer et al. 1998), MatchPlus (Gallant et al. 1992), the Learned Vector Space model (Caid et al. 1995), and Rungsawang's (1997) Distributional Semantics model. Latent Semantic Indexing (LSI) (Deerwester et al. 1990, Dumais 1994, Landauer et al. 1998, Husbands et al. 2000) is the most popular of these techniques. LSI has shown simulate human knowledge successfully (Landauer et al. 1998), and it has strong formal foundations (Baeza Yates & Ribiero Neto 1999). Latent Semantic Indexing has been reported to enhance performance for small, domain-specific collections. For general collections however, LSI acts in many ways as query expansion techniques, retrieving more documents, both relevant and irrelevant, thus improving Recall, but at the cost of low Precision.

For the purpose of studying synonym concepts, we wish to focus on one representative IR model that exploits synonyms sets, and we choose to investigate Latent

Semantic Indexing, due to its sound theoretical foundations, its ability to extract concept that resemble those used by humans, and its popularity in IR literature. Following we will describe the LSI model.

Latent Semantic Indexing was introduced in 1988. The main idea behind it is to map documents and query term vectors into a lower-dimensional space, where the dimensions of this space are orthogonal, and are treated as latent (or artificial) concepts. The claim is that by reducing the number of dimensions (from the total number of unique tokens to the much lower dimensions number), we reduce the noise, thus enable more effective retrieval. LSI is based on the more general text mining model, Latent Semantic Analysis (LSA) (Landauer et al. 1998). It takes an input the term-document matrix, $\vec{M}$, where each cell corresponds to the weight of that term in the specific document (different weighting schemes are possible; for a term that is not included in the document index the entry is zero). $\vec{M}$, a matrix of rank $t \times d$ (t represents the number of unique terms, and d is equal to the number of documents), then goes through Singular Value Decomposition (SVD). $\vec{M}$ is decomposed into three components: $\vec{M} = \vec{T}\vec{S}\vec{D}'$. The matrix $\vec{T}$ could be interpreted as a terms-concepts matrix; the matrix $\vec{D}'$ could be interpreted as concepts-documents matrix; and $\vec{S}$ is the $e \times e$ diagonal matrix of singular values (i.e. the artificial concepts), and $e = \min(t, d)$. With LSI, the matrix $\vec{S}$ is pruned, so only the k largest singular values are preserved, along with their corresponding vectors in $\vec{T}$ and $\vec{D}'$. When the pruned matrixes are multiplied, the result, $\vec{M}_k = \vec{T}_k \vec{S}_k \vec{D}'_k$, is the closet least squares approximation of $\vec{M}$. The number of dimensions, k, is a critical factor determining the performance of LSI – it should be small enough to reduce noise, but sufficiently large so that the conceptual space can accommodate the semantic patterns in the data. In a geometric interpretation, all documents and terms are treated as points in this semantic space. A user's query, $\vec{Q}$, which is submitted after the conceptual space is constructed, is projected into that space (the projected query $\vec{Q}_k = \vec{Q}' \vec{T}_k \vec{S}_k^{-1}$), and it too is represented as a point in that space. The relevance of documents to a query is calculated based on the distance in the SVD space, commonly as the dot product of the (normalized) query and document vectors (i.e. $Similarity(Q, D) = \left(\vec{Q}_k \vec{S}_k\right)\left(\vec{S}_k \vec{D}_k\right)$).

Since the introduction of the model in the late 80s, many studies have tested the appropriateness of the LSI model for enhancing retrieval effectiveness. Latent Semantic Indexing has been reported to address words ambiguity and enhance performance for mainly small, domain-specific collections, and in many cases its performances surpasses traditional keyword search by as much as 30% (Landauer et al. 1998). Experiments with the MED collection (1,033 documents) show small improvements in Precision in comparison to keyword search, and tests with the CISI collection (1,460 documents) show *no* improvements over term matching (Deerwester et al. 1990). LSI tests for the 9 collections used in TREC1 (of sizes 20k to 226k documents) show average performance levels, compared to the competing systems (Dumais 1993). (Nakov 2000) has tested LSI for a small collection and has shown significant Recall improvements. The studies reported above were conducted in very restrictive environments, where the number of documents is limited and the variability in topics is small. In these environments, LSI deals excellently with synonymy, and it has shown to yield significant improvements in Recall. For polysemy, however, LSI is much less effective, and in most tests it did not yield Precision improvements.

A crucial shortcoming of LSI is the model's sensitivity to the choices of its parameters. The most critical factor in LSI is the number of dimensions (i.e. concepts), and for practical application this parameter is determined through experimentation (Deerwester et al. 1990, Dumais 1993, Dumais 1994, Landauer et al. 1998, Nakov 2000). Other critical parameters determining the performance of LSI are the term weighing scheme employed for the input terms-documents matrix, and the choice on normalization of the document and query vectors. Unfortunately, there is no theory to guide LSI's settings; its usage is in many ways more an art than a science (Nakov 2000).

Because LSI is computationally intensive, most tests of LSI have been conducted in environments where both the number of documents and the variability in topics are limited. At pre-processing, the SVD process, at the heart of LSI, is computationally intensive, and the largest reported test of SVD was for a collection of less than 100,000 documents. The best algorithm for SVD computation has the complexity of

$O(k \times M^2 \times N + k \times N^3)$, where N is the number of documents, k is the number of dimensions, M is the number of unique terms (or tokens), and in most cases $k << M < N$ (Golub & van Loan 1993)[36]. It is not easy to scale-up LSI, and its adequacy for general collections is yet to be verified (Baeza Yates & Ribiero Neto 1999). In order to address LSI's scalability problem, two alternative techniques have been proposed in previous works: (a) decompose the collection into a set of smaller sub-collections; the query is then projected into each of the sub-collections' semantic space, and matched against documents in each of these spaces; or alternatively (b) compute SVD for just a random sample of the collection, and project the remaining documents into that space. These approaches have been explored empirically. In TREC1, a large and heterogeneous document collection was composed of nine distinct homogeneous collections, and LSI was applied separately for each collection. LSI's performance in TREC1 was average, when compared to other systems (Dumais 1992). In TREC2 and TREC3 there was no clear categorical partitioning of the collection, and LSI addressed the scalability issue by constructing the SVD space based on a sample of the documents (roughly 80,000, decomposed with a 199-dimensions SVD) and then projected the remaining documents, as well as the queries, onto that space. Precision levels were 5% better over term matching (Dumais 1993, 1994). Generally speaking, the techniques LSI has applied in TREC may not be appropriate for general collections for two reasons. First, a meaningful partitioning of the collections may not be available. Second, computing the SVD space based on a sample of the documents and folding-in the rest of the documents is only effective if the sampled documents constitute 50% of the collection or more (Dumais 1994), and for very large collections computing SVD for even half of the collections is not feasible.

One last limitation of LSI is that it is inefficient for matching queries to documents during runtime. For query-document matching, queries need to be projected onto the SVD space, and the query and document conceptual vectors are matched. For matching with LSI, an inverted file is not appropriate, since the conceptual document index includes values for almost all terms, and a query needs to be matched with indexes

---

[36] The complexity of SVD depends on the implementation algorithm. The complexity of the algorithm used in (Deerwester at al. 1990) was $O(N^2 \times k^3)$.

for the entire document collection[37] (Deerwester et al. 1990, Dumais 1994), making it significantly less efficient than the token-based model (the complexity of the process is linear with the total number of documents, N).

Hence, LSI is ineffective at both pre-processing and run-time, when compared to the token-based retrieval.

8.2 An Experimental Study of the Synonym-Based Retrieval

In the following section, we review our first-hand experimentation with Latent Semantic Indexing as a representative of retrieval models that are based on synonym set representations. The study is designed to measure both the effectiveness and efficiency of the model. In studying the model's effectiveness we will try to identify the critical factors determining retrieval Precision and Recall. Specifically we will explore the affect of (a) the number of SVD dimensions (i.e. concepts) in the semantic space, and (b) normalization of document and query vectors in the semantic space. Retrieval efficiency will be measured for both pre-processing (the generation of the semantic space) and run-time (projecting a query onto the semantic space and matching query to documents).

8.2.1 Implementation Procedure

We implemented LSI as follows. Pre-processing of documents and queries for all experiments was based on commonly used tokenizing techniques (as used for testing token-based representations and described in Chapter 6): stop-word removal with SMART's common words list (Ide & Salton 1971), stemming with Porter's algorithm (Porter 1980), removal of tokens that appear in few documents[38], and TF-IDF token weighting of documents' indexes. The pre-processed document-term matrix was used as an input for LSI.

Performing SVD on the matrix of 528 thousand documents by 72 thousand tokens is not possible, and the techniques explored previously in the literature for addressing the

---

[37] Rather than matched to only the documents containing the query terms, as is used in token-based retrieval.
[38] We pruned all tokens that appeared in less than five documents.

scalability problem – (a) performing SVD for a portion of the collection and 'folding in' the rest of the documents, and (b) utilizing a pre-existing decomposition of the collection - were not appropriate for our test collection. 'Folding in' is only effective when SVD is computed for over 50% of the collection and SVD was still not feasible for half our test collection, and the existed partitioning of the collection (based on the information sources) still yielded sub-collection that were too large. Hence, we were required to split the collection ourselves, and we arbitrarily decomposed the collection into 100 sub-collections of 5,280 documents each. SVD was performed on the complete set of documents (i.e. we did not fold-in additional documents), and Singular Value Decomposition (SVD) was performed using Matlab[39]. Each query was projected onto each of the 100 semantic spaces (for each of the sub-collections), and the similarity of query to documents was measured in those semantic spaces using the cosine measure, resulting in a ranked list of relevant documents.

8.2.2 Experiments

To test LSI and the parameters affecting the model's performance we designed two experiments:

- Experiment #1 designed to test the effect of the number of dimensions (i.e. number of concepts) employed. We were guided by previous research (suggesting 100-300 dimensions) and the available computational resources. We tested LSI when 150 and 300 dimensions were used in the SVD process, for each of the 100 sub-collections. In this test query and document indexes were *not* normalized prior to matching.

- Experiment #2 was designed to test the effect of vector normalization prior to matching. We tested two variations of LSI: in the first test document and query indexes were *not* normalized (as in Experiment #1); while in the second, once the semantic space was generated and queries were projected onto that space, document and query indexes vectors were normalized in L2 (so that the sum of squares of the conceptual query, $\vec{Q}_k \bullet \vec{S}_k$, and the conceptual document, $\vec{D}_k \bullet \vec{S}_k$, are each equal to

---

[39] Matlab is a commercial product by The MathWorks Inc. 3 Apple Hill Drive, Natick, MA 01760-2098, USA

one) prior to matching. We tested the effect of vector normalization for both 150 and 300 dimensions LSI.

8.2.3 Results and Analysis

The following results were obtained:

Experiment #1

The table below describes the result for Experiment #1 testing the effect of dimension number.

# of dimensions per sub-collection	Precision[10]	Precision[20]	Precision[30]	Recall[1000]
150 SVD dimensions	0.027	0.024	0.020	0.149
300 SVD dimensions	0.059	0.050	0.046	0.207

Table 8-1: results for Experiment #1: LSI performance as a factor of the number of SVD dimensions

The results in the table above indicate that, in general, the performance of LSI for the test collection is poor. In comparison, the performance of the traditional token-based model, based on the exact same pre-processing steps, was significantly higher (for instance, Precision[10] was 0.244, and Precision[20] was 0.204 for the token-based model). The number of dimensions has a significant effect on LSI performance, and employing more dimensions resulted in dramatic gains: Precision levels were roughly twice as high for 300 SVD dimensions (when compared to 150-dimension SVD), and Recall levels were almost 40% better[40].

We suspect that further improvements in performance could be obtained with more than 300 SVD dimensions.

---

[40] Statistical significance for the differences for all Precision and Recall measures is $P<0.01$.

<u>Experiment #2</u>

The results of the second experiment, testing the effect of vector normalization (for both 150 and 300 dimensions), are presented below.

# of dimensions per sub-collection	Normalization	Precision[10]	Precision[20]	Precision[30]	Recall[1000]
150	No	0.027	0.024	0.020	0.149
150	Yes	0.082	0.074	0.069	0.265
300	No	0.059	0.050	0.046	0.207
300	Yes	0.125	0.106	0.098	0.314

Table 8-2: results for Experiment #2: LSI performance as a factor of vector normalization.

The findings suggest that vector normalization has a substantial positive effect on LSI performance. With 150 dimensions, Precision levels are 3 times as high when normalization is used, and Recall levels are almost 80% higher[41]. With 300 dimensions, Precision levels are more than twice as high when normalization is used, and Recall levels are over 50% higher[42].

8.2.4 Discussion

In this chapter, we studied the Latent Semantic Indexing (LSI) retrieval model, and found that the model is computationally intensive and cannot easily scale-up for large collections. As approaches explored in past studies for scaling LSI were not appropriate for our large test collection, we resulted to de-composing the collection arbitrarily into 100 smaller sub-collections, performing SVD distinctively for each sub-collection. This approach addressed efficiency concerns, but resulted in poor effectiveness levels. The best Precision[10] results we obtained with LSI[43] was 0.159 (35% lower than the token-based model), and the best Recall levels were 0.366 (18% lower than the token-based

---

[41] Statistical significance for the differences for all Precision and Recall measures is P<0.001.
[42] Statistical significance for the differences for all Precision and Recall measures is P<0.001.
[43] These results were attained with 300 SVD dimensions, vector normalization, and query weighting.

model). In addition, we found that LSI is very sensitive to the model's parameters, specifically to the choice of vector normalization and the number of SVD dimensions.

In the future we plan to extend our study of Latent Semantic Indexing by exploring alternative realizations of the model, mainly through experimentation with (a) alternative pre-processing steps (document and query tokenizing), and (b) different number of SVD dimensions.

8.3 Conclusion

Concept-based representations try to address one of the most critical problems inhibiting the effectiveness of traditional retrieval systems - the inherent ambiguity of words. Specifically, representations based on synonym sets aim to resolve the problem of synonymy, which is associated with Recall losses. Various approaches for grouping terms into sets of similar meanings (i.e. synonym sets) have been proposed for addressing the problem of synonymy. Automatic extraction of synonyms sets could be based on either (a) clustering or (b) factor-analytic techniques. Both techniques have been explored extensively in the past, resulting commonly in Recall gains and Precision losses. In our experimental study, we explored the performance of the most popular of the factor-analytic approaches – Latent Semantic Indexing (LSI).

To date, LSI has been mainly applied to small or domain-dependent collections and its suitability for general collections has not been established. LSI is computationally expensive, and ad-hoc approaches for scaling-up LSI have resulted in effectiveness losses (Husbands et al. 2000). Decomposing of the collection and performing LSI for smaller sub-collections is an order of magnitude more efficient than LSI for the entire document collection. However, this technique results in poor effectiveness, and both Recall and Precision levels were significantly lower than those obtained with token-based representations.

Since alternative factor-analytic techniques have not been able to attain effectiveness levels beyond those reported for LSI, we argue that factor-analytic techniques for automatically constructing a semantic space are not appropriate for large and heterogeneous collections. The alternative approach for extracting and employing synonym concepts - term clustering for automatic construction of semantic resources that are used for query refinement - may enable Recall gains, but are, too, mainly appropriate for domain-specific collections.

We conclude that it is extremely difficult to automatically extract synonym concepts out of textual information, and design automatic systems that will exploit these conceptual structures for retrieval performance gains. At the current state of technology, fully automatic IR techniques that employ synonym concepts have not yet matured, and in most instances some human involvement is required in order to extract meaningful patterns from text. Thus, for general collections, where manual effort is not possible, synonyms-based IR is not appropriate. IR techniques based on synonyms, such as LSI, remain suitable for domain specific and restricted environments.

Our contribution in this chapter is in establishing the inappropriateness of LSI for general collections, and in validating LSI's acute sensitivity to the model's parameters. The tests of LSI serve to determine typical performance level for synonym-based retrieval.

Chapter 9: Topics in Information Retrieval

In this chapter, we explore the semantic units at the top category of our proposed framework – Topics – as illustrated below.

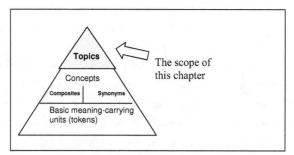

Diagram 9-1: the "Semantic Units Categorization" framework and the scope of this chapter (highlighted in yellow)

We try to address Research Question #1.4: What is the typical performance level for retrieval models that are based on **topics**? To address the question, we will:

- Review prior studies employing topic-based models to gauge at these models' performance, and identify a representative topic extraction technique.
- Conduct an empirical study of topics, extracted with the representative technique
  - o Study the effectiveness of topic-based retrieval, by exploring the effect of the techniques key parameters.
  - o Study the efficiency of topics extraction and matching techniques, to assess whether the techniques could scale up to general collections.

This chapter will continue as follows. In section 9.1 we describe the literature survey, in Section 9.2 we report on our empirical study, and we conclude the chapter in Section 9.3.

9.1 Topics in IR Literature

'Topics' are high-level concepts (also referred to as 'themes', 'categories', or 'classes'), and Chen (2001) suggests that they could be extracted by grouping documents into sets of shared meaning, where each set represents a unique topic. Three approaches to organizing documents into topically-coherent sets exist – (a) using structural information (i.e. metadata) associated with each document, and manually assigning the documents to categories (b) categorization, where documents are automatically assigned to pre-defined categories, and (c) classification, where the pre-defined categories do *not* exist, and classes formed through the automatic process of grouping the documents.

The first approach requires significant manual effort in tagging and manually classifying the documents, and is therefore not appropriate for large collections.

Categorization, the second approach, uses statistical techniques to develop the classifying model, based on a training set of documents (documents in the training set are pre-associated with categories). The model is then used to categorize new documents. This approach has been successfully applied for IR, for example by Chakrabarti et al. (1998). The limitations of automatic categorization are its reliance on the existence of a pre-defined category hierarchy, the fact that it imposes a structure on the collection (rather than reveals the underlying structure), and the need to use a training set. Due to these limitations, categorization is generally more appropriate for domain-specific and static collections, although it can be applied to general collections when a ready made classification scheme is adopted [such as the LookSmart web directory used in (Chen & Dumais 2000)].

Classification, the third approach, is completely automatic and seeks to discover the underlying structure in the collection. Classification is commonly done using clustering algorithms[44], which are scalable to very large collections. There are many possible clustering techniques, which differ in their effectiveness and efficiency, as well as in some of their key characteristics (for instance, the type of distance function used). A review of clustering techniques is beyond the scope of this paper and can be found in (Jain & Dubes 1988).

---

[44] Alternative approaches, such as Factor Analysis or Singular Value Decomposition, exist (see the survey in Part II, Chapter 8), but they are computationally expensive, thus not appropriate for large collections.

Both document categorization and classification have been extensively explored in IR [for a survey of categorization methods in IR see Yang (1998); for a survey of clustering methods see Willett (1988)], with several possible applications:

- Supporting the browsing search mode (i.e. navigating through subject categories), similar to the capabilities provided by some Web search engines, such as Yahoo! Category-driven browsing and Information Retrieval represent two different information access modes, thus browsing is outside the scope of this study.

- Classification of search results – organizing the documents returned to the user into coherent clusters helps users navigate their way in the retrieval result list, and reduces the cognitive effort a user has to expend in order to locate relevant resources. This approach has been extensively studied in recent years [for instance see Hearst et al. (1995), Sahami et al. (1998), Chen & Dumais (2000)], and is beginning to be used by commercial systems (for instance in Northern Light's search engine[45]). When combined with powerful visual representations, clustering of search results can considerably enhance the user experience and enable significantly faster access to relevant documents (Chen & Dumais 2000).

- Cluster-based retrieval – utilizing the topical organization of the complete collection to enhance retrieval performance. Cluster-based retrieval is based on the cluster-hypothesis, which states that "closely associated documents tend to be relevant to the same queries" (van Rijsbergen 1979), and assumes that relevant documents will concentrate in few clusters and that a query could automatically be associated with these clusters, so as to yield effectiveness gains. Cluster-based retrieval has been investigated in the past 30 years, and despite evidence suggesting its potential effectiveness, empirical studies with the model resulted often in effectiveness losses.

Out of the three applications described above, only cluster-based IR is directly related to this study. Category-driven browsing is not an IR application, and clustering of search results is a user-interface method (rather than an information retrieval model).

---

[45] http://www.northernlight.com/

Cluster-based IR, on the other hand, is a topic-based retrieval model, and will serve as the representative topic-based model in our investigation of semantic units. In the following sections we provide a formalize definition of the model and review prior works on cluster-based retrieval.

In cluster-based IR documents and queries are *not* indexed directly through topics, as topics are too broad to be used as indexing units and would not provide a clear distinction between relevant and irrelevant documents. Rather, topical organization of the corpus is employed in cluster-based IR to focus the matching process. The cluster-based model suggests the following steps: documents are initially indexed (commonly through tokens), based on document-document similarity the indexes are subject to clustering, and a representation (i.e. profile) for each cluster is computed. When a user submits a query, it is also indexed, and is matched with the documents in two subsequent steps: (a) the query is matched with cluster profiles, to determine the clusters most similar to the query, and a small set of clusters is selected, and (b) the query is matched with the documents in the selected clusters, and a ranked list of relevant documents is generated.

A formalized definition of this process will follow.
Initially, documents are indexed:

Let t be the number of index terms in the system and k_i be a generic index term.

$K = \{k_1, \cdots, k_t\}$ is the set of all index terms. A non-binary weight $w_{i,j} > 0$ is associated with each index term k_i of a document d_j. For an index term which does not appear in the document test, $w_{i,j} = 0$. The document d_j is associated an index term vector $\vec{d}_j$ represented by $\vec{d}_j = \left(w_{1,j}, w_{2,j}, \cdots, w_{t,j}\right)$. Further, let g_i be a function that returns the weight associated with the index term k_i in any t-dimensional vector (i.e., $g_i\left(\vec{d}_j\right) = w_{i,j}$).

Document indexes are then subject to clustering, and a profile is computed for each cluster

Let G be a cover of k clusters containing together N documents, and C be the set of clusters $C = \{C_1, \cdots, C_k\}$. Let C_m be the mth cluster in G. Let $P = \{P_1, \cdots, P_k\}$ be the set of profiles for C, and P_m be the profile of C_m, where P_m is a t-dimensional vector $\vec{p}_m$, represented by $\vec{p}_m = (w_{1,m}, w_{2,m}, \cdots, w_{t,m})$ (similarly to documents' indexes). A document d_j is associated with cluster C_m, $d_j \in C_m$, based on the similarity between the document and the cluster profile, $sim(d_j, p_m)$. A document may be associated with one or more clusters. In the simple case where clusters are exclusive and each document is associated with one cluster, $d_j \in C_m$, if $sim(d_j, p_m)$ is the maximum similarity over all profiles.

At run-time, when a query is submitted, it, too, is indexed

Let $w_{i,q}$ be the weight associated with the pair $[k_i, q]$, where $w_{i,q} \geq 0$. Then, the query vector $\vec{q}$ is defined as $\vec{q} = (w_{1,q}, w_{2,q}, \cdots, w_{t,q})$ where t is the total number of index terms in the system.

And the query is matched to documents in tow sub-sequent steps – first the query is matched to cluster profiles to determine the cluster/s most similar to the query

A query q_b is associated with one or more clusters, based on it's similarity to the clusters' profiles. Let h_b be the number of clusters associated with query q_b. Then q_b is associated with cluster C_m, $q_b \in C_m$, if the similarity between the query and the cluster profile, $sim(q_b, p_m)$, is amongst the h_b top similarities (i.e. $\max(sim(q_b, p_m))$, $m = 1 \ldots k$).

Second, the query is matched with all documents in each of the selected set of clusters (similarly to the way a query is matched with documents in the Vector-Space model; see Chapter 6).

Query q_b is associated with cluster C_m ($q_b \in C_m$). Let N_m be the set of documents in cluster C_m. The degree of similarity of the document d_j, $d_j \in N_m$, with regard to the query q as the correlation between the vectors $\vec{d}_j$ and $\vec{q}$. This correlation can be quantified several alternative measures, the most common being the *cosine of the angle* between these two vectors. That is,

$$sim(d_i, q) = \frac{\vec{d}_i \bullet \vec{q}}{|\vec{d}_i| \times |\vec{q}|} = \frac{\sum_{i=1}^{t} w_{i,j} \times w_{i,q}}{\sqrt{\sum_{i=1}^{t} w^2_{i,j}} \times \sqrt{\sum_{i=1}^{t} w^2_{i,q}}},$$

where $\left|\vec{d}_j\right|$ and $\left|\vec{q}\right|$ are the norms of the document and query vectors. The factor $\left|\vec{q}\right|$ does not affect the ranking because it is the same for all documents. The factor $\left|\vec{d}_j\right|$ provides a normalization in the space of the documents. Since $w_{i,j} \geq 0$ and $w_{i,q} \geq 0$, $sim(d_i, q)$ varies from 0 to +1.

Finally, a set of ranked documents (based on their similarity to the query) is returned.

Cluster-based retrieval is based on van Rijsbergen cluster hypothesis, suggesting that relevant documents will concentrate in few clusters, yet there is still major controversy in the literature as to the validity of the cluster hypothesis, and studies have provided ambiguous and inconclusive results. Jardine & van Rijsbergen (1971) and van Rijsbergen & Spark-Jones (1973) show some positive results, and Cutting et al. (1992) show that the hypothesis holds for the browsing task. However, Voorhees (1985) shows negative results. Shaw et al. (1997) also challenge the cluster-hypothesis, and show that results obtained by using random clusters are, in fact, no better than those obtained using standard clustering algorithms. More recent support for the clustering hypothesis is provided by results by Xu and Croft (1999) which have shown that for TREC queries, topical organization by global clustering does in fact concentrate most relevant document into a small number of sub-collections. These mixed results have been unable to validate the fundamental hypothesis underlying cluster-based retrieval.

The performance of cluster-based retrieval has been measured in previous studies through efficiency and effectiveness, and the results for each are reviewed below.

Much of the cluster-based IR research has focused on *efficiency*, by restricting the number of documents that have to be matched to the query. In order to achieve run-time efficiency, the collection is initially pre-processed using hierarchical clustering. At run-time, the query index is compared with clusters profiles by traversing down the cluster hierarchy, until the cluster(s) most similar to the query are identified. Efficiency is achieved by matching the query to only the documents in the clusters associated with it. The early experiments of Salton (1968) laid the ground for much of this work. Good (1958) and Fairthorne (1961) were the first to show that automatic classification could be useful in IR. Later works with cluster-based retrieval have established its appropriateness for enhancing run-time efficiency.

However, investigations into the effects of clustering on *effectiveness* of retrieval have yielded mixed or negative results. The cluster-based model does not prescribe the exact number of clusters that should be associated with a query, yet the common practice suggests that only one cluster be associated with each query. In an early work, Jardine & van Rijsbergen (1971), who worked with the small Cranfield collection,[46] argued that clustering has the *potential* to improve effectiveness if the optimal cluster is associated with the query. Croft (1980), using the same data collection, provided support for these findings by demonstrating that associating the query with optimal cluster could yield Precision improvement. Willett (1988) criticized these early findings for using the small and unrepresentative Cranfield collections, and for the fact that in these experiments only one small cluster is associated with each query (typically selecting only 2-3 documents for retrieval). Willett proceeded to conduct an extensive experiment of the model, where he obtained negative results. Results achieved at later studies seem to support Willett's argument. Cutting et al. (1992) state that cluster-based IR performance is indifferent (when compared to traditional Vector-Space IR model), Shaw et al. (1997) reveal poor performance for this approach, and further support for these negative results is given by Singhal and Pereira (1999), who claim that cluster-based IR has yielded results that are "negative to mixed at best". The current consensus in the field is that cluster-based retrieval is ineffective, and commercial retrieval systems nowadays do not employ this model (Cutting et al. 1992). It is still not clear, however, whether the model has the *potential* to enhance retrieval effectiveness (i.e. the difficulties are only in the realization of the model, as suggested by Jardine & van Rijsbergen 1971), or if the model is fundamentally flawed [i.e. the fundamental assumption underlying the model is not valid, as argued by Voorhees (1985) and Xu & Croft (1999)].

In the following section we will describe our first-hand experience with the cluster-based retrieval model, aimed to clarify these issues.

---

[46] Jardine & van Rijsbergen (1971) used a collection of 200 documents and 42 queries.

9.2 An Experimental Study of Topic-Based Retrieval

We designed an empirical study to investigate the cluster-based retrieval model and the reasons underlying its ineffectiveness. We address the concerns raised in Willett's extensive survey (1988). We test the model on a large scale test collection – the TREC database – which serves as a well-accepted benchmark in the field. In addition, rather than testing only the standard realization of the model where each query is associated with only one cluster (i.e. the common realization of the model), we explore alternative realizations of cluster-based retrieval where queries are associated with different number of clusters (from 1 to 30).

Since the effect of cluster-based model on retrieval efficiency is well-established, this study addresses the more problematic aspect of cluster-based IR: its contribution to enhancing retrieval effectiveness.

9.2.1 Experimental Design

Our study of cluster-based retrieval tests the effectiveness of the model, and in addition explores the model's underlying assumptions, namely the cluster hypothesis. It is easy to see that the validity of the clustering hypothesis depends to a great extent on the specific realization of the cluster-based model. For instance, the extent to which relevant documents will concentrate in few clusters depends on the clustering algorithm used for grouping the documents. In addition, the results depend on the specific document collection and the type of queries tested.

Our approach was to partition the cluster hypothesis into a series of more detailed assumptions, as suggested by Shaw et al. (1997), and to test each of the detailed assumptions distinctively. The series of detailed assumption underlying the cluster-based model is listed below.

- **Assumption 1** - If documents in a collection are mapped onto a conceptual space, the distribution of the documents will not be random. Thus the collection could be organized into clusters of documents, where documents within a cluster share similar meaning and documents in different clusters carry different meanings. This assumption has been studied and validated in the past [for instance see Shaw (1993)].

- **Assumption 2** - The clustering algorithm can reveal the inherent structure in the collection and produce topically-coherent sets of documents. Clustering algorithms have been employed for a variety of application, and in many cases show success in discovering structure inherent in the data. Van Risbergen (1979) suggests that many aspects of the clustering algorithm [such as the type of algorithm (hierarchical vs. flat), the type of distance measure used, and the method for calculating clusters profiles] do not have an effect on clustering performance. However, we argue that there is one aspect of clustering that does have an effect on cluster-based retrieval performance – the number of clusters used to decompose the collection. Clustering algorithm pre-determine the number of clusters to be used; if we assume that the collection is organized into classes of similar topics, the algorithms ability to reveal that structure will be largely depend on the extent to which the number of pre-set clusters match the number of topic classes in the collection. We are not aware of any empirical study exploring the effect of the number of clusters in the context of cluster-based retrieval, but experiments with Latent Semantic Indexing (LSI, a technique related to clustering, described in Chapter 8) show that the number of classes[47] used by the algorithm strongly influence retrieval performance (Husbands et al., 2000; Deerwester et al., 1990).

- **Assumption 3** - The documents relevant to a query will concentrate in very few clusters. The third assumption addresses the distribution of relevant documents, and has been explored with indecisive results [e.g. Xu & Croft (1999) obtained positive results, while Shaw et al. (1997) provide negative results].

- **Assumption 4** - The matching function will associate a query with relevant cluster(s) (i.e. the clusters containing the relevant documents). Commonly this is done by measuring the similarity of the query to the cluster profile, very much in the same way documents are matched to a query. The early experiments of Jardin & van Rijsbergen (1971) indicate that associating a query with the appropriate clusters might not be simple, and we suspect that due to the short length of the average query, automatic query-cluster association may be inaccurate.

---

[47] More accurately, 'dimensions', in LSI.

Each of these detailed assumptions rests on the preceding ones, and when all the assumptions hold, cluster-based retrieval should be able to enhance effectiveness. However, as discussed earlier, cluster-based IR has not been shown to provide effectiveness enhancements, suggesting that current realization of the cluster-based model might invalidate the assumptions listed above.

Our proposed approach is to study the validity of each assumption and its effect on retrieval performance, by testing empirically each assumption distinctively, as described in the following sections.

9.2.2 Implementation Procedure

Thus far, our discussion of clustering and its use in IR was very general and did not depend on any specific clustering technique. However, for testing and implementation, it is essential that we employ one specific algorithm, and we chose existing proven techniques for our tests. Below we shortly describe the possible clustering approaches, and justify our design choices.

There are basically two criteria for choosing a clustering technique: (a) the quality or effectiveness of clustering, and (b) the efficiency of the algorithm (van Rijsbergen 1979). The quality of clustering is measured by inter-cluster similarity (cohesiveness of clusters; $\sum_{i=1}^{k} \sum sim(d_j, p_i) \lor d_j \in C_i$) and intra-cluster similarity (the extent to which distinct clusters are different from one another; $\sum^{k} sim(p_i, p_j), p_i \neq p_j$). Efficiency of the algorithm is measured in terms of storage requirements and speed (or the algorithm complexity).

In principle, clustering has two steps: (a) indexing of documents[48], and calculating similarities between documents, and (b) organizing the documents into clusters, based on these similarities. We employed an indexing procedure similar to the one used for testing token-based representations and was described in Chapter 6[49]. In order to speed up

---

[48] According to Rasmussen (1992) the details of the indexing technique and the specific weighting scheme have little impact on clustering.

[49] The tokenizing procedure employed in our study was based on commonly used techniques: stop-word removal with SMART's common words list (Ide & Salton 1971), stemming with Porter's algorithm (Porter 1980), removal of tokens that appear in few documents, and TF-IDF token weighting.

document-document similarity calculations, we pruned all document indexes to include only the top terms[50]. The measure of similarity is designed to quantify the likeliness between documents, and is usually calculated by the cosine of the angle between the document index vectors (similar to similarity calculations for matching, as reviewed earlier), but alternative Cartesian measures (Euclidean, Manhattan, or Minkowski) are also possible. Since the type of similarity measure is unlikely to have an impact on clustering performance (van Rijsbergen 1979), for our implementation we employed a Euclidean similarity (or more accurately, distance) measure, where:

$$sim(d_i, d_j)^{-1} = dis(d_i, d_j) = \sqrt{\sum_{h=1}^{t} (d_{h,i} - d_{h,j})^2} \, .$$

Two main approaches for clustering are available: hierarchical and flat. With hierarchical clustering the clusters are organized in a tree structure, while in the flat organization is non-hierarchical. Hierarchical clustering is the most common technique for cluster-based IR, enabling efficient matching of query to clusters in run-time, by traversing the hierarchy[51]. The complexity of common hierarchical clustering algorithms is $O(N^2)$[52]. Since the usefulness of the model for enhancing run-time efficiency is well-established, and the type of clustering algorithm is unlikely to affect cluster-based retrieval performance (van Rijsbergen, 1979), we chose to use a flat clustering algorithm – K-means (MacQueen, 1967) - which enabled us to speed-up the process of organizing documents into topically-coherent clusters[53]. Below we describe the K-means algorithm:

1. Select k initial points in the tokens space to be used as initial clusters centers (i.e. profiles). The initial point could be specific documents, or an average of several documents' indexes.

2. Assign all documents to these initial points, based on their similarities to the profiles (each document is assigned to the most similar profile).

3. Re-compute the profile for each cluster.

4. Repeat steps 2-3, until the objective function is satisfied

---

[50] For each document index we kept only the terms with the highest weights, that together account for 80% of the total terms' weights. This process reduced the average index length from 138 tokens to 74 tokens.

[51] The complexity of matching query to clusters' profiles is O(Log K), where K is the number of clusters.

[52] Some hierarchical clustering algorithm are more efficient and achieve complexity of $O(N \log(N))$.

[53] The complexity of K-means is rectangular (i.e. $O(lkN)$; where N is the number of documents in the corpus, k is the number of clusters, and l is the number of iterations).

A number of parameters need to be pre-determined for the algorithm:

- Overlapping vs. exclusive clusters – we implemented a simple K-means, where clusters are exclusive.
- Cluster profile – several profile calculation methods are available:
  - Calculating a *centroid*, an average of the representations of all the documents that belong to the cluster.
  - Finding the *medoid*, the document with minimal distances to the rest of the documents in that cluster
  - Finding the *maximal predictor for a cluster*, where terms included in the profile predict the documents that are included in the cluster.

  Since there is no theory to support the selection of cluster profile calculation method, and retrieval effectiveness is unlikely to be effected by the choice of method (van Rijsbergen 1979), we chose to calculate the profile as the cluster centroid. For efficiency purposes, we pruned the centroid vector to include only the top terms[54].

- Number of clusters – there is no theory to guide this choice. To test the assumption on the effect of number of clusters (Assumption #2; see the discussion of cluster-based IR's underlying assumptions above), and we chose to study two different clustering algorithms – the first with 100 clusters, and the second with 200 clusters.
- Size of clusters – for the 100-cluster algorithm, minimum size was set to 2,000 documents and maximum size to 15,000 (cluster sizes for this case are listed in appendix 4). For the 200-cluster algorithm the allowed size was set to 1,000-10,000 documents (cluster sizes for this second case are listed in appendix 5). Clusters that evolved to smaller size than the minimum were terminated, and clusters larger than the maximum were split up[55].
- Objective function – we run the clustering program over several iterations, and employed both inter-cluster similarity and intra-cluster measures for deciding when to terminate the program.

---

[54] For each cluster centroid we kept only the terms with the highest weights, that together account for 80% of the total terms' weights.

[55] In the last iteration of clustering, clusters are not split or terminated, thus the resulting cluster sizes might exceed the limits we set. For instance, in our 200-clusters procedure, Cluster #169 includes only 890 documents, somewhat lower than our threshold.

9.2.3 Experiments

Four experiments were conducted in order to validate the assumptions underlying cluster-based retrieval. All four experiments used the same data set and employed similar measures of retrieval effectiveness.

- Experiment 1 – studied the performance of the cluster-based model, by restricting the query to different number of clusters. For this experiment the collection was decomposed into 100 clusters. While the cluster-based model does not prescribe the exact number of clusters (nor the portion of the collection) that should be associated with each query, it does suggest restricting the query to just few clusters. Thus, we tested the performance of cluster-based retrieval when 1/100, 5/100, 10/100, 20/100 and 30/100 of the clusters are associated with queries.
- Experiment 2 – investigated the effect of the number of clusters used in the clustering algorithm on retrieval effectiveness by comparing 100-cluster and 200-cluster models.
- Experiment 3 – investigated the distribution of relevant documents across clusters, and the effect of this distribution on retrieval effectiveness. For the third experiment we employed the 100-cluster corpus decomposition.
- Experiment 4 – studied the model's ability to associate a query with the relevant clusters, and the effect of the type of clusters associated with a query (relevant vs. irrelevant) on cluster-based IR effectiveness. This experiment, too, used the 100-cluster decomposition.

9.2.4 Results and Analysis

Experiment 1

Average performance levels, for the set of 100 queries, of cluster-based IR (retrieval with less than 100% of the collection), compared to the baseline Vector-Space model (retrieval with 100% of the collection, studied in Chapter 6), are presented in the graph below.

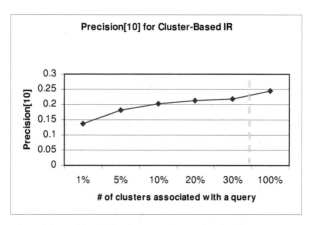

The graph illustrates how retrieval precision drops as fewer clusters are associated with a query. The optimum is achieved for the baseline Vector-Space model, when the entire collection is employed for query-document matching, and then precision declines to reach a minimum when just one percent of the collection is associated with each query.

The results for all the effectiveness measures we employed are presented in the table below.

Clusters per query	1/100	5/100	10/100	20/100	30/100	**100/100**
Precision[10]	0.136	0.181	0.203	0.214	0.219	**0.244**
Precision[20]	0.094	0.128	0.156	0.170	0.180	**0.204**
Precision[30]	0.078	0.105	0.126	0.148	0.156	**0.177**
Recall[1000]	0.155	0.233	0.269	0.314	0.352	**0.440**

Table 9-1: relevance measures for the cluster-based model, compared against the Vector-Space model

The results of the baseline Vector-Space model are presented in the right-most column in bold (100% of the collection used). Table 9-1 demonstrates how Precision and

Recall are both negatively affected by restricting the number of clusters the query is associated with. Thus, the cluster-based model results in effectiveness losses.

Experiment 2

When studying the effect of the clustering procedure on cluster-based IR, we found that the total number of clusters used for decomposing the collection has an effect on cluster-based IR performance. The results for Precision[10] are presented below.

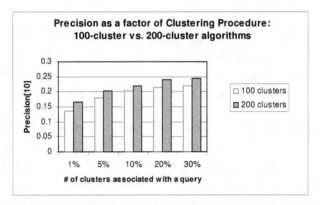

Diagram 9-3: Cluster-based IR Precision[10] when comparing two different types of clustering algorithms: a 100-cluster vs. a 200-cluster algorithm.

The graph illustrated that there is an evident effect for the number of clusters used, for all cases of the cluster-based model (when 1%, 5%, 10%, 20% and 30% of the collection is associated with the queries), and the 200-cluster procedure is superior to the 100-cluster procedure.

Results for all the effectiveness measures we employed are presented in the table below.

Clusters per query	The clustering algorithm	1%	5%	10%	20%	30%
Precision[10]	100 total clusters	0.136	0.181	0.203	0.214	0.219
	200 total clusters	0.166	0.204	0.219	0.241	0.245
	% difference	*+22.1%*	*+12.7%*	*+7.9%*	*+12.6%*	*+11.9%*
Precision[20]	100 total clusters	0.094	0.128	0.156	0.170	0.180
	200 total clusters	0.127	0.162	0.181	0.181	0.199
	% difference	*+33.9%*	*+26.6%*	*+15.7%*	*+12.1%*	*+10.3%*
Precision[30]	100 total clusters	0.078	0.105	0.126	0.148	0.156
	200 total clusters	0.102	0.134	0.152	0.168	0.174
	% difference	*+30.2%*	*+27.6%*	*+20.9%*	*+13.5%*	*+11.3%*
Recall[1000]	100 total clusters	0.155	0.233	0.269	0.314	0.352
	200 total clusters	0.214	0.297	0.338	0.375	0.391
	% difference	*+37.9%*	*+27.6%*	*+25.5%*	*+19.5%*	*+11.2%*

Table 9-2: Cluster-based IR performance when comparing two different types of clustering procedures: a 100-cluster vs. a 200-cluster algorithm.

The table presents significant differences in effectiveness – both Recall and Precision - based on the total number of clusters used for the clustering procedure.

Experiment 3

We examined how relevant documents are distributed in clusters (using a 100-cluster algorithm), and our results are presented below.

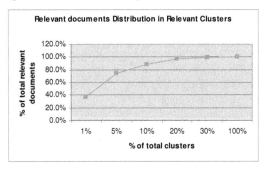

Diagram 9-4: distribution of relevant documents in most relevant clusters (for a 100-cluster clustering algorithm).

The results illustrate that on average relevant documents tend to be distributed in a relative small number of clusters (when selecting the most relevant clusters for each query, 10/100 of the clusters contained almost 90% of the relevant documents). However, when one cluster only is associated with each query (as suggested in most studies of cluster-based retrieval), only 40% of the relevant documents are available for matching.

The results reported above represent the *average* for all the queries tested in our experiment. A closer look at the data reveals differences between the queries – for some queries the relevant documents are concentrated in very few clusters (skewed distribution), while for other queries the distribution of relevant documents is spread more evenly between clusters (i.e. even distribution). In order to explore the effect of relevant documents distribution on cluster-based IR effectiveness, we compared two sets of queries – queries with skewed relevant document distribution across clusters against queries even distribution – and tested the effectiveness levels for the two query sets. The Precision[10] results for different cases of cluster-based IR (associating the query with different portion of the collection) are presented in the table below.

Clusters per query	2/100	5/100	10/100	20/100	30/100
Even distribution of relevant documents across clusters (50 queries)	0.128	0.152	0.196	0.200	0.202
Skewed distribution of relevant documents across clusters (50 queries)	0.202	0.210	0.290	0.228	0.236
% difference	*+58%*	*+38%*	*+48%*	*+14%*	*+17%*

Table 9-3: Precision[10] when comparing queries with an even distribution of relevant documents (relevant documents distributed across many clusters) against queries with skewed distribution of relevant documents (relevant documents are concentrated in few clusters), for different cases of cluster-based IR.

The table above demonstrates how the distribution of relevant documents across clusters effects Precision[10], and similar results were obtained for the other effectiveness measures. We notice that when only a few clusters are associated with the query, the effect of relevant document distribution is significant, but less so when a larger portion of the collection is associated with each query.

Experiment 4

In the fourth and last experiment, we employed a 100-cluster decomposition and studied the degree to which automatic query-cluster matching is able to associate a query with the relevant clusters (i.e. the clusters containing the largest number of relevant documents). When comparing the number of relevant documents in the most relevant clusters (from the results of Experiment 3) against the number of relevant documents in the clusters associated with the query (using automatic query-cluster matching), the following results were obtained.

Clusters per query	1/100	5/100	10/100	20/100	30/100
documents found in **most relevant clusters** as % of total relevant documents (Experiment 3 results)	37%	74%	88%	97%	99%
documents found in **clusters associated automatically with the query** as % of total relevant documents	19%	35%	44%	56%	65%

Table 9-4: distribution of relevant documents in clusters associated with a query, in comparison to the distribution in most relevant clusters. Results are based on 100-cluster clustering algorithm and are described for 5 different cases of cluster-based IR - when 1/100 of the collection is associated with each query, 5/100, 10/100, 20/100, and 30/100.

The results indicate that automatic query-cluster matching is inaccurate. The number of relevant documents contained in the clusters associated with a query is roughly half the number of relevant documents contained in the most relevant clusters. For instance, the ten clusters containing the most relevant documents account for 88% of the total number of relevant documents, while the ten clusters associated with the query account for, on average, only 44% of the total number of documents. Similar effect is obtained regardless of the type of cluster-based retrieval model (i.e. when a different number of clusters are associated with each query).

114

The results reported above represent the average for the entire set of one hundred queries tested in our experiment. A closer look at the data reveals differences between the queries – for some queries the automatically associated clusters contain many relevant documents, while for other queries the associated clusters contain very few relevant documents. In order to study how the ability to associate the query with appropriate clusters affects cluster-based IR performance, we separated the set of hundred queries into two equal groups – one containing queries with a high concentration of relevant documents in the clusters automatically associated with the query, while the other contained queries with a low concentration of relevant documents in the clusters associated with the queries. The table below describes our findings for different cases of cluster-based IR (associating the query with different portion of the collection).

Clusters per query	2/100	5/100	10/100	20/100	30/100
Low concentration of relevant documents in clusters associated with the query (50 queries)	0.074	0.136	0.170	0.184	0.212
High concentration of relevant documents in clusters associated with the query (50 queries)	0.256	0.226	0.316	0.244	0.226
% difference	*+246%*	*+66%*	*+86%*	*+33%*	*+7%*

Table 9-5: Precision[10] when comparing queries with low concentration of relevant documents in associated clusters against queries with a high concentration, for different cases of cluster-based IR (when 2/100, 5/100, 10/100, 20/100, and 30/100 of the collection are associated with each query).

Results show that the ability to associate the relevant documents to the queries is critical for attaining precision, when only a small portion of the collection is associated with each query (the difference between low and high concentration when 2/100 of the collection is associated with each query was 246%), and less critical when a large portion of the collection is associated with queries.

9.2.5 Efficiency Analysis

An analysis of efficiency for cluster-based retrieval provides the following data. Pre-processing for cluster-based IR includes document indexing (linear with N, the total number of documents in the collection), and clustering, which is rectangular for flat algorithms, such as K-means, and polynomial (complexity $O(N^2)$) for hierarchical algorithms). Run-time processing is more efficient than the Vector-Space model, as the query has to be matched to only documents in the clusters associated with it. The efficiency of associating the query with relevant clusters is correlated with the number of clusters, K ($O(\log(K))$ for hierarchical, and $O(K)$ for flat clustering). Matching of query to documents is linear in the number of documents included in relevant clusters.

9.2.6 Discussion

In this chapter we studied the cluster-based IR model, and found that restricting the number of clusters that are associated with each query results in performance losses – the smaller the portion of the collection that is associated with queries, the worse retrieval effectiveness is.

When examining the model's underlying assumptions and their effect on retrieval performance we found that:

- The effectiveness of cluster-based retrieval depends on the clustering algorithm's ability to reveal the collection's underlying structure. The number of clusters collection is decomposed into has an evident effect on retrieval effectiveness, and both Precision and Recall measures were higher when using a 200-cluster algorithm, in comparison to the baseline 100-cluster algorithm. The results of this study do not prescribe the appropriate number of clusters to be used, but it does provide strong evidence on the effect of the clustering procedure on cluster-based IR performance. Thus, it is possible that additional parameters of the clustering procedure, such as whether clusters overlap or are exclusive, may affect the model's performance.

- The distribution of documents that are relevant to a query over the clusters depends on the structure of the collection, the clustering algorithms ability to reveal that structure, and on the specific query. We studied this distribution and found that on average most of the relevant documents *are* distributed in very small number of clusters. This distribution seem to have a small effect on retrieval performance, especially in the cases when only a small portion of the collection is associated with each query.

- The association of appropriate clusters with a query using a standard realization of the cluster-based model is inaccurate, and the clusters that are associated with queries miss significant portion of the relevant documents. On average, the clusters automatically associated with queries contain only 50% of the relevant documents available in the most relevant clusters. This seems to be the model's weakest point, and the results we obtained invalidate the model's assumptions to a large extent. Furthermore, the ability to associate the relevant clusters with the query seems to have a dramatic effect on retrieval performance in the cases where a small portion of the collection is associated with the query.

To summarize, we found that standard realizations of the cluster-based model invalidate, at least to some extent, the model's underlying assumptions. The model's weakest link seems to be the difficulty in associating a query with the clusters containing the relevant documents. We believe that the cluster-based retrieval model has the potential to enhance retrieval effectiveness, but in order to attain that potential, a better way for automatically associating clusters with a query has to be found. A possible direction would be to involve the user in the process, or alternatively use automatic techniques to refine and expand the query. Also, the clustering algorithm employed, and specifically the number clusters chosen to decompose the collection, seem to have an effect on cluster-based retrieval effectiveness. However, determining the appropriate number of clusters would be difficult, and probably depend on the specific document collection.

In the future we plan to explore techniques for enhancing the cluster-based model's effectiveness by addressing the key parameters identified above. Specifically we will test the effect of the number of clusters the collection is de-composed into, and explore alternative methods for automatically associating queries with the most relevant clusters.

9.3 Conclusion

Topical organization through automatic classification of documents is efficient and could scale to very large collections. Classification has proved useful in information access for enabling category-driven browsing, and for clustering search results so that users could easily navigate their way in the retrieval result list. However, the retrieval model that is based on the topical organization of the entire corpus – cluster-based retrieval – has not proved effective for general text collections. The ineffectiveness of the cluster-based model is a long-standing problem in IR, and the analysis of previous works does not clarify whether the shortcoming of cluster-based retrieval are due to its theoretical foundations or caused by inappropriate realizations of the model. Our large-scale experimental study reveals that, to a large extent, the cluster hypothesis underlying the model holds, and that the model is limited by difficulties in realization, specifically in associating the query with the most relevant clusters. We believe that potentially, topic-based retrieval could yield effectiveness gains, however further research is warranted in order to substantiate this claim.

Our contribution in this chapter is in advancing the understanding of cluster-based retrieval and the factors inhibiting its performance. Our large-scale empirical study is the first to explore alternative realizations of the model, where queries are associated with a different number of clusters, thus demonstrating the correlation between the number of clusters associated with queries and retrieval effectiveness. We found that standard realizations of the model, where each query is associated with only one cluster, result in substantial effectiveness losses, suggesting that more clusters have to be associated with queries. Employing the alternative realizations of the model was also useful in the analysis of the cluster hypothesis' validity, and clarified the contradicting results to date – the assumption is valid to some extent, depending on the number of clusters that are associated with queries. In addition, to the best of our knowledge, this study provides the first empirical evidence for the effect of the clustering algorithm (and specifically, the number of clusters the collection is decomposed into) on retrieval effectiveness. Lastly, we were able to demonstrate the ineffectiveness of standard automatic query-cluster association, suggesting that it is *the* major factor inhibiting cluster-based retrieval's performance. The tests of cluster-based IR serve to determine typical performance level for topic-based retrieval.

Chapter 10: Part II Summary

Part II of this dissertation addressed the first research question, and tried to establish typical performance levels for the four types of semantic units of our proposed framework – Tokens, Composite Concepts, synonym Concepts, and Topics – and compare these performance levels. In order to attain this goal, we (a) surveyed the literature by mapping previous works to our framework's categories (based on the semantic units employed in representations), and studies the performance levels obtained for works in each category, and (b) conducted a large-scale empirical study to test the performance of a representative model from each of the framework's four categories.

Each of the four chapters of Part II was dedicated to one semantic unit category. In Chapter 6 we reviewed the use of 'Tokens' (i.e. basic meaning-carrying units) in IR, and reported the results of an empirical study using standard token indexing (i.e. token extraction and weighting) methods. In Chapter 7 we surveyed the use of 'Composite Concepts' in IR, and described our first-hand experimentation with statistical proximity models for extracting composites. In Chapter 8 we reviewed how 'Synonym Concepts' could be used in IR, and reported the results of a study of Latent Semantic Indexing (LSI). Finally, in Chapter 9 we surveyed the use of 'Topics' in information retrieval, and described our experiments with the cluster-based retrieval model.

The findings from the literature review and empirical tests were reported in chapters 6-9. Below we will summarize these findings and answer Research Question #1: How does the performance of retrieval model that are based on alternative artificial semantic units compare?

The most important finding from this part of the dissertation is that there are significant differences in performance for retrieval models that are based on different semantic units. Following we compare effectiveness (Precision and Recall) and efficiency levels for the different categories of semantic units. For our comparison, we employ the levels obtained for tokens as our baseline (Precision[10] level of 0.244, and

Recall[1000] level of 0.445; see details in Chapter 6), since the token indexing methods we used are the de-facto standard for retrieval systems.

Precision analysis reveals differences of over 40% between semantic units. Similar findings were observed for all Precision measures, and the figures presented in this section are based on Precision[10] results. Precision[10] for composite concepts were on average 14% higher than the token baseline, and for some cases (i.e. queries that contained high frequency of composites) were 41% higher (see details in Chapter 7). Synonym concepts (using Latent Semantic Indexing, and with optimal settings) performed poorly in our experiments (see details in Chapter 8) – 51% lower than the token baseline. Topic-based retrieval (with the cluster-based model; see details in Chapter 9) resulted in Precision losses – 10% loss when each query is associated with 20 out of the 200 clusters and 1% loss with 40/200 clusters. The diagram below compares the typical performance levels for the four categories of artificial semantic units.

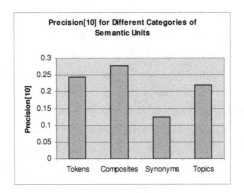

Diagram 10-1: typical Precision[10] levels for different categories of semantic units. Topic-based retrieval with 20/200 clusters per query.

We cannot compare these findings directly to previous studies, as there is no other study that isolates and compares the effect of semantic units; however, we can contrast our finding with the knowledge obtained through the literature analysis, as discussed following. Composites concepts were not compared previously to tokens on a well-established benchmark, but evidence from systems that employed this representation model [e.g. (Carmel et al. 2001)] corroborate our deduction that composites have the potential to enhance Precision. Synonym concepts have been reported to yield Precision levels that are equal to those of tokens [e.g. (Dumais 1992)]; however, most tests with synonyms were performed on rather small and homogeneous collections. Our tests revealed poor Precision levels for synonyms, and thus we conclude that synonyms are inappropriate for general collections. Lastly, previous studies on topic-based indexing suggest that the model has the potential to enhance Precision, but results in Precision losses in most any realization. Our experiments corroborate prior knowledge and we found that cluster-based retrieval is imprecise (see details in Chapter 9).

Recall analysis reveals significant differences of over 40% between the artificial semantic units. Recall[1000] for Composite concepts was on average 44% lower than the token baseline, and even the best performing queries (those with high composite frequencies) resulted in losses of almost 30% (see details in Chapter 7). Synonym concepts (with optimal settings) performed somewhat better than composites, but still resulted in substantial Recall losses of 29% compared to the token baseline (see details in Chapter 8). Topic-based retrieval (when each query is associated with 20 out of the 200 clusters) resulted in Recall losses of approximately 24% compared to the token baseline (see details in Chapter 9). The diagram below compares the typical Recall levels for the four categories of artificial semantic units.

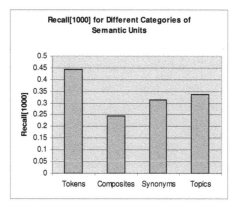

Diagram 10-2: typical Recall[1000] levels for different categories of semantic units. Topic-based retrieval with 20/200 clusters per query.

Similarly to Precision analysis, we cannot compare the Recall levels obtained in our experiments directly to previous studies, but we can contrast our finding with the knowledge obtained through the literature analysis. Recall levels of composites concepts were not compared previously to tokens on a well-established benchmark; however, Baeza-Yates and Ribiero-Neto (1999) corroborate our findings and suggest that indexing based on co-occurrence statistics (i.e. composite concepts) mostly addresses the problem of polysemy (i.e. one word referring to several concepts), thus can enhance Precision but not Recall. The results we obtained for Synonym concepts are the most surprising ones, as they contradict prior knowledge. Synonyms are intended to address the problem of synonymy (i.e. several words referring to the same concept) and enhance Recall, and previous works report on substantial Recall gains for this approach (e.g. (Landauer et al. 1998)). The low Recall levels we obtained for synonyms could be explained by the sensitivity of concept extraction method to the model's parameters and the fact that prior tests with Latent Semantic Indexing were performed on rather small and homogeneous collections, and thus are unrepresentative of the performance levels that are expected in general-collections retrieval. The Recall losses for topic-based retrieval are not surprising and corroborate previous knowledge, since the representative model tested – cluster-based retrieval – prescribes matching the query with only a small portion of the collection, and is intended to enhance Precision at the cost of Recall.

An analysis of the *efficiency* of semantic unit extraction and matching processes reveals that token-based retrieval is the most economical. Token based indexing is linear in the number of documents, and each document indexing is linear in the number of tokens; query-document matching is linear with the number of documents that contain query tokens. Composite concept extraction requires additional processing that is linear with the number of documents, and theoretically the indexing of each document is polynomial with the number of composites. Thus, techniques for simplifying the extraction process are required, for instance the linear algorithm we proposed in Chapter 7. Matching based on composites is theoretically as complex as token matching; although for our realizations, composite matching was more efficient as document composite indexes were significantly shorter than the token indexes. Synonym concepts extraction is inefficient, and the complexity of the Latent Semantic Indexing (LSI) approach we tested is $O(k \times M^2 \times N + k \times N^3)$, where N is the number of documents, k is the number of dimensions (i.e., concepts), M is the number of unique tokens. The complexity of LSI inhibits its use for large collections. Matching with synonyms, too, is less efficient than token matching, as the query has to be matched with all documents. Topic-based retrieval requires prior organization of the collection to clusters, which is linear (at best) with the number of documents, thus is scalable to very large collections. Topic-based matching is more efficient than token matching, as only a subset of the document set is matched with the query. Hence, topic-based retrieval offers efficient run-time processing, at the cost of additional pre-processing.

Overall, when we compare the *performance* of the different semantic units, token-based retrieval seems the most suitable for general collections, due to its simplicity and the inability of higher-level semantic units to provide substantial effectiveness improvements. Composites have provided some Precision gains and we believe that, with further improvements, could enable additional Precision increases. Early indications regarding the adoption of composite indexing by Web search engines (Pedersen 2003) provides additional support for composites potential to enhance Precision[56]. The main challenge for composite-based retrieval is in limiting the complexity of composite extraction and storage. Synonym-based retrieval was inefficient, provided disappointing effectiveness results, and its performance proved to be very sensitive to the model's parameters. Due to these limitations, we deem synonym-based retrieval unsuitable for general collections. Lastly, topical organization of the collection requires some additional pre-processing, but has the potential to improve Precision (at the cost of Recall losses). Further research on this model is warranted in order for cluster-based retrieval to attain its full potential. The inability of concept and topic based retrieval to provide substantial performance improvements over token-based retrieval demonstrate the difficulty in automatically extracting meaningful patterns from text. We believe that linguistic techniques and semantic resources may be required in order to generate more meaningful

---

[56] In very large collections, such as the World Wide Web, information searchers are often overloaded with a large number of results, and often explore only a very small subset of these results. Hence, IR systems for these environments, such as Web search engines, are interested mainly in enhancing Precision.

representations that will lead to improved retrieval; however, the great challenge with these approaches is scaling-up to general collections.

In order to compare the performance levels of the four semantic unit categories, we conducted four comprehensive sets of experiments that investigated one representative model from each category. These investigations have lead to some interesting findings, as summarized below.

Experiments with token-based representations (see Chapter 6) corroborated previous knowledge (e.g. the usefulness of token weighting), and were mainly used to establish a baseline to which the performance of alternative semantic units could be compared against.

Our study of composite concepts (see Chapter 7) is the first study of its kind to test the effect of composites in isolation. Our experiments reveal the model's sensitivity to several parameters, namely the number of unique concepts employed, and to a lesser extent – to the size of query indexes. The weighting scheme we tested for document indexes (i.e. TF-IDF), on the other hand, had little effect on performance. We proposed an efficient algorithm for addressing complexity of composite extraction, and our experiment provides the first empirical evidence for the usefulness of automatically extracted composite concepts in large and heterogeneous settings.

The findings from the experiments with synonym concepts based on LSI (see Chapter 8) contradict prior knowledge and result in both Precision and Recall losses when compared to token-based retrieval. Prior published works report successes for LSI, mainly in terms of Recall, and our findings challenge these previous studies. We suspect that two factors inhibited the performance of synonym-based retrieval with LSI: (a) we tested the approach for general collections, while most of the previous results were obtained for small and homogeneous collections, and (b) the model is very sensitive to the choice of parameters, and we explored only a portion of the parameter space. Our study of topics in IR using the cluster-based model (see Chapter 9) revealed the factors inhibiting the model's performance. Previous studies established the model's potential and reported on gaps between this potential and experimental results, but provided very little insight on the causes for cluster-based retrieval's inability to attain its potential. We found that, to a large extent, the cluster hypothesis underlying the model holds, and that the model is limited by difficulties in realization, specifically in associating the query with the most relevant clusters. In addition, our study is the first to explore alternative realizations of cluster-based IR, where queries are associated with a different number of clusters, thus demonstrating the correlation between the number of clusters associated with queries and retrieval effectiveness. Lastly, to the best of our knowledge, our study provides the first empirical evidence for the effect of the clustering algorithm (and specifically, the number of clusters the collection is decomposed into) on retrieval effectiveness.

Another noticeable finding from the studies of Part II is that, regardless of the semantic unit employed, the performance of a retrieval system that is based on classic methods (i.e. the Vector-Space model) is substantially inferior to the optimal performance levels reported in the literature. For example, the best retrieval systems that competed at the 8th Text Retrieval Conference (TREC8)[57] achieved Precision[30] levels of up to 0.4 (Spark-Jones 1999), roughly double the levels observed in our experiments. It is important to stress that our interest was not in developing the optimal retrieval system; rather, we were interested in isolating the effect of semantic units. Still, these gaps in performance levels are illuminating. The low performance levels obtained in our studies could be attributed to the fact that the systems competing at TREC included various features that were excluded from our realizations. First, we excluded features that were related to the user side, such as advanced interfaces and query refinements methods. The scope of this dissertation was restricted to extracting representations based solely on the document collection, while systems competing at TREC excluded advanced features on the user side. Second, since we were interested in isolating the effect of the semantic units, we employed a classic retrieval model. Most systems at TREC, however, employed more advanced retrieval models [e.g. the Probabilistic model (Robertson & Spark-Jones 1976)] and weighting schemes [e.g. BM25 (Robertson et al. 1998)]. We learn from these findings that, notwithstanding the importance of semantic units, other aspects of a

---

[57] TREC8, the 8th Text Retrieval Conference, was the last competition of the classic retrieval task (referred to as 'ad-hoc' retrieval. The testing of this type of information access method was discontinued in subsequent TRECs after improvements for ad-hoc retrieval have ceased.

retrieval system's design are essential for obtaining high performance levels. In Part IV, when we describe future research, we will discuss these additional aspects.

To summarize, the comparison of semantic unit performance revealed some significant differences. However, overall, concept and topic-based retrieval did not yield substantial improvements beyond the performance levels obtained for the traditional token-based retrieval model. We believe that the inability of artificial semantic representations to enhance performance substantially results from the inaccuracy in automatically extracting semantic units. We know that manually extracted semantic representations can enhance IR performance dramatically [e.g. see (Chen 2001) for a series of examples], thus the limitation of the artificial semantic approaches we've encountered is not in the semantic approach per-se, but rather in the accuracy of the automatic extraction process. In addition to comparing the performance of alternative semantic units, our extensive studies of each semantic unit revealed new findings, e.g. the factors inhibiting the effectiveness of cluster-based retrieval. In the concluding part of this dissertation – Part IV – we will discuss the limitation of our study and point to future research directions that could extend the work of this dissertation.

Part III – Combinations of Semantic Units

In this part of the dissertation, we try to address the second research question: "does the combination of two distinct artificial semantic units in one coherent retrieval model enable performance gains beyond the levels obtained for each semantic unit separately?" In Part II, we established typical performance levels for each distinct artificial semantic unit; now we intend to explore whether combining different semantic units in one retrieval model could enhance performance. To illustrate this idea we will repeat the analogy of cooking, or more specifically - barbequing a chicken (described in Chapter 4). In this analogy, in Part II we focused on the effect of spices on the taste, by studying four different categories of spices (garlic, honey, salt, and pepper) and fixing the rest of the ingredients chicken type and the cooking process. In Part III of this dissertation, we would like to investigate whether mixing the spices would result in a better product. Mixing the spices is challenging for two reasons. First, it is hard to predict which spices will go well together (e.g. honey and garlic) and what won't (e.g. salt and honey). Second, determining how to mix the two spices in the cooking process is not straightforward. Similarly, combining different semantic units, which traditionally are treated as substitutes, is challenging because (a) it is hard to predict which combinations will prove effective, and (b) it requires designing a retrieval model that combines the different types of semantic units. Existing IR models employ semantic units from only one category of our proposed framework – Tokens, Concepts, or Topics. *Interactions* between categories, though, are only used when representations of Tokens (i.e. token-based representations) are used as an input in the process of generating higher level representations (what we refer to as a 'bottom-up' approach, as illustrated below). For example, normally token-based representations are used as an input for extracting concepts (both synonyms sets and composite concepts), and these token-based representations are employed in the clustering of documents into topically coherent sets. However, to the best of our knowledge, prior work does not consider 'top-down' integration, where higher-level semantic units are used to re-define lower level units.

As argued in Chapter 4, we believe that such top-down integration has the potential to enhance retrieval performance beyond the levels obtained for each semantic unit separately. To demonstrate the logic in this argument, assume that semantic units in the top category of the "Semantic Unit Categorization" framework proposed in Part I - 'Topics' - are extracted and the collection is decomposed into topically coherent sets, where each document is associated with a topic. This organization provides semantic context and could now be used to better extract artificial semantic units at lower categories, for instance in the extraction of synonym concepts. Traditionally (i.e. with no combinations of semantic units), when a semantic space is generated for a heterogeneous collection and synonyms sets are extracted, tokens that have several meanings may confound the automatic extraction process. For instance, the token 'state' may be associated into the same synonym set as tokens describing a *country* (e.g. 'federation', 'kingdom', 'nation'), as well as tokens describing a *condition* (e.g. 'situation', 'position', 'status'), forming the ambiguous synonyms set {state, federation, situation, kingdom, position, nation, status}. Now assume that we combine different semantic units in one coherent retrieval model, and prior to generating the semantic space we organize the collection into topically-coherent set. This organization is likely to group documents describing *a country* into one set, and documents describing *a condition* into another document set. Now, if we were to produce a distinct semantic space for each topically-coherent set, the generated synonym sets will not be ambiguous – in the set describing *a country* we will extract the synonym set {state, federation, kingdom, nation}, while in the set describing *a condition* we will extract the synonym set {state, situation, position, status}.

Part III of our research is the first exploration into an uncharted domain, where we try to combine distinct semantic units into a coherent retrieval model. Our aim here is twofold: (1) to design a novel retrieval model by exploring the interplay between semantic units from different categories, and (2) to study the extent to which a novel retrieval model, integrating semantic units from different categories, could yield effectiveness enhancements beyond the performance levels of retrieval models that are based on semantic units from a single category.

A comprehensive evaluation of all possible interactions between the semantic units reviewed on Part II is clearly beyond the scope of this dissertation; hence, our experimental studies will explore only a subset of the possible interactions. We believe that the set of interaction explored is large enough to provide evidence as to the value of interactions between retrieval models across categories.

We will explore two types of semantic unit combinations. In the first type (described in Chapters 11-13), we organize the collection into topically-coherent sub-collection to provide a semantic context, and employ that semantic context to re-define the lower-level semantic units – tokens (described in Chapter 11), composite concepts (described in Chapter 12), and synonym concepts (described in Chapter 13). The topical organization could be utilized for re-defining the lower-level semantic units in two ways: (a) in indexing, by re-selecting the semantic units or by re-assigning weights, based on the topical organization, and (b) by utilizing the contextual information to modify the matching process. In the first three chapters of Part III, we explore different approaches for utilizing the contextual information. In Chapter 11, we re-weight tokens based on topical organization, and proposed a modified matching process; in Chapter 12 we explore a novel matching process based on composite concepts; and in Chapter 13 we use the topical organization for both extracting synonym concepts and query-documents matching with synonym representations. The second type, explored in Chapter 14 and 15, proposes a simpler combination of semantic units, where query-document matching is based on two types of indexes. In Chapter 14 query and document indexes of both tokens and composites are used for matching, and in Chapter 15 we proposed an integrated matching process of token and synonym-based indexes.

For the experiments of Part III we will employ the same test collection (TREC database; disks 4 and 5) and same performance measures used in Part II (Precision[10], Precision[20], Precision[30], and Recall[1000]).

The extraction of concepts and topics requires a pre-processing where tokens are extracted and are employed to index documents. In order to 'level the playing field', we used the same token extraction pre-processing steps (based on the tokenizing procedure described in Chapter 6) in the implementations of all the different retrieval models.

Part III will continue as follows: in Chapter 11 we design a retrieval model that exploits the interaction between 'Topics' and 'Tokens'; in Chapter 12 we design a retrieval model by integrating semantic units from 'Topics' and 'Composite Concepts' categories; in Chapter 13 we develop a retrieval model that combines semantic units from 'Topics' and 'Synonym Concepts' categories; in Chapter 14 we integrate token-based and composite-based matching; and in Chapter 15 we integrate token-based and synonym-based matching. In each of these chapters, we describe the retrieval model we developed, as well as the results of an empirical study evaluating the performance of the model. Finally, we will conclude Part III of the dissertation in Chapter 16 by summarizing the findings and drawing conclusions.

The diagram below illustrates the correspondence between the chapters of Part III and the "Semantic Unit Categorization framework" (introduced in Part I).

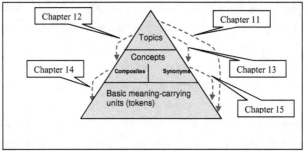

Diagram III-a: the "Semantic Unit Categorization framework", the interplay between semantic units from distinct categories (illustrated by blue arrows), and the corresponding chapters of Part III

Chapter 11: Exploring the Interplay between 'Topics' and 'Tokens'

In this section we will try to address Research Question #2.1: Could 'Topics' and 'Tokens' be integrated into one coherent retrieval model? And if yes – how will the performance of the combined model compare to the performance of 'Topics' and 'Tokens'-based models? To address the question, we will:

- Propose a novel retrieval model that combines topical organization of the collection and token-based retrieval. We will employ the semantic context provided by the topical organization to re-design the indexing and matching processes of token-based retrieval.
- Conduct an empirical study of the proposed model, based on the representative techniques for token and topics based retrieval (described in Chapters 6 and 9 respectively).
  - o Study the effectiveness of the model, by exploring the effect of key parameters.
  - o Study the efficiency of the proposed model.
  - o Compare the performance of the combined model to that of token-based and topic-based retrieval.

This chapter will continue as follows. In Section 11.1 we will develop the novel retrieval model, and in Section 11.2 we will report the finding from an empirical study that investigated one realization of the model proposed in Section 11.1.

11.1 A Novel Retrieval Model Combining Topics and Tokens

The development of the combined retrieval model begins at two starting points: (a) token-based retrieval, specifically the Vector-Space model (reviewed in Chapter 6), and (b) cluster-based retrieval (reviewed in Chapter 9). In the following sections we will recap some of the important point for each of these models, and then proceed to discuss the combination of the models.

132

11.1.1 Recap: Token-Based Retrieval

Retrieval based on tokens, and specifically the Vector-Space model (Salton et al. 1975), prescribes the following steps: (1) producing token-based indexes for documents (and later, at run-time, for queries) by extracting tokens and assigning weight to tokens in the indexes, and (2) matching the query and document indexes, to produce a ranked list of 'assumed-to-be relevant' documents.

Token extraction (or 'tokenizing') is based on Luhn's (1958) principles for identifying meaning-carrying units. Tokenizing commonly includes the following processes: removal of high-frequency terms (through a stop-word list), stemming, and removal of low-frequency terms.

Two factors determine retrieval effectiveness: exhaustivity and specificity. Indexing *exhaustivity* is defined as the number of different topics indexed, and is usually associated with Recall. Indexing *specificity* is defined as the ability of the index to describe topics precisely, and is associated with Precision.

Weighting schemes are employed to assign weights to index terms, and these schemes try to balance exhaustivity and specificity. Exhaustivity is commonly addressed through a local (to the document) factor in the weighting scheme, usually the frequency of the terms in the document (or the normalized frequency). Specificity is commonly addressed through a global factor, correlated with the frequency of the term in the entire collection. The local factor is positively correlated with the weight, while the global factor is negatively correlated with the weight. Different weighting schemes have been proposed in the past, and the de-facto standard is Term-Frequency Inverse-Document-Frequency (TF-IDF), defined formally below:

Let N be the total number of documents in the collection and n_i be the number of documents in which the index term k_i appears. Let $freq_{i,j}$ be the raw frequency of term k_i in the document d_j (i.e., the number of times the term k_i is mentioned in the text of the document d_j). Then, the normalized frequency $f_{i,j}$ of term k_i in the document d_j is given by $f_{i,j} = \dfrac{freq_{i,j}}{\max_l freq_{i,j}}$, and is referred to as the *Term Frequency, TF,* factor. The maximum, $\max_l freq_{i,j}$, is computed over all terms which are mentioned in the text of the document d_j. If the term k_i does not appear in the document d_j then $f_{i,j} = 0$. The *Inverse Document Frequency* factor, *IDF,* for k_i is given by $IDF_i = \log \dfrac{N}{n_i}$. The best known term-weighting scheme use weights which are given by

$$w_{i,j} = TF \times IDF = f_{i,j} \times \log \frac{N}{n_i}.$$

The first component of TF-IDT, TF, is calculated as the relative frequency of the specific token in the document and is associated with exhaustivity; the second component, IDF, is calculated as the relative frequency of the token in the entire collection and is associated with specificity.

Document indexes are pre-processed, and query is indexed at run-time. The calculation of query-document similarity performed based on the cosine of the angle between the vector indexes.

Token-based retrieval, and specifically the Vector-Space model, is the ad-hoc standard for commercial retrieval systems, and to date the majority of retrieval systems for general collections are based on this model. Recently, with the rapid explosion of information and the increasing usage of retrieval systems, traditional token-based models have been criticized for returning too much irrelevant information.

11.1.2 Recap: Cluster-Based Retrieval

Cluster-based retrieval (van Rijsbergen 1979) employs a topical organization of the collection to enhance retrieval performance. The cluster-based model is an extension to the Vector-Space retrieval model, and employs similar procedures for indexing documents and queries and for measuring query-document similarity. Cluster-based retrieval deviated from the Vector-Space model by decomposing the collection into topically coherent clusters (in a pre-process), and then, in run-time, matching the query against documents in two subsequent steps: (1) the query is associated with only few clusters (based on its similarity to the clusters' profiles), and (2) the query is matched to documents contained in the restricted set of clusters associated with the query. Cluster-based retrieval was shown to have the potential to enhance Precision (at the cost of Recall losses); however, to data, experiments with the model resulted in Precision losses.

11.1.3 Combining Token-Based and Cluster-Based Retrieval

We argue that the organization of documents into topically-coherent sets, employed in the cluster-based model, provides semantic context that could be used to adjust the indexing and matching processes. We introduce two principles that we argue are necessary for topic-based retrieval: (a) cluster based weighting, and (b) cluster-based matching. We will describe these principles below.

11.1.3.1 Cluster-Based Weighting

As mentioned in Section 11.1.1, the indexing process is influenced by two critical factors: exhaustivity and specificity. While exhaustivity is a local factor and is not likely to be affected by the decomposition of the document collection into clusters, specificity is highly dependent on our definition of "the collection". In the cluster-based model the collection is decomposed into sub-collections (i.e. clusters), and in the case where the query is associated with one or few clusters, these clusters are used as the complete set of documents to be matched to the query (i.e. the selected clusters form "the collection" for matching purposes). We argue then that the use of only a small set of documents as candidates for retrieval should have implications for the indexing process, namely it should change our view of specificity.

To illustrate this idea consider a document index, D, that contains 20 index terms: a-t, where a and b appear frequently in the collection, thus their specificity is small (they are not useful in discriminating document D from other documents), and this is reflected in the terms weights in D. Now assume that this document was clustered into a set of documents that share the index terms c-t (but not a or b). In the case where this cluster is the only cluster associated with the query, "the collection" is composed of only the documents in that cluster. In this scenario the specificity of index terms a and b is now much higher, since they are useful in discriminating document D from the rest of the documents in the cluster, and the weight of these terms in D should increase.

In the commonly used TF-IDF weighting scheme, the IDF component (calculated as $IDF_i = \log\dfrac{N}{n_i}$, where N is the total number of documents in the collection and n_i is the number of documents in which the index term k_i appears) is associated with the specificity factor. We argue that when the collection is decomposed into topically-coherent clusters, D needs to be modified, such that $IDF *_i = \log\dfrac{N^*}{n^*_i}$, where N^* is equal to the total number of documents in the clusters associated with the query, and n^*_i is equal to the total number of documents in the selected clusters containing the index term i. We term this principle *Cluster-Based Weighting*, and propose that it should be utilized in cluster-based retrieval to modify the weighting of tokens in document and query indexes.

11.1.3.2 Cluster-Based Matching

Consider the matching process in cluster-based retrieval, as illustrated below.

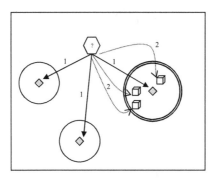

Diagram 11-1: matching process in cluster-based retrieval. The question mark represents a query and the circles represent clusters. Diamond shapes at the clusters' profiles, and boxes represent documents. The solid arrows represent the initial matching of query to clusters, and the dotted lines represent the subsequent matching of query to documents in the most relevant clusters.

In cluster-based retrieval, initially the query is matched with cluster profiles (see bold arrows in the diagram above), and the cluster/s most similar to the query is selected (the double-circled cluster). Then, the query is matched against documents in the selected cluster/s (dotted arrows), to find the most similar documents. Hence, the relevance of a document, D, to a query, Q, $R(Q, D)$, is calculated by the similarity of the two, $sim(Q, D)$, thus $R(Q, D) = sim(Q, D)$. The additional information regarding the topical organization of the collection is only employed to restrict the number of clusters, but not to judge the similarity of a document to the query.

We argue that the additional information available through the topical organization of the corpus - namely (a) the similarity of the query to the cluster profile, $sim(Q, P)$[58], and (b) the similarity of the cluster profile to the document, $sim(P, D)$[59] - could be utilized in estimating the relevance of a document to a query. The diagram below illustrates the additional information that clustering makes available, and that could possibly be utilized in matching.

---

[58] Information of query-profile similarity, $sim(Q, P)$, is readily available, as it is used in cluster-based retrieval to restrict the number of clusters that are associated with a query.
[59] Information of profile-document similarities, $sim(P, D)$, is readily available as it is calculated for the clustering procedure.

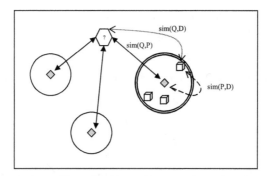

Diagram 11-2: information that could be exploited for matching: query-document *sim*(Q,D) employed in the traditional cluster-based retrieval model for evaluating a document's relevance, and the additional information available through the topical-organization of the collection: query-profile similarity *sim*(Q,P), and profile-document similarity *sim*(P,D). Circles represent clusters, diamonds represent cluster profiles, boxes represent documents, and the question mark represents the query.

Since the calculation of similarity of a document to a query provides us with only an approximation of how relevant the document is to the user's query, we conjecture that by employing the additional information available through clustering, we could attain a better estimate of the document's relevancy to a query.

To demonstrate how this additional information could become useful, we will provide some examples. First, we will demonstrate the potential usefulness of the similarity between a the cluster profile and a document, $sim(D,P)$. Consider the simple case, where two documents d_1 and d_2 belong to the same cluster, $d_1, d_2 \in C_1$, where P_1 is the profile of the cluster, and the similarity of the query to the two documents is equal (i.e., $sim(Q,d_1) = sim(Q,d_2)$). A possible way of discriminating between the two documents would be to consider their distance from the cluster profile. Since the cluster represents a semantic region with its center at the profile, and the query was associated with the cluster based on its similarity to the profile, it is reasonable to assume that the similarity of a document to the cluster profile conveys meaning. Hence, if document d_1 is closer to the profile, $sim(P_1, d_1) > sim(P_1, d_2)$ then we would deduce that d_1 is more relevant to the query, even though the similarity of the query to both documents is similar.

Second, we will demonstrate the potential usefulness of the similarity between a query and the cluster profile, $sim(Q, P)$. Consider the case where two documents d_1 and d_2 belong to two different clusters, $d_1 \in C_1$ and $d_2 \in C_2$, and both documents are within the same distance to the query (i.e. $sim(Q, d_1) = sim(Q, d_2)$), as illustrated below.

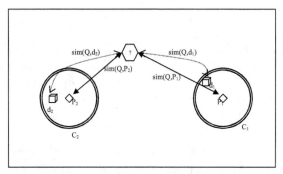

Diagram 11-3: demonstrating the potential usefulness of query-profile similarity. The case where two documents d_1 and d_2 belong to two different clusters, $d_1 \in C_1$ and $d_2 \in C_2$, and both documents are within the same distance to the query (i.e. $sim(Q, d_1) = sim(Q, d_2)$). The profile of the cluster containing document d_2, P_2, is more similar to the query than the profile of the cluster containing document d_1, P_1, (i.e., $sim(Q, P_1) < sim(Q, P_2)$).

In this case, we could utilize the similarity of a query to the clusters' profiles, P_1 and P_2 respectively, to discriminate between the two documents. Specifically, if the profile of the cluster containing document d_2, P_2, is more similar to the query than the profile of the cluster containing document d_1, P_1, (i.e., $sim(Q, P_1) < sim(Q, P_2)$), then it is likely that d_2 is more relevant to the query than d_1. The diagram above illustrates this case.

The two extreme cases described above exemplify clear cases where the additional information available through the topical organizational of the collection - query-profile and profile-document similarities – could be utilized to better estimate the relevance of a document to a user's query. For the more common cases, where the similarity between a query and two documents is not equal, it is less clear how the additional information could be utilized, although it is very likely that the relevance of a document to a query, $R(Q, D)$, is dependent on the three similarities described above, and $R(Q, D) = f(sim(Q, P), sim(Q, D), sim(P, D))$, where f represents some unknown function. We term this principle '*cluster-based matching*'.

Defining the exact form of function f is beyond the scope of this study; however, we believe that a case-based approach for matching is appropriate, where a set of rules would discriminate between each pair of documents. Below we roughly sketch such a scheme:

- o If the two documents belong to the same cluster, compare their similarities to the query.
  - If the similarity is equal (or very close to equal), employ the profile-document similarity to discriminate between the documents (as exemplified in the first case above).
  - Else, the relevance of a document to a query will be determined to a large extent by query-document similarity (possibly with some weight given to profile-document similarity)
- o If the documents belong to different clusters, compare their similarities to the query.
  - If the similarity is equal (or very close to equal), employ the query-profile similarity to discriminate between the documents (as exemplified in the second case above).
  - Else, the relevance of a document to a query will be determined to a large extent by query-document similarity. Query-profile might still be weighted in the relevance function, depending on the positioning of the clusters in the semantic space

- If the two clusters C_1 and C_2 containing the documents d_1 and d_2, (i.e., $d_1 \in C_1$ and $d_2 \in C_2$) are very close to one another, the relevance of a document will largely depend on his similarity to the query

- Else (the two clusters C_1 and C_2 are remote), query-profile similarity, as well as query-document similarity, could be employed to evaluate relevance.

The description of the scheme above is not intended as a definition of the relevance function, but merely as an example realization of the 'cluster-based matching' principle, illustrating the way in which the three similarity measures – query-document, query-profile, and profile-document – could be employed to evaluate a document's relevance to a query.

11.1.4 A Retrieval Model Combining Token-Based and Cluster-Based Representations

We propose a novel retrieval model, which explores the interplay between token-based and cluster-based representations, as an extension to the cluster-based retrieval model. In this novel model token-based indexing and token-based query-document matching are adjusted to reflect the topical organization of the collection. The extensions to the cluster-based model comprise of the two principles proposed in the sections above - cluster-based weighting and cluster-based matching. In cluster-based weighting, topical organization of documents is employed to re-index the documents, so that tokens' weights in the index are adjusted. In cluster-based matching, matching of query and documents token indexes is amended, so as to utilize the additional information available through the corpus' topical organization.

11.2 An Exploratory Empirical Evaluation of the Model Combining Topics and Tokens

In this section we describe an exploratory empirical test of the two principles proposed above: cluster-based weighting and cluster-based matching. The principles are conceptual, and many possible realizations of these principles exist. An extensive evaluation of each principle was not feasible within the restricted scope of this dissertation, thus our exploratory study will test only simplified realizations of cluster-based weighting and cluster-based matching. The aim of this study is to investigate the effect of each principle in isolation, and then test the interaction between the two principles.

11.2.1 Experimental Design

We conducted three experiments, as follows:

- o Experiment 1: designed to test the effect of **cluster-based weighting** (where the IDF factor in the TF-IDF weighting scheme is adjusted to reflect that only a restricted set of the clusters are associated with the query). We will compare cluster-based weighting against the traditional cluster-based model (where the IDF factor is calculated per the entire collection).

- o Experiment 2: designed to test the effect of **cluster-based matching** (where additional information – specifically query-profile and profile-document similarities – is employed for matching). We will compare cluster-based matching against the traditional cluster-based model (where only query-document similarity is used for matching).

- o Experiment 3: designed to test the interactions between cluster-based weighting and cluster-based matching, We will compare the performance of the model including the two principles against cluster-based weighting (from Experiment 1), and cluster-based matching (from Experiment 2).

In order to test the effect of the principles described above, we compare two realizations of cluster-based retrieval – the traditional vs. modified based on the principle explored – and test their effectiveness (employing both Recall and Precision measures) for the set of 100 queries. To analyze the data we compare the averages - $\mu 1$ for the traditional model and $\mu 2$ for the modified model - over all queries, and pose the null hypothesis: $\mu 2 < \mu 1$. Statistical significance for rejecting the null hypothesis is based on a one-sided t-test, where equal variance is not assumed.

11.2.2 Implementation Procedure

The starting point for all three experiments was the traditional cluster-based model, with tokenizing and 100-clustering for pre-processing (see details in Chapter 9). For all experiments, document indexes were weighted and query indexes un-weighted, and we explored alternative realizations of cluster-based retrieval when the query is associated with 1 out of the total 100 clusters, 5, 10, 20, and 30 clusters.

As discussed above, we only tested simplified realizations for each principle, as described in the following section.

Cluster-based weighting proposes that the weighting scheme be adjusted so "the collection" is defined by the documents in the restricted set of clusters associated with the query. However, for practical reasons it is important that the index terms weights be calculated in advance, and not during querying time. While the traditional TF-IDF weights are calculated prior to querying, cluster-based weights depends on the query (and the clusters associated with the query), and could not be calculated in advance. This problem could be resolved if only one cluster is associated with the query, and the IDF component is calculated in advance for document indexes to reflect specificity for that one cluster. We term this simplified version of cluster-based weighting '*One Cluster TF-IDF*', and we employed this simplified realization for our experiments. However, in Chapter 9 we proposed that in optimal realizations of cluster-based retrieval a query should be associated with several clusters (roughly 10% of the total number of clusters in the collection), rather than with only one cluster. Applying the cluster-based weighting principle in that case would require heavy computations at run-time, and thus is not appropriate. A possible solution would be to use one-cluster TF-IDF (where weights are calculated prior to matching), even though the weights will reflect specificity for one cluster. We believe that when few clusters are associated with the query, one-cluster TF-IDF will perform better than the traditional corpus-based weighting, but this scheme will become less effective in cases where many clusters are associated with each query.

In our discussion of cluster-based matching above, we proposed the general relevance function $R(Q,D) = f(sim(Q,P), sim(Q,D), sim(P,D))$, where f represents some unknown function. We suggested that a case-based approach is appropriate for employing the additional query-profile and profile-document similarities (i.e., $sim(Q,P)$ and $sim(D,P)$ respectively) in relevance calculations. However, in this exploratory investigation of cluster-based matching we will test the simplest additive functions, without distinguishing between different cases, as follows:

- $f_1 = sim(Q,D)$; standard matching used in the traditional cluster-based model, and will serve as the baseline for comparisons.
- $f_2 = sim(Q,D) + sim(Q,P)$; similarity between query to document, plus query-profile similarity.
- $f_3 = sim(Q,D) + sim(P,D)$; similarity between query to document, plus profile-document similarity.
- $f_4 = sim(Q,D) + sim(Q,P) + sim(P,D)$; similarity between query to document, plus query-profile and profile-document similarities.

11.2.3 Results and Analysis

Below we present the results of the three experiments.

Experiment 1

The first experiment investigated the effect of cluster-based weighting (or more specifically, one-cluster TF-IDF), and the results for all effectiveness measures employed are presented below:

Measure	Weighting	1/100	5 / 100	10 / 100	20 / 100	30 / 100
Precision[10]	Standard	0.136	0.181	0.203	0.214	0.219
	Cluster-based	0.167	0.210	0.240	0.224	0.231
	% improvement	22.8%	16%	18.2%	4.7%	5.5%
Precision[20]	Standard	0.095	0.128	0.156	0.170	0.180
	Cluster-based	0.123	0.167	0.182	0.181	0.188
	% improvement	29.6%	30.5%	16.7%	6.5%	4.4%
Precision[30]	Standard	0.078	0.105	0.126	0.148	0.156
	Cluster-based	0.104	0.140	0.156	0.160	0.162
	% improvement	32.7%	33.3%	23.8%	8.1%	3.8%
Recall[1000]	Standard	0.155	0.233	0.269	0.314	0.352
	Cluster-based	0.169	0.244	0.283	0.318	0.350
	% improvement	9%	4.7%	5.2%	1.3%	-0.5%

Table 11-1: the effect of one-cluster weighting.

For all measures and all realizations of cluster-based retrieval, results for the cluster-based weighting scheme are superior to the traditional cluster-based model. The effect of cluster-based weighting is more evident when few clusters are associated with queries. With 1/100 clusters per query Precision gains are 23%-33%[60], and Recall gains are 9%. With 5/100 clusters per query, Precision gains are in the 16-34% range[61], and Recall gains are minor (roughly 4%). With 10/100 clusters per query Precision gains are roughly 20%[62], and then the gains grow smaller as more clusters are associated with each query.

The results for the Precision[20] measure, for alternative realizations of cluster-based IR, are illustrated in the diagram below:

---

[60] With 1/100 clusters per query, Precision gains for Precision[10] are 23% (insignificant), for Precision[20] are 30% (P< 0.12; insignificant), and for Precision[30] are 33% (P<0.098). Statistical significance is based on a one-sided t-test, where equal variance is not assumed.

[61] With 5/100 clusters per query, Precision gains for Precision[10] are 16% (insignificant), for Precision[20] are 31% (P< 0.06), and for Precision[30] are 34% (P<0.04).

[62] With 10/100 clusters per query, Precision gains for Precision[10] are 18% (insignificant), for Precision[20] are 17% (insignificant), and for Precision[30] are 24% (P<0.10).

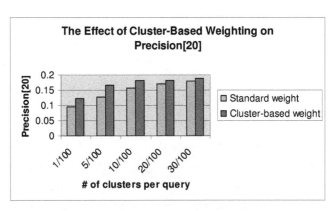

Diagram 11-4: comparing Precision[20] for one-cluster TF-IDF against the traditional
cluster-based model

The diagram clearly demonstrates the superiority of one-cluster weighting for all
realizations of cluster-based retrieval.

An interesting finding is that the effect of restricting the number of clusters
associated with each query when cluster-based weighting is employed is different from
the effect observed for traditional weighting (see Chapter 9). While in traditional cluster-
based retrieval performance drops as fewer clusters are employed, with one-cluster TF-
IDF optimal performance levels are obtained with 10/100 clusters per query (higher than
the results obtained for 20/100 and 30/100 clusters per query).

The initial results obtained in this experiment are very encouraging, especially
when considering that we only used a very simple realization of cluster-based weighting -
one-cluster TF-IDF. It is expected, thus, that better results may be obtained with a
complete realization of the principle, when the index terms are weighted based on the
complete set of clusters associated with the query.

<u>Experiment 2</u>

This experiment investigated the effect of cluster-based matching, and tested the performance of the following relevance functions:

- $f_1 = sim(Q, D)$; standard matching (the baseline)
- $f_2 = sim(Q, D) + sim(Q, P)$
- $f_3 = sim(Q, D) + sim(P, D)$
- $f_4 = sim(Q, D) + sim(Q, P) + sim(P, D)$

In order to gain some initial understanding on the behaviour of these functions we first tested their performance when employing the entire set of 100 clusters (i.e. for the Vector-Space model, rather than for the cluster-based model); the following results were obtained:

Measure \ Matching	f_1	f_2	f_3	f_4
Precision[10]	0.244	0.231	0.073	0.071
Precision[20]	0.204	0.169	0.064	0.063
Precision[30]	0.177	0.140	0.058	0.055
Recall[1000]	0.440	0.440	0.440	0.440

Table 11-2: effectiveness measures for alternative realizations of cluster-based matching, when employing the entire set of 100 clusters (i.e., vector-space model). The best results for each measure are shaded in gray.

The results presented in the table above demonstrate that Recall is almost not affected by cluster-based matching. As for Precision - the inclusion of a profile-document similarity, $sim(P, D)$, (see functions f_3 and f_4) results in substantial losses (approximately 70% Precision losses), and thus is not beneficial; on the other hand, the inclusion of a query-profile similarity, $sim(Q, P)$ (see function f_2), results in smaller losses (5%-20% Precision losses), and thus may hold some potential.

We proceeded to explore the effect of cluster-based matching on the cluster-based retrieval model (i.e. when less than 100/100 clusters are associated with each cluster). Based on the results obtained for the entire collection (see above), we decided to discard the less promising functions - f_3 and f_4 - and to study in more detail the more promising function f_2. We introduced two new variations of f_2, exploring linear combinations of $sim(Q, P)$ and $sim(P, D)$, as follows:

- $f_5 = 2 \times sim(Q,D) + sim(Q,P)$, and

- $f_6 = sim(Q,D) + 2 \times sim(Q,P)$.

The results are presented below.

Measure	Matching	5 / 100	10 / 100	20 / 100	30 / 100
Precision[10]	$f_1 = sim(Q,D)$ (baseline)	0.181	0.203	0.214	0.219
	$f_2 = sim(Q,D) + sim(Q,P)$	0.182	0.187	0.208	0.209
	$f_5 = 2 \times sim(Q,D) + sim(Q,P)$	0.185	0.193	0.214	0.208
	$f_6 = sim(Q,D) + 2 \times sim(Q,P)$	0.171	0.175	0.177	0.177
Precision[20]	$f_1 = sim(Q,D)$ (baseline)	0.128	0.156	0.170	0.180
	$f_2 = sim(Q,D) + sim(Q,P)$	0.128	0.144	0.155	0.158
	$f_5 = 2 \times sim(Q,D) + sim(Q,P)$	0.130	0.150	0.160	0.165
	$f_6 = sim(Q,D) + 2 \times sim(Q,P)$	0.123	0.129	0.131	0.128
Precision[30]	$f_1 = sim(Q,D)$ (baseline)	0.105	0.126	0.148	0.156
	$f_2 = sim(Q,D) + sim(Q,P)$	0.103	0.115	0.126	0.128
	$f_5 = 2 \times sim(Q,D) + sim(Q,P)$	0.107	0.122	0.136	0.138
	$f_6 = sim(Q,D) + 2 \times sim(Q,P)$	0.100	0.105	0.105	0.102

Table 11-3: the effect of cluster-based matching on cluster-based retrieval. The best results for each measure and for each realization of cluster-based retrieval (based on the number of clusters per query) are shaded in gray.

The results reveal that out of the restricted set of the relevance functions explored in this experiment, in most realizations of cluster-based retrieval (with 10/100, 20/100, and 30/100 clusters per query) the traditional relevance function (based on query-document similarity) performs best. Alternative functions - $f_2 = sim(Q,D) + sim(Q,P)$, $f_5 = 2 \times sim(Q,D) + sim(Q,P)$, and $f_6 = sim(Q,D) + 2 \times sim(Q,P)$ - perform comparatively only when few 5/100 clusters are employed (in these cases f_6 is optimal and it slightly surpasses the performance of the traditional matching function).

These results are somewhat discouraging, as they give negative indication for the value of cluster-based matching. We believe that more complete realizations of the principle, perhaps based on the case approach proposed earlier, will prove more useful.

Experiment 3

The third and final experiment of this study investigated the interaction effect of cluster-based weighting and cluster-based matching, based on the simple realizations tested in Experiment 1 (i.e. one-cluster TF-IDF) and Experiment 2 (i.e. linear combination of $sim(Q,D)$ and $sim(Q,P)$). The table below demonstrated the interaction between the two effects.

Measure	Weighting	Matching	5 / 100	10 / 100	20 / 100	30 / 100
Precision[10]	Standard	$f_1 = sim(Q,D)$; standard	0.181	0.203	0.214	0.219
		$f_2 = sim(Q,D) + sim(Q,P)$	0.182	0.187	0.208	0.209
		$f_5 = 2 \times sim(Q,D) + sim(Q,P)$	0.185	0.193	0.214	0.208
		$f_6 = sim(Q,D) + 2 \times sim(Q,P)$	0.171	0.175	0.177	0.177
	Cluster-based	$f_1 = sim(Q,D)$; standard	0.210	0.240	0.224	0.231
		$f_2 = sim(Q,D) + sim(Q,P)$	0.214	0.246	0.259	0.240
		$f_5 = 2 \times sim(Q,D) + sim(Q,P)$	0.213	0.242	0.259	0.233
		$f_6 = sim(Q,D) + 2 \times sim(Q,P)$	0.225	0.232	0.245	0.250
Precision[20]	Standard	$f_1 = sim(Q,D)$; standard	0.128	0.156	0.170	0.180
		$f_2 = sim(Q,D) + sim(Q,P)$	0.128	0.144	0.155	0.158
		$f_5 = 2 \times sim(Q,D) + sim(Q,P)$	0.130	0.150	0.160	0.165
		$f_6 = sim(Q,D) + 2 \times sim(Q,P)$	0.123	0.129	0.131	0.128
	Cluster-based	$f_1 = sim(Q,D)$; standard	0.167	0.182	0.181	0.188
		$f_2 = sim(Q,D) + sim(Q,P)$	0.169	0.185	0.213	0.193
		$f_5 = 2 \times sim(Q,D) + sim(Q,P)$	0.168	0.182	0.213	0.191
		$f_6 = sim(Q,D) + 2 \times sim(Q,P)$	0.170	0.192	0.202	0.200
Precision[30]	Standard	$f_1 = sim(Q,D)$; standard	0.105	0.126	0.148	0.156
		$f_2 = sim(Q,D) + sim(Q,P)$	0.103	0.115	0.126	0.128
		$f_5 = 2 \times sim(Q,D) + sim(Q,P)$	0.107	0.122	0.136	0.138
		$f_6 = sim(Q,D) + 2 \times sim(Q,P)$	0.100	0.105	0.105	0.102
	Cluster-based	$f_1 = sim(Q,D)$; standard	0.140	0.156	0.160	0.162
		$f_2 = sim(Q,D) + sim(Q,P)$	0.144	0.158	0.185	0.168
		$f_5 = 2 \times sim(Q,D) + sim(Q,P)$	0.142	0.157	0.185	0.164
		$f_6 = sim(Q,D) + 2 \times sim(Q,P)$	0.147	0.159	0.175	0.174

Table 11-4: the interaction between the effects of the cluster-based weighting and cluster-based matching on alternative realizations of cluster-based retrieval. In gray – the best results for each measure and for each cluster-based retrieval realization.

Based on the results presented above, we make several observations:

- For all Precision measures and for all realizations of cluster-based retrieval (i.e. 5/100, 10/100, etc.), the model combining of the two principles - cluster-based weighting and cluster-based matching - yields the best results.

- For all Precision measures, the model combining the two principles is substantially superior to traditional cluster-based model. With 5/100 clusters per query, the optimal realizations of the model combining cluster-based weighting and matching yields results higher by 24%-40% than the traditional cluster-based model; with 10/100 and 20/100 clusters, the results are 21%-26% higher, and when 30/100 clusters are selected, the results are 11%-14% higher than the traditional cluster-based model.

- For all Precision measures, the optimal realization of the model combining the two principles (using the f_2 or f_5 functions; with 20/100 clusters per query) is superior to the classical token-based model by 4%-6%[63]. Thus it is possible to attain minor Precision gains, while improving run-time efficiency.

- For the model combining of the two principles, among the alternative realizations of cluster-based matching there is no one dominant function, although $f_6 = sim(Q,D) + 2 \times sim(Q,P)$ is optimal in most cases. Performance gains for the model combining of the two principles, with f_6 and one-cluster TF-IDF, results in Precision gains beyond the traditional cluster-based model, as follows: 14-24% gains for Precision[10][64], 11-33% gains for Precision[20][65], and 12-40% gains for Precision[30] [66]. The results achieved with f_6 may suggest that $sim(Q,P)$, in addition to the commonly used $sim(Q,D)$, is important for predicting the relevance of a document, when employed in combination with cluster-based weighting.

---

[63] Precision[10] is 6.1% higher; Precision[20] is 4.4% higher; and Precision[30] is 4.5% higher. These differences are statistically insignificant.

[64] Precision gains and statistical significance for Precision[10]: 5/100 clusters – 24% (P<0.11); 10/00 clusters – 15% (insignificant); 20/100 clusters – 14% (insignificant); 30/100 clusters – 14% (insignificant);

[65] Precision gains and statistical significance for Precision[20]: 5/100 clusters – 33% (P<0.05); 10/00 clusters – 22% (P<0.1); 20/100 clusters – 19% (insignificant); 30/100 clusters – 11% (insignificant).

[66] Precision gains and statistical significance for Precision[30]: 5/100 clusters – 40% (P<0.03); 10/00 clusters – 28% (P<0.06); 20/100 clusters – 18% (insignificant); 30/100 clusters – 12% (insignificant).

To illustrate the interactions between cluster-based matching [with $f_6 = sim(Q,D) + 2 \times sim(Q,P)$] and cluster-based weighting (with one-cluster TF-IDF), the following diagram is presented.

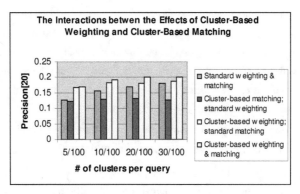

Diagram 11-5: interaction effects between cluster-based weighting (realized with one-cluster TF-IDF) and cluster-based matching (realized with $f_6 = sim(Q,D) + 2 \times sim(Q,P)$) for the extended cluster-model, with Precision[20] measure, at alternative realizations of cluster-based IR.

The diagram above illustrates the interaction effects of cluster-based matching and cluster-based weighting. The model combining the two principles yields superior Precision[20] levels to any partial model. Similar effects were observed for the other measures: Precision[10], Precision[30], and Recall[1000].

Efficiency Analysis

For pre-processing both clustering and token indexing extraction are linear processes[67], and thus the combination of Topics and Tokens could scale to very large collections. For matching at run-time, token matching is based on an inverted matrix and the process is linear with the number of documents that contain query terms. Cluster-

---

[67] Actually, clustering complexity is rectangular. For instance the complexity of K-means clustering is $O(lkN)$, where N is the number of documents in the collection, k is the number of clusters, and l is the number of iterations.

based retrieval improves run-time efficiency by restricting query-document matching to only documents in the clusters associated with the query.

However, the extensions proposed in this chapter require additional processing.

Cluster-based weighting suggests that document and query indexes be re-weighted after documents are organized into topically coherent clusters, and re-weighting is linear in the number of documents in the corpus, N. Theoretically, re-weighting should occur at run-time, after the most relevant clusters are associated with queries, but this may have a substantial negative impact on run-time efficiency. Alternatively, simplified realizations of the cluster-based weighting principle, such as one-cluster TF-IDF proposed here, may enable to perform re-weighting at pre-processing.

Cluster-based matching suggests that additional information – specifically query-profile and profile-document similarities be employed for estimating the relevance of a document to a specific query. The additional information is readily available, as it used for the clustering algorithm (i.e. profile-document similarities) and restricting queries to the most relevant clusters (i.e. query-profile similarity). Cluster-based matching suggests that this information be employed at run-time but does not prescribe a specific function. The complexity of this process will depend on the exact form of the relevance function. The simplified realization explored in this study – linear combinations of query-profile and query-document similarities – is uncomplicated and will have only a negligible effect on efficiency.

11.2.4 Discussion

The results from the three experiments reported above are in general positive, and suggest that the principles proposed in Section 11.1 – cluster-based weighting and cluster-based matching – can enhance the performance of cluster-based retrieval. In these exploratory experiments we implemented and tested only very simple realizations of the proposed principles, yet we were able to achieve significant effectiveness gains. One-cluster TF-IDF, the simplified realization of cluster-based weighting, yields significant Precision gains, while cluster-based matching, with the simplified realization $f_6 = sim(Q,D) + 2 \times sim(Q,P)$, results in some Precision losses. However, when cluster-based matching is combined with cluster-based weighting, the interaction effect yields the optimal Precision levels. Recall was not affected by the proposed principles.

When compared to the classic token-based model, our best realization of the combined model resulted is minor improvements.

Another interesting finding is that the behaviour of cluster-based weighting differs from traditional cluster-based retrieval, and that in some cases restricting the number of clusters per query actually results in effectiveness gains. For the traditional cluster-based retrieval model, early works suggested the potential of clusters' restriction for retrieval effectiveness, yet results obtained to date associate cluster restriction with effectiveness losses (see Chapter 9). Our findings for cluster-based weighting strengthen the claim that cluster restriction could potentially yield effectiveness gains.

In the future we plan to explore more complete realizations of cluster-based weighting and matching, and test those realizations empirically. Specifically, additional research is warranted for:

- Cluster-based weighting – in the current implementation, only a simple realization of this principle was tested, one-cluster TF-IDF. In order to adjust the indexing process to the set of clusters associated with each query, "the collection" should be defined by the set of documents in these associated clusters, and the IDF factor in the weighting scheme applied to indexes should be adjusted to reflect that definition of "the collection".

- Cluster-based matching – this study was limited to the exploration of simple linear combinations of the three similarity measures: query-profile, query-document, and profile-document, for evaluating the relevance of a document to a query. Future research should investigate a case-based approach, where the additional information (i.e. query-profile and profile-document similarities) is only employed in cases where query-document similarity is not sufficient to distinguish the relevant documents (see our discussion in Section 11.1).

In addition, in the future we plan to explore the effect of the clustering algorithm used for decomposing the collection into the topical clusters. Since the focus of this study was not on the clustering procedure, only one possible implementation for the clustering algorithm was explored. Some possible modifications of the clustering procedure include the use of: different clustering technique, different similarity measure, overlapping clusters, a different number of clusters, and a different method for calculating cluster profile. In Chapter 9, we demonstrated the effect of the clustering procedure, and specifically the number of clusters, on the performance of cluster-based retrieval; thus, is it reasonable to believe that this procedure may also affect the performance of the two principles introduced in this chapter: cluster-based weighting and cluster-based matching.

11.3 Conclusion

In this chapter we studied the interaction between conceptual structures from two classes of the Semantic Units Categorization framework – topics and basic meaning-carrying units (or tokens). Specifically, we explored how the cluster-based retrieval model could be modified such that the indexing and matching processes, which employ token-based representations, will be adapted based on the topical organization of the collection. We proposed two principles: cluster-based weighting and cluster-based matching, which suggest fundamental modifications to cluster based retrieval. We conducted an exploratory empirical study of the proposed principles with simplified realizations, to obtain positive results, and we believe that more complete realizations of the principles will yield further improvements. This study reveals how the interplay between topical organization and token-based indexing and matching could result in effectiveness improvements.

Our contribution in this chapter is three fold. First, conceptual contribution in developing a novel retrieval model, based on two newly proposed principles; second, in the empirical testing of this novel model, providing evidence for its effectiveness; and third, in demonstrating how the interplay between conceptual structures based on topics and tokens could be utilized in the design of effective retrieval models, and thus opening the door for further studies on Topics-Tokens interaction.

Chapter 12: Exploring the Interplay between 'Topics' and 'Composite Concepts'

In this chapter we will try to address Research Question #2.2: Could 'Topics' and 'Composite Concepts' be integrated into one coherent retrieval model? And, if yes, how will the performance of the combined model compare to the performance of the separate 'Topics" and 'Composite Concepts'-based models? To address the question, we will:

- Propose a novel retrieval model that combines topical organization of the collection and composite-based retrieval. We will employ the semantic context provided by the topical organization to re-design matching processes in composite-based retrieval.

- Conduct an empirical study of the proposed model, based on the representative techniques for composite-based and topics-based retrieval (described in Chapters 7 and 9 respectively).
  - o Study the effectiveness of the model, by exploring the effect of key parameters.
  - o Study the efficiency of the proposed model.
  - o Compare the performance of the combined model to that of composite-based and topic-based retrieval.

This chapter will continue as follows. In Section 12.1 we will develop the novel retrieval model, and in Section 12.2 we will report the finding from an empirical study that investigated one realization of the model proposed in Section 12.1.

12.1 Cluster-Based Retrieval with Composite-Based Representations

The development of the proposed retrieval model begins at two starting points: (a) cluster-based retrieval (reviewed in Chapter 9), and (b) indexing through composite concepts (reviewed in Chapter 7). In the following sections we will recap some of the important point for each of these models, and then proceed to discuss the combination of the models

12.1.1 Recap: Cluster-Based Retrieval

Cluster-based retrieval (van Rijsbergen 1979) employs a topical organization of the collection to enhance retrieval performance (namely Precision), and is based on the cluster hypothesis stating that documents relevant to a query will tend to concentrate in few clusters. In cluster-based IR the document collection is pre-processed and decomposed into topically coherent clusters, and then, in run-time, matching the query against documents in two subsequent steps: (1) the query is associated with only few clusters (based on its similarity to the clusters' profiles), and (2) the query is matched to documents contained in the restricted set of clusters associated with the query. Cluster-based retrieval suggests that query is restricted to only few clusters, but does not pre-scribe the exact number of clusters. Cluster-based retrieval was shown to have the potential to enhance Precision (at the cost of Recall losses); however, to data, experiments with the model resulted in Precision losses (see our literature review in Chapter 9).

12.1.2 Recap: Retrieval with Composite Concepts

In the statistical approach to extracting composite concepts investigated in this thesis (see Chapter 7), composites are obtained by grouping sets of token that appear together in the text (i.e. they co-appear within a pre-set proximity window). Documents, as well as queries, are indexed through these co-occurrence sets, and matching is based on query-document similarity of the composite-based indexes. The most simple and widely deployed form of composite concepts is phrases, and phrase indexing is reported to improve Precision by 2-4%. Generally speaking, more complex forms of composites have not been adopted for general purpose retrieval systems, due to the complexity of composite extraction, indexing, and matching processes. However, there is evidence to suggest that indexing through composite concepts is now being adopted by general purpose commercial retrieval systems (Pedersen 2003).

12.1.3 Combining Cluster-Based and Composite-Based Retrieval

We propose that if the cluster hypothesis holds and relevant documents do concentrate in few clusters, matching the query to documents could be based on composite concepts indexes (rather than token indexes). Cluster-based retrieval has the potential to improve retrieval Precision (by associating queries with only clusters that contain high concentration of relevant documents), but at the cost of Recall losses (since the clusters not associated with queries also contain some relevant documents); however, experiments with the model have resulted in Precision losses. Composite-based retrieval has shown to be more precise than the traditional token-based retrieval (see our results in Chapter 7). Thus, there is reason to believe that defining the semantic space based on composite concepts (rather than tokens) and applying cluster-based retrieval in that space will enable to attain cluster-based IR's full potential and result in Precision gains.

Possibly, composite concepts could be employed in three different processes of cluster-based retrieval:

- At pre-processing: the organization of the collection into topically–coherent clusters could be based on composite concepts, where document-document similarities are calculated with documents' composite indexes.

- At run-time: restriction of the number of clusters associated with the query is done by comparing the similarity of the query and clusters' profiles. Query-cluster similarity could possible be calculated based on composite indexes.

- At run-time: matching the query to all documents in the restricted set of clusters could be done based on query and documents composite concepts indexes.

In the study reported below, we've employed composite indexes only for run-time (i.e. matching) processes. Details on the specific realization employed for our experimental study and the findings from that study are provided in the following sections.

12.2 An Exploratory Empirical Evaluation of the Model Combining Topics and Composite Concepts

In this section we describe an exploratory empirical test of the model combining composite-based indexing and matching with cluster-based retrieval. In Section 12.1.3 we've listed several possible combinations of cluster-based and composite-based retrieval. In the model, we explore here composite-based indexes for documents, cluster profiles, and queries are employed in the two-stage matching process (i.e. query-profile and then query-document similarities are calculated with composite concepts indexes). However, pre-processing and the organization of the collection into topically-coherent clusters for our study were performed in the traditional manner, employing token indexes.

12.2.1 Experimental Design

In this initial exploratory study of the combined model there are many interesting questions to explore. Following we identify the two most critical issues worth investigating. First, we would like to study the model's effectiveness (when compared to the traditional cluster-based model with token indexes) and learn whether the semantic units employed to construct the semantic space – composites vs. tokens - affect the performance of cluster-based retrieval. Experiments with composite-based retrieval in Chapter 7 reveal that the model yields Precision gains over token-based retrieval when the entire collection is employed for matching, and it would be interesting to explore whether similar gains could be obtained when only portion of the collection is used for matching. Second, the effect of clusters' restriction is critical. While for the traditional cluster-based model (with token indexes) cluster restriction was shown to have the potential to enhance retrieval, in practice this potential is yet to be attained. We suspect that employing composite concepts to define the semantic space may influence the behavior of cluster-based retrieval, such that cluster' restriction may not result in Precision losses, and intend to test this effect.

We conducted two experiments, as follows, in order to test the questions raised above:

- Experiment 1: designed to test the performance of the combined model for alternative realizations of cluster-based IR (where 1, 5, 10, 20, and 30 of the total 100 clusters are associated with each query). We will test the **effect of the semantic unit employed** to construct the conceptual space by comparing the performance of composite against token indexes, for cluster-based retrieval.
- Experiment 2: designed to test the **effect of cluster-restriction** by analyzing how the performance of cluster-based IR with composites is affected with the number of clusters associated with queries. We will compare this affect to the effect observed for cluster-based IR with tokens (based on the results obtained in the experiments in Chapter 9).

In order to test the effects described above we study the combination of cluster-based with composite concepts retrieval, when different number of clusters are associated with each query – 1, 5, 10, 20, and 30 out of the total 10 clusters. The baselines for our comparison will be the two distinct retrieval models – the traditional cluster-based IR (with token indexes, as described in Chapter 9) and composite-based retrieval (described in Chapter 7).

In the two experiments we will employ the effectiveness measures used throughout this dissertation: Precision[10], Precision[20], Precision[30], and Recall[1000].

We take a similar approach to the one proposed for the composite concepts study in Chapter 7, and use only queries that have at least one composite concept in their index. 91 queries (of the total 100 queries available) were used, and are listed in Appendix 3.

12.2.2 Implementation Procedure

The starting point for the two experiments was the 100-cluster topical organization (using documents' token indexes and the K-means clustering algorithm, as described in Chapter 9) and composite concepts indexes for both documents and queries (two-term, symmetric, intransitive, proximity-based co-occurrence sets, extracted with the lenient lower cut-off threshold, as described in Chapter 7). Thus, clusters were defined based on the traditional token representations, while matching was performed based on composite representations. Composite concept indexes for cluster profiles were generated similarly to token profile indexes, where the profiles is calculated as the centroid for all documents in that cluster. Matching was performed in two steps, by first comparing query and clusters-profile composite indexes to select the most relevant clusters, and then matching queries composite indexes with the composite indexes of documents in the restricted set of clusters associated with the query. Similarities – query-profile and query-document – were calculated as the cosine of the angle between the two composite vector indexes. In alignment with the other experiments in this thesis, document indexes were TF-IDF weighted and query indexes un-weighted.

12.2.3 Results and Analysis

Below we present the results of the two experiments in this study.

Experiment 1

The first experiment investigated the effect of the semantic unit employed for cluster-based retrieval, and compared the performance of the combined model introduced above (i.e. cluster-based retrieval with composite concepts) to traditional cluster-based retrieval (with token representations). The results for all effectiveness measures employed are presented below:

Measure	Semantic Unit	1/100	5/100	10/100	20/100	30/100
Precision[10]	Tokens	0.136	0.181	0.203	0.214	0.219
	Composites	0.197	0.276	0.275	0.276	0.279
	Difference	45%	52%	35%	29%	27%
Precision[20]	Tokens	0.094	0.128	0.156	0.17	0.18
	Composites	0.135	0.198	0.200	0.206	0.207
	Difference	43%	55%	28%	21%	15%
Precision[30]	Tokens	0.078	0.105	0.126	0.148	0.156
	Composites	0.110	0.168	0.169	0.177	0.179
	Difference	41%	60%	34%	19%	15%
Recall[1000]	Tokens	0.155	0.233	0.269	0.314	0.352
	Composites	0.234	0.243	0.242	0.243	0.247
	Difference	51%	4%	-10%	-23%	-30%

Table 12-1 – the effect of the semantic unit used for representations on the performance of cluster-based retrieval. Results for alternative realizations of cluster-based retrieval, with 1, 5, 10, 20, and 30 clusters per query, out of the total 100 clusters.

For all realizations of cluster-based retrieval, composite concepts representations perform substantially better than token representations – when many clusters are associated with each query the gains are in the 15%-30% range, and when only few clusters are associated with each query Precision gains reach 60%. The diagram below presents the results for Precision[10].

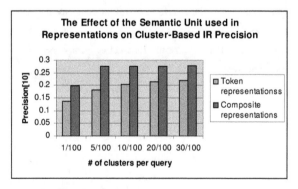

Diagram 12-1 – the effect of the semantic unit used for representations on Precision[10] for cluster-based retrieval. Results for alternative realizations of cluster-based retrieval, with 1, 5, 10, 20, and 30 clusters per query, out of the total 100 clusters.

This result is very interesting, as when query is matched with all documents in the collection (i.e. no cluster-restriction) the Precision gains for composites over tokens are significantly lower (14%) than the gains obtained when few clusters are associated with the query (as reported above). Furthermore, Precision[10] for composite concepts with only 5 clusters per query is 0.276, 13% higher than that obtained for token-based retrieval with no cluster restriction, indicating that cluster-based retrieval could be used to enhance Precision (at least when indexing is based on composite concepts).

Recall is higher for token representations when many clusters are associated with the query, while higher for composite representations with few clusters per query. This is due to the fact that while with tokens representations Recall decreases as fewer clusters are associated with a query, with composite representations Recall levels remain at the same level regardless of the number of clusters associated with queries. The effect of cluster restriction of Recall is illustrated below.

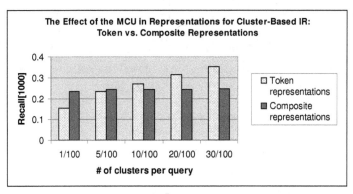

Diagram 12-2 – the effect of the semantic unit used for representations on Recall[1000] for cluster-based retrieval. Results for alternative realizations of cluster-based retrieval, with 1, 5, 10, 20, and 30 clusters per query, out of the total 100 clusters.

Experiment 2

The second experiment in this study investigated the effect of clusters' restriction on composite-based retrieval, and explored whether the behavior of composite-based representation is similar to that of token-based retrieval. To investigate the behavior of cluster restriction we calculated, for each of the measures, the performance level at different cluster-restriction cases – with 1, 5, 10, 20, and, 30 clusters per query – as a percentage of the performance level when clusters are associated with the query (i.e. no cluster restriction). The results of Experiment 2 are presented below.

Clusters per query	Semantic Unit	1/100	5/100	10/100	20/100	30/100
Precision[10]	Tokens	0.136	0.181	0.203	0.214	0.219
	% of all	56%	74%	83%	88%	90%
	Composites	0.197	0.276	0.275	0.276	0.279
	% of all	71%	99%	99%	99%	100%
Precision[20]	Tokens	0.094	0.128	0.156	0.17	0.18
	% of all	46%	63%	76%	83%	88%
	Composites	0.135	0.198	0.200	0.206	0.207
	% of all	66%	97%	98%	101%	101%
Precision[30]	Tokens	0.078	0.105	0.126	0.148	0.156
	% of all	44%	59%	71%	84%	88%
	Composites	0.110	0.168	0.169	0.177	0.179
	% of all	61%	93%	94%	98%	100%
Recall[1000]	Tokens	0.155	0.233	0.269	0.314	0.352
	% of all	35%	53%	61%	71%	80%
	Composites	0.234	0.243	0.242	0.243	0.247
	% of all	95%	98%	98%	98%	100%

Table 12-2 – the effect of cluster restriction on the performance of composite-based retrieval, when compared to the effect on token-based retrieval. Results for alternative realizations of cluster-based retrieval, with 1, 5, 10, 20, and 30 clusters per query, out of the total 100 clusters. In all cases, document indexes are TF-IDF weighted and query indexes are un-weighted.

The table above illustrates that cluster restriction hardly effects retrieval with composite representations, while it has a substantial negative impact on token-based retrieval. Precision for composite concepts remains in the 93%-99% (as a percent of the levels with no cluster-restriction) when query is restricted down to 5 clusters, and is in the 61%-71% range with only one cluster per query. For comparison consider the case where queries are restricted to 5 clusters – in that case Precision[10] losses for composite representations are only 1%, while the losses for retrieval with token representations average at 26%. The effect of cluster restriction on Precision[10] is illustrated in the diagram below.

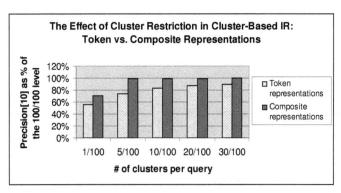

Diagram 12-3 – the effect of cluster restriction on Precision[10] for composite-based retrieval, when compared to the effect on token-based retrieval. Results for alternative realizations of cluster-based retrieval, with 1, 5, 10, 20, and 30 clusters per query, out of the total 100 clusters.

Recall for composite concepts is affected similarly by cluster restriction, and when the query is restricted down to only one cluster, still Recall losses are merely 5% (in comparison, restricting the query to only one cluster results in 65% Recall losses for token representations). The affect of cluster restriction on Recall is illustrated below.

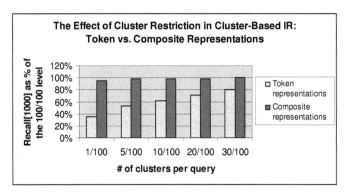

Diagram 12-4 – the effect of cluster restriction on Recall[1000] for composite-based retrieval, when compared to the effect on token-based retrieval. Results for alternative realizations of cluster-based retrieval, with 1, 5, 10, 20, and 30 clusters per query, out of the total 100 clusters.

Efficiency Analysis

For pre-processing both clustering and composite concept extraction are linear processes[68], and thus the combined approach could scale to very large collections.

For matching at run-time composites matching is similar to token matching, as in both cases an inverted matrix could be used, and the process is linear with the number of documents that contain query terms. Cluster-based retrieval for composites improves run-time efficiency as the query is only matched to documents in the most relevant clusters, as in the traditional cluster-based retrieval model.

12.2.4 Discussion

The results of the two experiments described in the previous section demonstrate the viability of the combination of topic-based and composite-based retrieval models. Results of Experiment 1 reveal that cluster-based retrieval with composite concepts is substantially more effective than the traditional cluster-based model (which is based on token representations), especially when few clusters are associated with each query. The gains for composite concepts in cluster-based retrieval – up to 60% in Precision and 51% in Recall – are significantly higher than the gains obtained for composites (over token representation) when query is not restricted and matched against the entire set of documents (see results of Chapter 7).

From Experiment 2 we learn that cluster restriction hardly affects the composite-based model, and retrieval with only 5 clusters per query out of the set of 100 clusters results in minor Precision and Recall losses (1% for Precision[10] and 2% for Recall[1000]). Hence, cluster-based IR with composite representations could yield significant run-time efficiency gains (by restricting query-document matching 5% of the collection), with practically no effectiveness losses when compared to composite based retrieval with matching over all documents in the corpus.

---

[68] Actually, clustering complexity is rectangular. For instance the complexity of K-means clustering is $O(lkN)$, where N is the number of documents in the collection, k is the number of clusters, and l is the number of iterations.

Cluster-based IR with composite representations differs from the traditional cluster-based model (with token representations) in that two matching processes – query-profile and query-documents – are based on the similarities of composite concepts indexes, rather then token representations. The superiority of composite-based query-documents matching was already demonstrated in Chapter 7, resulting in 14% gains over token representation. The additional gains (up to 60%) available with cluster restriction are attributed to query-profile similarity, and cluster association to query based on composite concept indexes seems to be substantially more accurate and association based on token indexes. The minor Recall losses when query is associated with 5% of the total clusters (merely 2%) support this conclusion, as they demonstrate that query-cluster association based on composite indexes select the clusters that contain a large portion of the total relevant documents available in the collection.

Our combination of cluster-based retrieval with composite concepts representations proposed to modify the two-step matching process of cluster-based retrieval, so it is based on composite concepts representations. However, the combination of the two retrieval models could go beyond that, so that two additional processes are modified. First, composite-based indexes of documents could be used for decomposing the collection into topically coherent clusters (i.e. document-document similarities for the clustering algorithm will be based on composite indexes). Second, composite concept representations could be adjusted once documents are assigned to topic-specific clusters, very much in the same way token representations were adjusted to accommodate for topical organization of the corpus in Chapter 11[69]. In the future we plan to explore how alternative combinations of cluster-based retrieval and composite concept representations, as suggested above, could affect retrieval performance.

---

[69] In chapter 11 we proposed that the topical organization of the collection should impact both the weighting and matching processes, and proposed two principles for cluster-based retrieval – 'cluster-based weighting'
and 'cluster-based matching'.

12.3 Conclusion

In this chapter, we studied the interaction between semantic units from two categories of the proposed framework – topics and composite concepts. Specifically, we explored the combination of cluster-based retrieval with statistical co-occurrence proximity model. We proposed that the two-step matching process of cluster-based retrieval – query-profile and query-document matching – be based on composite concept representations, rather than on token representations.

We conducted an exploratory empirical study of the proposed combined model, to obtain positive results – the combined model performed substantially better than traditional (i.e. using token representations) cluster-based retrieval. When compared to the composite-based retrieval model (with no cluster restriction), the combined model) resulted in similar effectiveness levels, while providing substantial run-time efficiency gains. We believe that fuller combination of the two models (as suggested in Section 12.2.4) will yield further improvements.

Our contribution in this chapter is three fold. First, conceptual contribution in proposing a retrieval model that combines cluster-based retrieval with composite concepts representations; second, in the empirical testing of this novel model, providing empirical evidence for its effectiveness; and third, in demonstrating how the interplay between semantic units of two different types - topics and composite concepts - could be utilized in the design of effective retrieval models, and thus opening the door for further studies on Topics-Composites interaction.

Chapter 13: Exploring the Interplay between 'Topics' and 'Synonym Concepts'

In this chapter we will try to address Research Question #2.3: Could 'Topics' and 'Synonym Concepts' be integrated into one coherent retrieval model? And if yes – how will the performance of the combined model compare to the performance of the separate 'Topics' and 'Synonym Concepts'-based models? To address the question, we will:

- Propose a novel retrieval model that combines topical organization of the collection and synonym-based retrieval. We will employ the semantic context provided by the topical organization to re-design the indexing and matching processes of synonym-based retrieval.

- Conduct an empirical study of the proposed model, based on the representative techniques for synonym-based and topics-based retrieval (described in Chapters 8 and 9 respectively).
  - o Study the effectiveness of the model, by exploring the effect of key parameters.
  - o Study the efficiency of the proposed model.
  - o Compare the performance of the combined model to that of synonym-based and topic-based retrieval.

This chapter will continue as follows. In Section 13.1 we will develop the novel retrieval model, and in Section 13.2 we will report the finding from an empirical study that investigated one realization of the model proposed in Section 13.1.

13.1 Latent Semantic Indexing in Topically-Coherent Sub-Collections

In this section we will propose several combinations of a synonym-based model – Latent Semantic Indexing (LSI) – and topic-based retrieval. The development of the combined retrieval models begin at two starting points: (a) Synonym-based retrieval through Latent Semantic Indexing (LSI; reviewed in Chapter 8), and (b) topic-based retrieval (reviewed in Chapter 9). In the following sections we will recap some of the important point for each of these models, and then proceed to discuss the combination of the models.

13.1.1 Recap: Latent Semantic Indexing (LSI)

LSI (Deerwester et al. 1990, Dumais 1994, Landauer et al. 1998, Husbands et al. 2000) is an extension to the vector-space model where a factor-analytic technique - Singular Value Decomposition (SVD) - is used to extract the main factors (i.e., synonym concepts) (see our review in Chapter 8). The semantic space is represented through these orthogonal factors, and information elements - documents and queries – are mapped onto that space, so that query-document similarity is calculated based on their positioning in the conceptual space. LSI has shown simulate human knowledge successfully (Landauer et al. 1998), and has strong formal foundations (Baeza Yates & Ribiero Neto 1999). Latent Semantic Indexing has been reported to enhance performance for small, domain-specific collections, and in many cases its performances surpasses traditional keyword search by as much as 30% (Landauer et al. 1998). For general collections, LSI acts in many ways as query expansion techniques, retrieving more documents, both relevant and irrelevant, thus improving Recall, but at the cost of low Precision. Several factors inhibit LSI's performance in general collections:

- LSI is very sensitive to the model's parameters, specifically to the number of vectors (i.e. concepts) and the choice of vector normalization (as we have established in Chapter 8).

- The core process of LSI – Singular Value Decomposition - is computationally expensive, and it cannot scale to large collections (the largest LSI processing reported in the literature was for 100,000 documents). To address the scalability problem of LSI, two alternative techniques have been previously proposed: (a) compute SVD for just a random sample of the collection, and project the remaining documents into that space, or alternatively (b) decompose the collection into a set of smaller sub-collections; the query is than projected into each of the sub-collections, and matched against all documents. The first approach is effective only if the sampled documents constitute 50% of the collection or more (Dumais 1994), making it inappropriate for very large collections. The latter approach was investigated in Chapter 8, resulting in poor performance.

- LSI is inadequate for heterogeneous collections. LSI is interpreted as a technique for revealing the latent semantic structure in a collection, based on the patterns of words usage. This might work quite well when the document collection is homogeneous. For example, in a Computer Science document collection, the terms 'virus', 'worm', and 'Trojan horse' may exhibit similar co-occurrence patterns, and thus identified as referring to the same concept. In a Health Science collection, on the other hand, the term 'virus', might share co-occurrence patterns with 'germ', thus indicate that the two terms refer to the same concept. However, in a heterogeneous collection, concept discovery is much more complicated. Consider the examples given above. Now assume that the two distinct collections are merged in to one heterogeneous collection, and are subject to Latent Semantic Analysis. The term 'virus' now shares patterns with two completely unrelated terms: 'Trojan horse' and 'germ', and the system is likely to wrongly associate all three terms with the one artificial concept. Hence, LSI's performance is expected to suffer when applied to a heterogeneous collection.

- LSI is inefficient at run-time, since the use of an inverted matrix for query-document matching is not feasible[70] (Deerwester et al. 1990, Dumais 1994).

13.1.2 Recap: Topic-Based Retrieval

Automatic identification of topics in large collections could be achieved through classification, which is commonly done using clustering algorithms[71] that are scalable to very large collections[72]. The adequacy of clustering algorithm for decomposing a

---

[70] An inverted matrix is used in the token-based vector-space model to restrict query matching to only the documents containing query terms.

[71] Alternative approaches, such as Factor Analysis or Singular Value Decomposition, exist (see the survey in Part II, Chapter 8), but they are computationally expensive, thus not appropriate for large collections.

[72] The complexity of some clustering algorithms, such as K-means (MacQueen 1967) is rectangular (i.e., $O(lkN)$; where N is the number of documents in the collection k is the number of clusters, and l is the number of iterations)

document collection into meaning sharing clusters has been well established in the literature (Willett 1988, Jain & Dubes 1988).

Topical organization is utilized in cluster-based retrieval (van Rijsbergen 1979) to enhance retrieval performance. Cluster-based retrieval is based on the cluster hypothesis, stating that documents relevant to a query will tend to concentrate in few clusters (see our review in Chapter 9). In cluster-based IR, the document collection is pre-processed and decomposed into topically coherent clusters, and then, in run-time, matching the query against documents in two subsequent steps: (1) the query is associated with only few clusters (based on its similarity to the clusters' profiles), and (2) the query is matched to documents contained in the restricted set of clusters associated with the query. Cluster-based retrieval provides efficiency gains at run time, and was shown to have the potential to enhance Precision (at the cost of Recall losses). However, to data, experiments with the model resulted in Precision losses (see our literature review in Chapter 9).

In Chapter 11 of this dissertation we proposed that the cluster-based model be extended to include two new principles – cluster-based weighting and cluster-based matching. While cluster-based retrieval suggests that the set of documents for query matching be restricted, it does *not* prescribe any modifications to indexing and query-document similarity calculation. The two extensions introduced in Chapter 11 suggest that both indexing (or more specifically index term weighting) and matching processes be adjusted to accommodate the topical organization of the collection. Our experiments revealed that, even with simplified realizations of the principles, cluster-based weighting results in effectiveness gains, and the combination of the two principles results in even further gains.

13.1.3 Combining Synonym-Based and Topic-Based Retrieval

We propose three levels for combining LSI with topic-based retrieval, as follows. First, topical organization of the collection could be utilized to provide high-level context for the LSI process, as proposed by Dumais (1994). To demonstrate this idea, consider a heterogeneous collection, which includes both computer-related and medical texts. As illustrated earlier, in such a collection LSI might associate the terms 'virus' with both 'germ' (from the medical literature) and 'Trojan horse' (from the computer-related literature), treating them as synonyms of the same concept. Pre-clustering of the documents might assign documents describing the different topics to distinct clusters. Performing LSI on the medical cluster will associate 'virus' with only medical synonyms, while LSI in the computer cluster will associate 'virus' with purely computer-related synonyms. Thus pre-clustering of the collection may help address the problem of polysemy, and enhance retrieval Precision. Inspired by Dumais' conjecture, we propose a model, '*Topic-LSI*', where LSI is augmented with a pre-processing phase (after standard keyword indexing, and before the SVD process) in which the document collection is clustered into topically coherent sub-collections (or clusters), thus providing a high-level context. Next, SVD is performed for each sub-collection. Thus, concept extraction is performed separately for each knowledge domain. 'Topic-LSI' addresses two of LSI's limitations mentioned above – it enables to use LSI for very large[73], as well as for heterogeneous, collections.

A second combination of topics and synonyms is possible by utilizing the topical organization of the collection to restrict the number of clusters associated with the query (similarly to cluster-based retrieval), such that (a) cluster profiles are projected onto the semantic space and query-profile similarity is performed in that space, to restrict the set of clusters associated with the query (similarly to cluster-based retrieval), and (b) the query is projected only onto the semantic spaces of the restricted clusters, and query-document similarity is calculated in that semantic space (similarly to LSI). We refer to this combined retrieval model '*Cluster-based LSI*'. This combined model could improve LSI run-time efficiency (since the query is only matched with documents in the restricted set of clusters), thus addressing the fourth of LSI's limitations discussed above, and has the potential to improve Precision, since the selected clusters usually will include a high concentration of relevant documents.

---

[73] For very large collections, the core process of LSI, SVD, in itself might not be adequate, while Topic-LSI offers a viable solution, as clustering is significantly more efficient than SVD. Thus the combined approach, where clustering is first utilized to reduce the dimensionality of the problem, is bound to reduce the solution's complexity.

Lastly, a more complex combination of LSI and cluster-based retrieval could be achieved by including the two additional principles proposed in Chapter 11 – cluster-based weighting and cluster-based matching. Cluster-based weighting suggests that the weighting of index terms be adjusted to accommodate for the fact that only few clusters are associated with the query. In LSI, document indexes are not weighted directly; rather weighting of index terms is performed as a pre-process to LSI. Hence, we propose that for cluster-based LSI, document indexes be weighted, prior to Singular Value Decomposition (SVD), so the global factor in the weighting scheme (the IDF factor in Term-Frequency-Inverse-Document-Frequency) will reflect the fact that "the collection" for matching purposes includes only documents in the clusters associated with the query. Cluster-based matching suggests that query-profile and document-profile could be utilized to estimate the relevancy of a document to a query. We will employ this principle in LSI's semantic space, so that the similarities - $S(Q, D)$, $S(Q, P)$, and $S(P, D)$ - are all measured in that space.

We plan to explore the three levels combinations between LSI and topic-based IR proposed above – topic-LSI, cluster-based LSI, and cluster-based LSI with cluster-based weighting and matching – as described below.

13.2 An Exploratory Empirical Evaluation of LSI with Topic-Based Retrieval

In Section 13.1.3 we proposed a general approach for combining LSI and topic-based retrieval, based on three levels on integration. In this section we describe the design and results of a set of experiments that test the performance of these three combined models.

13.2.1 Experimental Design and Implementation Procedure

In this initial exploratory study of the combined models there are many interesting questions to explore. Following, we identify the most critical issues worth investigating.

First, for testing topic-LSI, where LSI is performed distinctively for topically-coherent clusters, we would like to study the model's sensitivity to the critical LSI parameters identified in Chapter 8 (the number of SVD dimensions and vector normalization) and to the critical factor of the topical decomposition process identified in Chapter 9 (i.e. the number of clusters, or topics, the collection is decomposed into). Then, we will test the effect of topical organization on LSI by comparing topic-LSI to LSI for arbitrary decomposition (described in Chapter 8).

Second, for testing cluster-based LSI, where queries are restricted to only a small set of clusters (as in cluster-based retrieval), we will test the sensitivity of the integrated model to the critical parameters of cluster-based IR (i.e. the number of clusters each query is restricted to). We will test the effect of query restriction by comparing topic-LSI to cluster-based LSI. We will also test the effect of the semantic unit employed to construct the semantic space by comparing cluster-based LSI with the traditional (token-based) cluster-based retrieval.

Finally, we will test the effect of cluster-based weighting and cluster-based matching on cluster-based LSI.

Te baseline for comparing the integrated models were the two distinct retrieval models: (1) LSI with an arbitrary decomposition of the collection (as described in Chapter 8), and (2) cluster-based retrieval, where clustering is performed with K-means (MacQueen, 1967), Euclidean document-document distance measure, and cluster cetroids as profiles (as described in Chapter 9).

Below we describe the experiments in more detail.

Topic-LSI was studies in experiments 1-3. The collection was decomposed into 100 topically-coherent clusters of varying sizes (ranging from 2,000 to 15,000; see list of cluster sizes in appendix 4), using the clustering procedure employed for cluster-based retrieval, as described above. Singular value decomposition (SVD) was performed distinctively for each cluster, on the complete set of documents in that cluster (i.e. we did not fold-in additional documents), using Matlab[74]. **Experiment 1** tested the model's sensitivity to LSI's parameters, as follows. To test the effect of the number of SVD dimensions (or factors), we tested two values: 150 and 300 average dimensions. The clusters are un-even, and we wanted the number of dimensions to be correlated with the size of the sub-collection. We, thus, set the number of dimensions in sub-collection i to equal $N_i \times r \times k_{avg} / N$ (where N_i is the size of cluster i, r is the number of clusters, k_{avg} is the average number of dimensions per cluster, and N is the collection's size), ensuring the *average* size is 150 and 300. The effect of query weighting was tested by comparing TF-IDF weighted and un-weighted (using raw terms' frequencies in the index, instead of weights) queries. The effect of vector normalization in the SVD space was tested by comparing two alternative query-document matching schemes. In one the un-normalized query and document vectors are matched using the cosine function. In the alternative scheme, the vectors are normalized in L2 (so that the sum of squares of the conceptual query, $\vec{Q}_k \bullet \vec{S}_k$, and the conceptual document, $\vec{D}_k \bullet \vec{S}_k$, are each equal to one) prior to matching. In **Experiment 2** we studied the effect of the number of topics (or clusters) the collection is decomposed into on Topic-LSI. We compared two variations of Topic-LSI: in then first we employed 100 topics, while in the second we used 200 clusters of sizes 1,000-10,000 (see list of clusters' sizes in Appendix 5). In **Experiment 3** we tested the effect of topical organization by comparing the performance of LSI with random corpus decomposition (tested in Chapter 8) to LSI with topically coherent decomposition (i.e. Topic-LSI). For both cases we employed 100 sub-collections decomposition, and performed LSI with 300 SVD dimensions and query weighting. Since vector normalization had a different effect on the models compared, we chose to compare the best variation of each model – LSI in random decomposition with vector normalization against Topic-LSI with un-normalized vectors.

Cluster-Based LSI was studied in experiments 4 and 5. In this model each query was associated to a restricted set of clusters, based on the similarity of cluster profile to the query vector. Both query and profile vectors were projected onto LSI's semantic

---

[74] Matlab is a commercial product by The MathWorks Inc., 3 Apple Hill Drive, Natick, MA 01760-2098, USA

space, and their similarity was calculated in that space using the cosine measure. Then query-documents distance was measured in the SVD space, similarly to standard LSI.

Experiment 4 tested the effect of the semantic unit employed to construct the semantic space, by comparing cluster-based LSI with the traditional (token-based) cluster-based retrieval (based on results obtained in Chapter 9). For both models the collection was decomposed into 200 topically-coherent clusters, and query vectors were un-weighted. For cluster-based LSI we employed a 300-dimension SVD process, with no vector normalization. **Experiment 5** tested the effect of restricting the number of clusters associated with the query by comparing cluster-based LSI to Topic-LSI. For both models, we employed a 200-cluster corpus decomposition, and LSI was performed with 300 SVD dimensions, and un-normalized vectors. For cluster-based LSI we restricted queries to 1, 2, 10, 20, 30, 40, and 60 out of the total 200 clusters.

Experiment 6-8 tested the effect of cluster-based weighting and matching on cluster-based LSI. **Experiment 6** tested a simple realization of cluster-based weighting – one-cluster weighting – where document indexes weights for LSI are calculated as though the collections includes that cluster alone (as described in Chapter 11), prior to SVD processing. **Experiment 7** tested the one simple realization of cluster-based matching that performed best in Chapter 11 studies, where the relevancy of a document to a query is estimated based on the sum of query-profile and query-document similarities (i.e., $f_2 = sim(Q,D) + sim(Q,P)$). **Experiment 8** tested the combined effect of cluster-based weighting and matching on cluster-based LSI. These experiments were performed with 100-clusters corpus decomposition, LSI with 150 SVD dimensions, un-weighted query indexes, and un-normalized vectors, and query-clusters association of 10, 20, and 30 out of the total 100 clusters.

In all three experiments we employed the effectiveness measures used throughout this dissertation: Precision[10], Precision[20], Precision[30], and Recall[1000].

13.2.2 Results and Analysis

The initial set of experiments studies the performance of Topic-LSI, using a 100-clusrter corpus decomposition.

The first experiment investigated the sensitivity of Topic-LSI to LSI' critical parameters - the number of SVD dimensions, and vector normalization. Our findings are summarized in the table below.

Average # of dimensions per cluster	150	150	300	300
Normalization	No	Yes	No	Yes
Precision[10]	0.148	0.073	0.189	0.107
Precision[20]	0.129	0.062	0.176	0.086
Precision[30]	0.117	0.056	0.157	0.080
Recall [1000]	0.319	0.226	0.355	0.281

Table 13-1: Sensitivity of Topic-LSI to LSI's parameters. Corpus decomposition with 100 clusters.
Optimal results are shaded in gray.

The table above demonstrates that Topic-LSI is very sensitive to LSI's parameters. Precision for 300 SVD dimensions surpass that of 150 dimensions by 27%-46%, and Recall is better by 11%-24%, and this effect is similar to the effect observed for traditional LSI. Vector normalization has a substantial negative effect on both Precision and Recall, resulting in 30%-50% losses, and this effect is opposite to the effect observed for traditional LSI. We are unsure why the topical-coherency of the sub-collection should influence the effect of vector normalization. Overall, the optimal performance levels were obtained for 300 SVD dimensions and un-normalized vectors.

Experiment 2

The second experiment investigated the sensitivity of Topic-LSI to the number of cluster the collection is decomposed into. When comparing Topic-LSI with 100 and 200-cluster corpus decomposition, using the optimal setting revealed above (300 SVD dimensions, and un-normalized vectors), the following results were obtained.

# of clusters in corpus	100	200	difference
Precision[10]	0.189	0.237	25%
Precision[20]	0.176	0.206	17%
Precision[30]	0.157	0.179	14%
Recall[1000]	0.355	0.377	6%

Table 13-2: Sensitivity of Topic-LSI to the number of clusters the corpus is decomposed into.

The table above demonstrates that employing 200-cluster decomposition results in Precision and Recall gains over the 100-cluster decomposition. These findings support the findings in Chapter 9, suggesting that the effectiveness of topic-based IR depends on the number of topics used.

Experiment 3

The third and last experiment of Topic-LSI investigated the effect of topical organization on LSI effectiveness by comparing LSI in arbitrarily-decomposed clusters to LSI in topically-coherent clusters. For both cases we employed 100 sub-collections decomposition, and performed LSI with 300 SVD dimensions and query weighting. Since vector normalization had a different effect on the models compared, we chose to compare the best variation of each model – LSI in random decomposition with vector normalization against Topic-LSI with un-normalized vectors. Our results are presented below.

Measure	LSI in arbitrarily-generated clusters	Topic-LSI (LSI in topically-coherent clusters)	Difference
Precision[10]	0.125	0.189	51%
Precision[20]	0.106	0.176	66%
Precision[30]	0.098	0.157	60%
Recall[1000]	0.314	0.355	13%

Table 13-3: The effect of topical organization of LSI

The table above demonstrates that topical organization of the sub-collections effect LSI Precision significantly (by 51%-60%), and Recall is affected to a lesser extent[75].

The next set of experiments studies Cluster-Based LSI, where Topic-LSI is complemented with restricting the number of clusters per query.

---

[75] Recall[1000] for Topic-LSI is 13% higher.

<u>Experiment 4</u>

The fourth experiment investigated the effect of the semantic unit employed to construct the semantic space on cluster-based IR, by comparing cluster-based LSI against the traditional (token-based) cluster-based retrieval (based on results obtained in Chapter 9). For both models the collection was decomposed into 200 topically-coherent clusters. For cluster-based LSI we employed a 300-dimension SVD process, with no vector normalization. The results are presented below.

clusters per query	Semantic unit	2/200	10/200	20/200	40/200	60/200
Precision[10]	Tokens	0.166	0.204	0.219	0.241	0.245
	Synonyms	0.162	0.223	0.228	0.241	0.240
Precision[20]	Tokens	0.127	0.162	0.181	0.181	0.199
	Synonyms	0.136	0.179	0.188	0.203	0.207
Precision[30]	Tokens	0.102	0.134	0.152	0.168	0.174
	Synonyms	0.112	0.151	0.159	0.172	0.178
Recall[1000]	Tokens	0.214	0.297	0.338	0.375	0.391
	Synonyms	0.086	0.112	0.123	0.146	0.150

Table 13-5: The effect of the semantic unit employed to construct the semantic space on cluster-based IR. Using 200-cluster decomposition and un-weighted query. LSI with 300-dimension SVD process, and no vector normalization. Results for 5 alternative realizations of cluster-based IR (with 2, 10, 20, 30, and 60 clusters per query out of the total 200 clusters).

The results reveal that there is no significant difference in Precision for cluster-based retrieval between token and synonym concepts representations; although in most cases, cluster-based LSI is superior to the traditional cluster-based model. Recall, surprisingly, is substantially lower for cluster-based LSI.

<u>Experiment 5</u>

The fifth experiment investigated the effect restricting the number of clusters associated with the query, by comparing Topic-LSI and cluster-based LSI. For both models, we employed a 200-cluster corpus decomposition, and LSI was performed with 300 SVD dimensions, and un-normalized vectors. For cluster-based LSI we restricted queries to 1, 2, 10, 20, 30, 40, and 60 out of the total 200 clusters. The results of this experiment are illustrated in the diagram below.

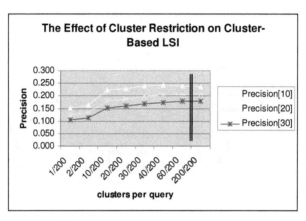

Diagram 13-1: The effect of cluster restriction on Precision of cluster-based LSI. Using 200-cluster decomposition and LSI with 300 SVD dimensions, un-weighted query index, and un-normalized vectors.

Since it is well established that cluster restriction results in Recall losses, we focused our analysis on Precision. We observe that for all Precision measures performance levels remain constant when less clusters are associated with each query, down to 30/200 clusters; further restriction on the number of clusters results in minor Precision losses down to 10/200 clusters; restricting the number of clusters beyond that point results in substantial losses.

The diagram below illustrates the effect of cluster restriction on Precision[10] for cluster-based LSI, when compared to the effect on standard (i.e., using token representations) cluster-based retrieval.

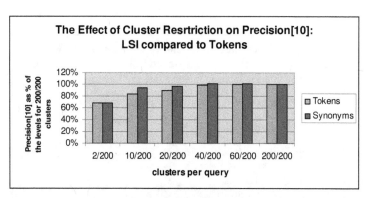

The Effect of Cluster Resrtriction on Precision[10]:
LSI compared to Tokens

Diagram 13-2: The effect of cluster restriction on Precision[10] for cluster-based LSI, when compared to the effect on standard cluster-based retrieval. Using 200-cluster decomposition, and LSI with 300 SVD dimensions, un-weighted query index, and un-normalized vectors.

We notice that the effect of cluster restriction in cluster-based LSI is very similar to the effect in standard cluster-based retrieval.

The next set of experiments studied cluster-based weighting and matching for cluster-based LSI. For experiments 6-8, we employed a 100-cluster decomposition and performed LSI with 150 SVD dimensions, and un-normalized query vectors.

Experiment 6

The sixth experiment tested a simple realization of cluster-based weighting – one-cluster weighting – where document indexes weights for LSI are calculated as though the collections includes that cluster alone (as described in Chapter 11), prior to SVD processing. Our results indicate that cluster-based weighting has a substantial negative effect on Precision (15%-32% losses) and minor positive effect of Recall (3%-6% gains). The effect of cluster-based weighting for cluster-based IR in LSI's conceptual space was opposite to the effect observed for token representations (where one-cluster weighting improved effectiveness significantly).

Experiment 7

The seventh experiment tested the realization of cluster-based matching that performed best in Chapter 11 studies, where the relevancy of a document to a query is estimated based on the sum of query-profile and query-document similarities (i.e. $f_2 = sim(Q,D) + sim(Q,P)$). We found that this simple realization of cluster-based matching had no effect on the performance of cluster-based LSI, and effectiveness levels almost identical to the traditional matching (i.e. where relevance is estimated solely on query-document similarity).

Experiment 8

The last experiment of this chapter tested the combined effect of cluster-based weighting and matching on cluster-based LSI. The results reveal that, the combination of cluster-based weighting and cluster-based matching had little effect, and its performance levels were very similar to those obtained with only cluster-based weighting.

Efficiency Analysis

During pre-processing, LSI requires significant computational resources and is restricted to small and medium-size collections due to the complexity of its core process – Singular Value Decomposition (SVD). SVD's complexity is $O(s \times M^2 \times N + s \times N^3)$, where N is the number of documents, s is the number of dimensions, M is the number of unique terms (or tokens), and in most cases $s \ll M < N$ (Golub & van Loan 1993). Topical decomposition of the corpus is significantly less complex that LSI, yet requires substantial processing (for instance the complexity of K-means clustering is rectangular, $O(lkN)$, where N is the number of documents in the collection, k is the number of clusters, and l is the number of iterations). When clustering precedes LSI and LSI is calculated distinctively for each cluster (assuming k clusters of average size N/k), the complexity of LSI is $O\left(k \times \left(s \times M^2 \times \dfrac{N}{k} + s \times \left(\dfrac{N}{k}\right)^3\right)\right)$. Hence, the combined clustering-LSI processing could scale to very large collections.

For run-time, LSI is more complex than traditional token-based matching, since queries have to b projected onto the semantic space and the use of an inverted matrix is not feasible (Deerwester et al. 1990, Dumais 1994). Restricting query to only a few clusters requires query-profile matching, but is substantially more efficient since it restricts query-document matching to only documents in the most relevant clusters. Hence, complementing LSI with cluster-based retrieval compensates for LSI run-time inefficiency.

13.2.3 Discussion

The results of the eight experiments described in the previous section demonstrate the viability of the combination of topic-based and synonym-based retrieval models.

Results of experiment with Topic-LSI (experiments 1-3) reveal that topical pre-organization of the collection enhances the Precision of synonym-based retrieval (specifically, LSI) significantly, and results in moderate Recall gains. Topic-LSI is very sensitive to the type of topical corpus decomposition (specifically, the number of topically-coherent clusters employed) as well as to LSI parameters (mainly the number of SVD dimensions and vector normalization). Another interesting finding is that while LSI proved to be significantly less effective than token-based retrieval (see results of Chapter 8), Topic-LSI performs as well as token-based retrieval.

When Topic-LSI is complemented with cluster-based retrieval, i.e. restricting the query to only the most relevant clusters (referred to as 'cluster-based LSI', and studies in experiments 4 and 5), we observed degradation in effectiveness, as fewer clusters were associated with queries. This effect, as well as the performance levels, was very similar to those observed for standard (i.e. with token representations) cluster-based retrieval.

Cluster-based weighting and cluster-based matching, studies in experiments 6-8, showed almost not impact on cluster-based LSI.

The most important findings of this study is that providing context for synonym-based retrieval, by decomposing the collection into topically-coherent clusters and performing concept extraction within each cluster, improves the performance of synonym-based retrieval significantly. Furthermore, LSI, which has been traditionally been associated with Precision losses (see for instance our experiments in Chapter 8), could actually match the performance of token-based retrieval, when used with prior topical organization of the collection. Given the sensitivity of the combined model - 'Topic-LSI' - to the model's parameters and the fact that we explored only a very limited set of parameter's settings, we believe that Topic-LSI performance could potentially surpass the performance of token-based retrieval.

In the experiments reported above we explored three levels of integration between the Topics and Synonym categories, and for each of these integration levels we explored only few realizations. Given the sensitivity of the models to their parameters, further explorations are warranted in order to attain the full potential of Topic-Synonym combination. In the future we plan to study the performance of the combined models with alternative realizations.

13.3 Conclusion

In this chapter we studied the interaction between semantic units from two categories of our proposed framework – topics and synonym concepts. Specifically, we explored the combination of Latent Semantic Indexing (LSI) with topical organization of the collection (through clustering) and query-cluster restriction. We proposed three different levels for complementing LSI based on the topical organization of the corpus: (1) Topic-LSI (where LSI is performed within topically-coherent clusters), (2) cluster-based LSI (where, in addition, queries are restricted to only few clusters), and (3) complementing cluster-based LSI with cluster-based weighting and cluster-based matching.

We conducted an exploratory empirical study of the proposed combinations to obtain encouraging results. Topic-LSI addressed the two most critical limitations of LSI - inability to scale to large collections, and inappropriateness for heterogeneous collections - and showed significant effectiveness gains over LSI. Cluster-based LSI addressed an additional limitation of LSI – run-time complexity – and suggested that the matching process could be made more efficient by restricting query-document matching to only documents in the most relevant clusters, with minor impact on effectiveness (e.g. with only 10 out of the total 200 clusters per query, Precision[10] is merely 6% lower that the level obtained for the entire 200 clusters). Hence, this study reveals how the interplay between topical organization and synonym concept representations could result in performance improvements.

Our contribution in this chapter is three fold. First, conceptual contribution in proposing a retrieval models that combine Latent Semantic Indexing with topical corpus decomposition; second, in the empirical testing of this novel models, providing evidence for its effectiveness; and third, in demonstrating how the interplay between meaning-carrying units of different granularities - topics and synonym concepts - could be utilized in the design of effective retrieval models, and thus opening the door for further studies on Topics-Synonyms interaction.

Chapter 14: Exploring the Interplay between 'Composite Concepts' and 'Tokens'

In this chapter we will try to address Research Question #2.4: Could 'Tokens' and 'Composite Concepts' be integrated into one coherent retrieval model? And if yes – how will the performance of the combined model compare to the performance of token-based and composite-based models? To address the question, we will:

- Propose a novel retrieval model that combines token-based and composite-based retrieval. We will index documents and queries through both tokens and composites, and will assess query-document relevance based on the token-based and composite-based index similarities.

- Conduct an empirical study of the proposed model, based on the representative techniques for token-based and composite-based retrieval (described in Chapters 6 and 7 respectively).

  - Study the effectiveness of the model, by exploring the effect of key parameters.
  - Study the efficiency of the proposed model.
  - Compare the performance of the combined model to that of token-based and composite-based retrieval.

This chapter will continue as follows. In Section 14.1 we will develop the novel retrieval model, and in Section 14.2 we will report the finding from an empirical study that investigated one realization of the model proposed in Section 14.1.

14.1 Matching Query to Documents Using Token-Based and Composites-Based Representations

The development of the retrieval model begins at two starting points: (a) traditional token-based retrieval (reviewed in Chapter 6), and (b) indexing through composite concepts (reviewed in Chapter 7). In the following sections we will recap some of the important point for each of these models, and then proceed to discuss the integration of the models

14.1.1 Recap: Token-Based Retrieval

Retrieval based on tokens, and specifically the Vector-Space model (Salton & Lesk 1971), prescribes the following steps: (1) producing token-based indexes for documents (and later, at run-time, for queries) by extracting tokens and assigning weight to tokens in the indexes, and (2) matching the query and document indexes, to produce a ranked list of 'assumed-to-be relevant' documents.

Token extraction (or 'tokenizing') is based on Luhn's (1958) principles for identifying meaning-carrying units (and pruning all words that do not carry distinct meaning), and commonly includes the following processes: removal of high-frequency terms (through a stop-word list), stemming, and removal of low-frequency terms. The indexing is completed by assigning weights to tokens in document and query indexes to reflect their resolving power, and the most popular weighting scheme is TF-IDF.

Matching is restricted to the documents containing query terms (through the use of an inverted matrix), and query-document similarity is estimated based on the cosine of the angle between the two vector indexes.

Token-based retrieval, and specifically the Vector-Space model, is the ad-hoc standard for commercial retrieval systems, and to date the majority of retrieval systems for general collections are based on these models. Recently, with the rapid explosion of information and the increasing usage of retrieval systems, traditional token-based models have been criticized for returning too much irrelevant information.

14.1.2 Recap: Retrieval with Composite Concepts

In the statistical approach to extracting composite concepts investigated in this thesis (see Chapter 7), composites are obtained by grouping sets of token that appear together in the text (i.e. they co-appear within a pre-set proximity window). Documents, as well as queries, are indexed through these co-occurrence sets, and matching is based on query-document similarity of the composite-based indexes. The most simple and widely deployed form of composite concepts is phrases, and phrase indexing is reported to improve Precision by 2-4%. Generally speaking, more complex forms of composites have not been adopted for general purpose retrieval systems, due to the complexity of composite extraction, indexing, and matching processes. However, there is evidence to suggest that indexing through composite concepts is now being adopted by general purpose commercial retrieval systems (Pedersen 2003).

14.1.3 Integrating Token-Based and Composite-Based Retrieval

We propose that token and composite concepts representations capture different semantic aspects, thus estimating query-document similarity based on both types of representations may lead to more accurate results. We suggest a simple integration of token-based and composite-based retrieval, where indexing and matching is performed separately for each model, and then the matching results (i.e. query-document similarities) are combined into a single measure. We do not claim to prescribe the relative importance of token-based or composite-based matching, hence we propose the general similarity function, S(Query, Document), that is a linear combination of the token-based ($S_{Token}(Query, Document)$) and composite-based ($S_{Composite}(Query, ocument)$) similarities. Hence,

$$S(Query, Document) = \alpha \times S_{Token}(Query, Document) + (1 - \alpha) \times S_{Composite}(Query, Document)$$

$\alpha=1$ represents only token-based similarity, and $\alpha=0$ represents a similarity measure that is based solely on composite indexes.

In the following section we describe the specific realization employed for our experimental study, and report on the findings from that study.

14.2 An Exploratory Empirical Evaluation of Integrating Token-Based and Composites-Based Matching

14.2.1 Experimental Design

In this initial exploratory study model integrating token-based and composite-based matching, we study the extent to which a combined similarity function can enhance retrieval effectiveness. We investigate alternative combinations of the function

$$S(Query, Document) = \alpha \times S_{Token}(Query, Document) + (1 - \alpha) \times S_{Composite}(Query, Document)$$

by exploring different α values. We compare the performance of the combined model to the performance of the two distinct models – token-based and composite-based retrieval.

Since we established earlier that composite-based retrieval is mostly useful in Precision, in our experiment here we employ only Precision measures: Precision[10], Precision[20], and Precision[30]. To test the significance of the improvements provided by the combined model we use a one-sided t-test, where equal variance is not assumed.

We take a similar approach to the one proposed for the composite concepts study in Chapter 7, and use only queries that have at least one composite concept in their index. 91 queries were used, and are listed in Appendix 3.

14.2.2 Implementation Procedure

Token-based matching and indexing was performed using the standard tokenizing techniques employed in the experiments in Chapter 6: stop-word removal with SMART's common words list (Ide & Salton 1971) and stemming with Porter's algorithm (Porter 1980), leaving 443,826 unique tokens. We pruned infrequent tokens that appeared in les than 6 documents, arriving at 72,354 unique tokens[76]. Document indexes were then weighted using the TF-IDF scheme.

Composite-based indexing and matching was based on the procedure described in Chapter 7: we took as an input the set of tokens extracted for token-based indexing (see description above), and then extracted two-term, symmetric, intransitive, proximity-based co-occurrence sets, using the lenient lower cut-off threshold (removing concepts that

---

[76] The resulting average document index included 138 tokens.

appeared in less than 6 documents), resulting in 1,046,135 unique concepts[77]. The frequency of concepts was based on the proximity of the co-occurring terms, within the same sentence and across sentences (employing the exact scheme employed in Chapter 7 experiments). Document indexes were then weighted using the TF-IDF scheme. As in the other studies in this dissertation, query indexes remained un-weighted.

14.2.3 Results and Analysis

The graph below presents Precision levels for the combined approach, using different α values: 1 (tokens only), 0.75, 0.5, 0.33 (the optimal value), 0.25, and 0 (composites only)

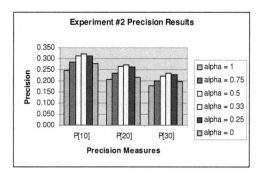

Diagram 14-1: Precision levels for alternative combinations of token-based and composite-based matching

The graph illustrates how query-document similarity calculations that are based on both token and composite matching are more precise than similarity calculation based on either of these models distinctively, and reach an optimum at $\alpha = 0.33$ (giving 33% weight to tokens and 67% weight to composite concepts). The table below compares the performance of the combined model to that of the distinct models.

---

[77] The resulting average document index included 73 concepts.

	Precision[10]	Precision[20]	Precision[30]
Tokens & Composites (α=0.33)	0.322	0.273	0.233
Tokens & Composites vs. Tokens	+30.8%	+31.9%	+30.3%
Tokens & Composites vs. Composites	+16.3%	+32.6%	+29.7%

Table 14-1: comparing Precision levels for the combined model (with α=0.33) against the distinct token-based and composite-based models.

The optimal tokens and relations combination (obtained with α set to 0.33) produced substantially better results than the token-based matching (with Precision levels over 30% higher[78]) and composite-based matching (with Precision levels 16%-30% higher[79]).

The complexity of the combined approach is equal to the sum of the complexities of the distinct token-based and composite-based models. At pre-processing the complexity of the indexing process is linear with the total number of documents in the corpus, and at run-time matching is linear with the number of documents that contain query terms. Hence, although the combined approach is scalable to general collections, it is still more complex than the complexity of either of the two distinct models.

14.2.4 Discussion

The results of the experiment described in the previous section demonstrate the viability of the combination of token-based and composite-based retrieval models, as matching based on the two models resulted in significant Precision gains.

It is very interesting to note that a simple integration of matching data from two models that perform similarly, results in Precision levels that surpass substantially the

---

[78] Statistical significance was as follows: p = 0.031 for Precision[10], p = 0.025 for Precision[20], and p = 0.025 for Precision[30].

[79] Statistical significance was as follows: p = 0.150 (insignificant) for Precision[10], p = 0.027 for Precision[20], and p = 0.040 for Precision[30].

performance levels of the distinct models. If tokens and composites were to represent similar semantics, than the combination should not have performed better than the distinct models. We deduce then that token and composites capture different semantics aspects, thus corroborating the "Semantic Unit Categorization" framework introduced in Part1 of this dissertation.

14.3 Conclusion

In this chapter we studied the interaction between semantic units from two categories of our proposed framework – tokens and composite concepts. Specifically, we explored how a matching function that builds token-based and composite-based similarity measures could enhance retrieval performance.

We conducted an exploratory empirical study of the proposed integrative model, to obtain positive results – the combined model performed substantially better than either of the two distinct models, resulting in Precision gains of up to 32%. Thus, this study reveals how the interplay between token and composite concept representations could result in performance improvements.

We obtained optimal performance levels for the combined model with the similarity function:

$$S(Query, Document) = 0.33 \times S_{Token}(Query, Document) + 0.67 \times S_{Composite}(Query, Document)$$

It is possible that for different collections, different α values will prove optimal.

Our contribution in this chapter is in providing the first strong evidence for the value of integrating token-based and composite-based matching. We hope that this study will open the door for further studies on Token-Composites interaction.

Chapter 15: Exploring the Interplay between 'Synonym Concepts' and 'Tokens'

In this chapter we will try to address Research Question #2.5: Could 'Tokens' and 'Synonym Concepts' be integrated into one coherent retrieval model? And if yes – how will the performance of the combined model compare to the performance of token-based and synonym-based models? To address the question, we will:

- Propose a novel retrieval model that combines token-based and composite-based retrieval. We will index documents and queries through both tokens and synonyms, and will assess query-document relevance based on the token-based and synonyms -based index similarities.

- Conduct an empirical study of the proposed model, based on the representative techniques for token-based and synonyms -based retrieval (described in Chapters 6 and 8 respectively).
  - Study the effectiveness of the model, by exploring the effect of key parameters.
  - Study the efficiency of the proposed model.
  - Compare the performance of the combined model to that of token-based and synonyms -based retrieval.

This chapter will continue as follows. In Section 15.1 we will develop the novel retrieval model, and in Section 15.2 we will report the finding from an empirical study that investigated one realization of the model proposed in Section 15.1.

15.1 Matching Query to Documents Using Token-Based and Synonyms-Based Representations

The development of the retrieval model begins at two starting points: (a) traditional token-based retrieval (specifically, the Vector-Space model, reviewed in Chapter 6), and (b) indexing through synonym concepts (specifically, Latent Semantic Indexing, reviewed in Chapter 8). In the following sections we will recap some of the important point for each of these models, and then proceed to discuss the integration of the models

15.1.1 Recap: Token-Based Retrieval

Retrieval based on tokens, and specifically the Vector-Space model (Salton & Lesk 1971), prescribes the following steps: (1) producing token-based indexes for documents (and later, at run-time, for queries) by extracting tokens and assigning weight to tokens in the indexes, and (2) matching the query and document indexes, to produce a ranked list of 'assumed-to-be relevant' documents.

Token extraction (or 'tokenizing') is based on Luhn's (1958) principles for identifying meaning-carrying units (and pruning all words that do not carry distinct meaning), and commonly includes the following processes: removal of high-frequency terms (through a stop-word list), stemming, and removal of low-frequency terms. The indexing is completed by assigning weights to tokens in document and query indexes to reflect their resolving power, and the most popular weighting scheme is TF-IDF.

Matching is restricted to the documents containing query terms (through the use of an inverted matrix), and query-document similarity is estimated based on the cosine of the angle between the two vector indexes.

Token-based retrieval, and specifically the vector-space model, is the ad-hoc standard for commercial retrieval systems, and to date the majority of retrieval systems for general collections are based on these models. Recently, with the rapid explosion of information and the increasing usage of retrieval systems, traditional token-based models have been criticized for returning too much irrelevant information.

15.1.2 Recap: Retrieval with Synonym Concepts

Latent Semantic Indexing (LSI) is the most popular retrieval model that employs synonym-based representations, mainly due to its strong theoretical foundations (Baeza Yates & Ribiero Neto 1999. LSI (Deerwester et al. 1990, Dumais 1994, Landauer et al. 1998, Husbands et al. 2000) is an extension to the Vector-Space model where factor-analytic techniques are used to extract the main factors that represent synonym concepts (see our review in Chapter 8). The semantic space is represented through these orthogonal factors, and information elements - documents and queries – are mapped onto that space, so that query-document similarity is calculated based on their positioning in the conceptual space. LSI has shown simulate human knowledge successfully (Landauer et al. 1998). Latent Semantic Indexing has been reported to enhance performance for small, domain-specific collections, and in many cases its performances surpasses traditional keyword search by as much as 30% (Landauer et al. 1998). For general collections, LSI acts in many ways as query expansion techniques, retrieving more documents, both relevant and irrelevant, thus improving Recall, but at the cost of low Precision.

15.1.3 Integrating Token-Based and Synonym-Based Retrieval

We propose that token and synonym concepts representations capture different semantic aspects, thus estimating query-document similarity based on both types of representations may lead to more accurate results. We suggest a simple integration of token-based and synonym retrieval where indexing and matching is performed separately for each model, and then the matching results (i.e. query-document similarities) are combined into a single measure. We do not claim to prescribe the relative importance of token-based or synonym-based matching, hence we propose the general similarity function, S(Query, Document), that is a linear combination of the token-based ($S_{Token}(Query, Document)$) and synonym-based ($S_{Synonym}(Query, Document)$) similarities. Hence:

$$S(Query, Document) = \alpha \times S_{Token}(Query, Document) + (1 - \alpha) \times S_{Synonym}(Query, Document).$$

$\alpha=1$ represents only token-based similarity, and $\alpha=0$ represents a similarity measure that is based solely on synonym indexes.

In the following section we describe the specific realization employed for our experimental study, and report on the findings from that study.

15.2 An Exploratory Empirical Evaluation of Integrating Token-Based and Synonyms-Based Matching

15.2.1 Experimental Design

In this initial exploratory study model integrating token-based and synonym-based matching, we study the extent to which a combined similarity function can enhance retrieval effectiveness. We investigate alternative combinations of the function

$$S(Query, Document) = \alpha \times S_{Token}(Query, Document) + (1 - \alpha) \times S_{Synonym}(Query, Document)$$

by exploring different α values. We compare the performance of the combined model to the performance of the two distinct models – token-based and synonym-based retrieval.

In our experiment here we employ effectiveness measures used throughout this study: Precision[10], Precision[20], and Precision[30], and Recall[1000].

15.2.2 Implementation Procedure

Token-based matching and indexing was performed used the standard tokenizing techniques employed in the experiments in Chapter 6: stop-word removal with SMART's common words list (Ide & Salton 1971) and stemming with Porter's algorithm (Porter 1980), leaving 443,826 unique tokens. We pruned infrequent tokens that appeared in les than 6 documents, arriving at 72,354 unique tokens[80]. Document indexes were then weighted using the TF-IDF scheme. Query-document similarity was calculated using the cosine function.

The tokenizing procedure and the document-token matrix generated for token-based retrieval was used as the input for constructing a (synonym-based) semantic space. Since Latent Semantic Indexing was not scalable to our test collection, we arbitrarily decomposed the corpus into 100 sub-collections (as described in Chapter 8). Singular Value Decomposition (SVD) was performed distinctively for each sub-collection, with 300 dimensions, using Matlab[81]. Each query was projected onto each of the 100 semantic

---

[80] The resulting average document index included 138 tokens.
[81] Matlab is a commercial product by The MathWorks Inc., 3 Apple Hill Drive, Natick, MA 01760-2098, USA

196

spaces (one for each sub-collection), and query-documents similarity was measured in that space by normalizing both vectors and using the cosine function.

In both cases - token-based and synonym-based indexing - queries indexes were not weighted (i.e. the query index included the frequency of terms).

Once token-based and synonym-based similarities were obtained, they were integrated. For integration we explored alternative α values – from $\alpha=0$ (only synonym-based similarity) to $\alpha=1$ (only token-based similarity).

15.2.3 Results and Analysis

When testing the performance for different value of α we obtained the best results at $\alpha=0.86$. The table below compares the performance of the combined model at the optimal level to that of the distinct models.

Tokens & Synonyms ($\alpha=0.86$)	Precision[10]	Precision[20]	Precision[30]	Recall[1000]
Average	0.255	0.205	0.174	0.437
Tokens & Synonyms vs. Tokens	+4.5%	+0.2%	-1.5%	-1.9%
Tokens & Synonyms vs. Synonyms	+104.0%	+93.8%	+78.5%	+39.0%

Table 15-1: comparing Precision levels for the combined model (with $\alpha=0.86$) against the distinct token-based and synonym-based models.

The optimal tokens and relations combination (obtained with α set to 0.86) produced similar results to those obtained with token-based matching, and substantially better results than pure synonym-based retrieval (Precision 80%-100% higher and Recall roughly 40% higher).

The complexity of the combined approach is equal to the sum of the complexities of the distinct token-based and synonym-based models. At pre-processing the complexity of token-based indexing is linear with the total number of documents in the corpus, and

197

LSI complexity is $O(s \times M^2 \times N + s \times N^3)$, where N is the number of documents, s is the number of dimensions, M is the number of unique terms, and in most cases $s << M < N$ (Golub & van Loan 1993).

At run-time, token-based matching is linear with the number of documents that contain query terms, and LSI matching is linear with the total number of documents in the collection.

15.2.4 Discussion

LSI with arbitrary decomposition of the collection performs poorly, as demonstrated in Chapter 8. Combining LSI matching with token-based matching improved dramatically the performance of LSI, but did not yield gains beyond the performance levels of token-based matching. LSI is very sensitive to the model's parameters and we believe that if LSI is set-up optimally it could reach the performance levels of token-based models [as has been argued by (Landauer et al. 1998)], and thus the integration of LSI-based and token-based matching could yield performance levels that would surpass those of the distinct models.

15.3 Conclusion

In this chapter we studied the interaction between semantic units from two categories of our proposed framework – tokens and synonym concepts. Specifically, we explored how a matching function that builds token-based and synonym-based similarity measures could enhance retrieval performance.

We conducted an exploratory empirical study of the proposed integrative model, and obtained optimal performance levels for the combined model with the similarity function:

$$S(Query, Document) = 0.86 \times S_{Token}(Query, Document) + 0.14 \times S_{Composite}(Query, Document)$$

It is possible that for different collections, different α values will prove optimal. This integration was able to improve on LSI-based matching substantially, but did not yield performance improvements over token-based retrieval.

Our contribution in this chapter is in exploring a novel approach for synonym-token integration, and revealing its limitations.

Chapter 16: Part III Summary

Part III of this dissertation addressed the second research question, and tried to establish whether the interplay between semantic units from distinct categories could provide performance gains (beyond the performance levels obtained for each semantic unit separately). In order to attain this goal, we (a) designed novel retrieval models by exploring the interplay between semantic units from different categories, and (b) operationalized the novel model (based on the typical realization for each semantic unit category described in Part II) and tested it empirically on the same large-scale benchmark used earlier in this research. As in Part II, we employed the following representative models for each of the semantic unit categories:

- 'Tokens' – tokenizing based on the classical methods of removal of high-frequency terms, stemming, and removal of low frequency terms. Tokens were weighted based on Term-Frequency Inverse-Document-Frequency' (TF-IDF) scheme.

- Composite Concepts: extracting two-token co-occurrence sets using statistical proximity models.

- Synonym Concepts: by using Latent Semantic Indexing (LSI), where factor-analytic techniques are employed to construct a semantic space of lower dimensions.

- Topics: cluster-based retrieval, where topical organization of the collection is employed to restrict the set of documents a query is matched against.

Empirical testing was performed with the same collection employed for Part II tests: the TREC database (disks #4 and #5) and 100 queries.

Each of the four chapters of Part III was dedicated to one type of combination of semantic units. In Chapter 11 we proposed how topical organization of the collection could be used to revise the indexing and matching processes in token based retrieval. We proposed two new principles - 'cluster-based weighting' and cluster-based matching' – and tested them empirically to demonstrate their viability. In Chapter 12 we proposed that cluster-based retrieval employ composite concepts indexes for the matching process (in two steps: matching a query to clusters, and matching a query to documents in these clusters). Results from this study demonstrate significant Precision gains over the standard (token-based) cluster-based retrieval model. In Chapter 13 we proposed that topical organization of the collection be used in concurrence with synonym-based retrieval (i.e. Latent Semantic Indexing; LSI) in two ways. First, in a model named 'Topic LSI', synonym concepts are extracted within topically coherent clusters, results in substantial performance gains over the synonym-based model explored in Chapter 8 (where synonym concepts are extracted within arbitrary clusters). Second, on top of the extraction of concepts within the topical clusters, topical organization is employed to restrict the number of clusters associated with a query (referred to as 'Cluster-Based LSI'), to produce slight improvements over traditional (token-based) cluster-based retrieval. In Chapter 14 we proposed that token-based and composite-based retrieval be integrated, such that the matching process is based on both token and composite indexes, and tested the model to show significant improvements over the individual token-based and composite-based retrieval. Lastly, in Chapter 15 we proposed that token-based and synonym-based retrieval be integrated, such that the matching process is based on both token and synonym indexes, and tested the model to show minor improvements over the retrieval model of the individual units.

The findings from the empirical tests were reported in chapters 11-15. Below we will summarize these findings and answer Research Question #2: does the combination of two distinct artificial semantic units in one coherent retrieval model enable performance gains beyond the levels obtained for each semantic unit separately? We will start by highlighting the most important findings from each chapter of Part III, and then continue to generalize from the specific findings to broader conclusions.

In Chapter 11 we explored topic-token combination and introduced two extensions to the cluster-based model. 'Cluster-based Weighting' suggested that once documents are assigned to a specific cluster, the indexing process be adjusted (or more precisely suggest that the token-weighting process change). 'Cluster-Based Matching' proposed that the additional information available through clustering (i.e., query-profile and profile-document similarities) be employed in the matching process. For each of these two theoretical principles we proposed a simple realization, and tested that realization empirically. Cluster-based weighting showed significant performance improvements (especially when few clusters are associated with the query), and when complemented with cluster-based matching additional performance gains were obtained. Furthermore, when the two proposed principles were employed, cluster restriction resulted in Precision gains, and performance levels with 10/100 clusters per query were 15% higher than those with no cluster restriction (i.e. the classic Vector-Space model).

In Chapter 12 we explored topic-composite combination and proposed that the two-step matching process of cluster-based retrieval be based on composite concept indexes (instead of token-based indexes) for both documents and queries. Two interesting results were obtained: first, cluster-based IR with composites is significantly more effective than the traditional token-based model (with Precision gains of 60% and Recall gains of 50%); second, cluster restriction hardly affects performance of composite-based retrieval (very differently from the results observed for the traditional token-based model), and when only 5/100 clusters are associated with the query performance is similar (i.e., Precision loss of 1% and Recall loss of 2%) to that obtained with no cluster restriction.

In Chapter 13 we explored topic-synonym combination and proposed that the semantic space for LSI be generated in topically coherent clusters (referred to as 'Topic-LSI'), thus addressing two of LSI's main limitations: (a) scalability, and (b) homogeneity of the sub-collection. Topic-LSI outperformed traditional LSI (where the document corpus was arbitrarily decomposed into sub-collection) substantially, resulting in 51%-66% Precision gains and 13% Recall gains). We then proposed to extend this model and employ the topical organization to restrict the number of cluster associated with each query (i.e., cluster-based retrieval in LSI's semantic space, referred to as 'Cluster-Based LSI'), thus addressing an additional limitation of LSI – run-time efficiency. Cluster-restriction in the LSI space resulted in Precision losses (6%-19% losses with 10/200 clusters per query), very similar to the affect of cluster restriction on token-based retrieval.

In Chapter 14 we explored Token-Composite interaction, and proposed that the matching process (i.e., estimating document's relevancy to a query) be based on both token and composite indexes, and tested the model to show significant improvements over the individual token-based and composite-based retrieval. We obtained best performance levels for the combined model with the similarity function:

$$S(Query, Document) = 0.33 \times S_{Token}(Query, Document) + 0.67 \times S_{Composite}(Query, Document)$$

With the above function, the combined model performed 30%-32% better than token-based retrieval and 16%-33% better than composite-based retrieval.

In Chapter 15, we explored token-synonym combination and proposed that the matching process (i.e. estimating document's relevancy to a query) be based on both token and synonym indexes, and tested the model to show some improvements over the individual token-based and synonym-based retrieval. We obtained best performance levels for the combined model with the similarity function:

$$S(Query, Document) = 0.86 \times S_{Token}(Query, Document) + 0.14 \times S_{Composite}(Query, Document).$$

With the above function, the combined model performed similarly to token-based retrieval[82] and substantially better (i.e. 78%-105% in Precision; 39% in Recall) than composite-based retrieval. The Token-Synonym combination was the least successful of all the combinations explored in this Part, probably due to the difficulties associated with synonym concept extraction (discussed in Chapter 8).

Efficiency analysis revealed that the complexity of the combined model is determined by the complexity of the distinct models that are combined. Hence, models including Tokens, Composites, or Topics could scale-up to general collections, while models that are based on Synonyms are substantially less efficient.

The review of the novel models introduced in Part III of this dissertation and the performance gains obtained with simple realizations of the combined models allow us to answer Research Question 2 with positively – yes, different semantic units could be combined into one coherent retrieval model, and the combination can enhance performance.

In Part III we proposed two types of semantic unit combinations: in Chapter 11-13 we employed a topical organization of the collection to modify indexing and matching process of token-based, composite-based, and synonym–based retrieval. In chapters 11 (i.e. 'cluster-based weighting' for tokens) and 13 (i.e. 'Topic-LSI') we demonstrated how the indexing process could be adjusted, based on the collection's topical organization, to result in significant Precision gains and minor Recall improvements. In chapters 11 (i.e. 'cluster-based matching'), 12 (i.e. cluster-based retrieval with composites), and 13 (i.e.

---

[82] The highest gains for the combined model were obtained for Precision[10] – 4.5%.

'Cluster-Based LSI') we demonstrated how the matching process - for tokens, composites, and synonyms - could be adjusted, based on the collection's topical organization, to result in some performance gains. There various ways to utilize the topical organization in adjusting indexing and matching processes, and in chapters 11-13 we only explored few of these possibly integrations. However, at least one generalization could be made – it seems from our experiments that the true value of topical organization could be extracted by *re-indexing* the documents within topically-coherent clusters.

An additional type of integration was explored in chapters 14 and 15, where indexing and matching were performed separately for each semantic unit, and then the query-document similarity measures were combined. This type of integration proved very useful for combining token-based and composite-based retrieval.

A comprehensive evaluation of all possible interactions between the semantic units reviewed on Part II was clearly beyond the scope of this dissertation; hence, our experimental studies explored only a subset of the possible interactions. We believe that the set of interaction explored is large enough to provide evidence as to the value of interactions between retrieval models across categories. Additional interactions, e.g., forming Composites of Synonym Sets, could be explored in future studies.

To summarize, we found that semantic units from distinct categories could be combined into a coherent retrieval model, and that this combination can result in substantial performance gains. Although the combination of semantic units could result in improved retrieval, the inaccuracy of the automatic extraction process (for all semantic units), identified in the concluding chapter of Part II, impede the performance of the combined models. As a result, the performance levels we obtained with the combined models are still substantially lower than the levels reported for state-of-the-art systems (Spark-Jones 1999). The studies in this chapter provide an initial exploration into the area of semantic unit combination. Alternative realizations of the combinations we explored, or different types of combinations, are possible and have the potential to improve retrieval performance beyond the levels we obtained. We hope that the approach proposed in Part III will open the door for future studies on semantic unit combination. In the concluding part of this dissertation – Part IV – we will discuss the limitation of our study and point to future research directions that could extend the work of this dissertation.

Part IV – Thesis Conclusion

The fourth and final part of this research includes two chapters. In Chapter 17, we will recall the problem definition and the two main research question posed at the onset of this dissertation, recall the findings from the nine studies of this dissertation (four in Part II and five in Part III), and then discuss the findings and highlight the contribution of this research. In Chapter 18, we will conclude the thesis by discussing its limitations and pointing to some possible future research directions.

Chapter 17: Thesis Summary

17.1 Recap: Introduction and Motivation

The growing amount of textual information produced in organizations coupled with the increasing significance of information for planning and decision making purposes, call for effective techniques for accessing textual information. One of the most critical problems impeding the performance of text retrieval systems is the gap between the way in which users think about information (through semantic representations) and the form of text documents (natural language). Bridging that gap requires that users' information needs, as well as the documents, be represented through semantic units. The goal of this dissertation was to explore the extent to which semantic units employed in retrieval models affect the performance of retrieval systems. We focused on large and heterogeneous collections, thus we restricted our investigations to semantic units that could be extracted using completely automatic techniques – i.e. artificial semantic units.

Design Research is interested in studying Constructs, Models, Methods, and Instantiations; however, the field of IR is predominantly concerned with the study of algorithms (i.e. Methods) and the construction of systems (i.e. Instantiations). Addressing the key problem of information retrieval and bridging the gap between semantic representations and words require that we study the semantic units (i.e. Constructs) that are at the core of the representations. To date, a large-scale evaluation of the effect of artificial semantic units on retrieval performance has not been taken. We have argued that establishing the effect of automatically-generated semantic units on IR performance is an essential step towards resolving the problem of word ambiguity.

We use the term 'Artificial Semantics' throughout this thesis in a restrictive sense, to refer to patterns that are extracted from text using domain-independent and scalable methods. This view of Artificial Semantics is predominantly statistical, and excludes methods that are based on linguistic analysis, which are domain specific.

17.2 Recap: Research Questions and Method

This dissertation posed two main research questions concerning the effect of artificial semantic units of retrieval performance. Since the conceptual modelling approach is not popular in IR, and there exists no clear definition of semantic units, we initially developed a classification of artificial semantic units – 'Tokens', 'Composite Concepts', 'Synonym Concepts', and 'Topics'. Later, we employed that framework to guide our studies.

The first question was: "How does the performance of retrieval model that are based on alternative artificial semantic units compare?" Our method for establishing typical performance levels for each category of semantic units was based on two steps: (1) mapping prior works in the field to the proposed framework categories and studying the results in these studies, and then (2) conducting a series of empirical studies to isolate the effect of the semantic units by fixing the Models, Methods, Instantiations, and the test bed. We tested one representative extraction technique for each semantic unit, and conducted an in-depth study of that technique by investigating the key parameters affecting its performance. We chose the following representative models for each semantic unit (see Part II for justification on our choices):

- Tokens: extracted through standard procedure, including the removal of high-frequency words using a stop-word list, stemming words to their root form, and the removal of low-frequency words. The tokens extracted to test token-based models also served as the starting point for extracting higher-order semantic units.

- Composite Concepts: extracted two-token, symmetric, co-occurrence sets using statistical proximity models (and measuring proximity within and across sentences).

- Synonym Concepts: extracted using Latent Semantic Indexing (LSI), where factor-analytic technique (i.e. Singular Value Decomposition) is employed to construct a semantic space of lower dimensions, and each dimension is interpreted as a synonym concept.

- Topics: extracted through document clustering. The topical organization of the collection was employed to restrict the set of documents a query is matched against (i.e. the cluster-based retrieval model).

Once typical performance levels were established, we compared these levels to draw conclusions about the suitability of each semantic unit for general-collection text retrieval.

The second research question we posed was: "Does the combination of two distinct artificial semantic units in one coherent retrieval model enable performance gains beyond the levels obtained for each semantic unit separately?" The combination of distinct semantic units is challenging, as (a) it is not clear what combination will work, as illustrated in the chicken barbeque and spices analogy, and (b) semantic units could not be integrated haphazardly, and the design of a coherent retrieval model that combines different form of representation requires a deep understanding of each representation as well as a strong sense of intuition. To address the second research question, we built on the same representative techniques employed for the first research question, proposed novel retrieval models that combine semantic units from distinct categories into a coherent retrieval models, and tested these novel models empirically on the TREC benchmark.

17.3 Recap: Key Findings

Below we will recall the key findings from this research.

17.3.1 Key Findings: Typical Performance Levels for Semantic Units

The major findings from Part II of the dissertation were that there are significant differences in performance for different semantic units. In addition to comparing the performance of alternative semantic units, our extensive studies uncovered the advantages and limitations of each semantic unit. Following we highlight some of the key findings from these studies.

- Tokens (reviewed in Chapter 6): the typical performance levels, which were used as a baseline for the other semantic units, were Precision[10]=0.244 and Recall[1000]=0.445. We found that token-based retrieval is relatively insensitive to the choice of parameters. These findings are inline with results of recent TREC conferences, which suggest that additional improvements for token-based retrieval have largely ceased, with the different tokenizing techniques generally producing similar results (Voorhees & Harman 1999, 2000).

- Composite Concepts (reviewed in Chapter 7): composites have provided some Precision gains over tokens (on average=14%; for a subset of the queries = 41%). To the best of our knowledge, this was the first study to isolate and test the effect of composites. Our experiments reveal the model's sensitivity to several parameters, namely the number of unique concepts employed, and to a lesser extent – to the size of query indexes. The weighting scheme we tested for document indexes (i.e. TF-IDF), on the other hand, had little effect on performance. Based on the high sensitivity of composite-based retrieval to the model's parameters, the positive results we obtained with only a simple realization of the model, and the fact that this model has not been explored extensively in IR, we believe that additional Precision enhancements are possible with alternative realizations of the model. The main challenge for composite-based retrieval is in limiting the complexity of composite extraction and storage, and in our study we proposed an efficient algorithm for addressing complexity of composite extraction. In summary, our experiment provides the first empirical evidence for the usefulness of automatically extracted composite concepts in large and heterogeneous settings.

- Synonym Concepts (reviewed in Chapter 8): synonym-based retrieval was substantially less efficient that token-based retrieval and provided disappointing effectiveness results. Findings from our experiments contradict prior knowledge and result in both Precision and Recall losses when compared to token-based retrieval. Prior published works report successes for LSI, mainly in terms of Recall, and our findings challenge these previous studies. We suspect that two factors inhibited the performance of synonym-based retrieval with LSI: (a) we tested the approach for general collections, while most of the previous results were obtained for small and homogeneous collections, and (b) the model is very sensitive to the choice of parameters, and we explored only a portion of the parameter space. Based on our study, we conclude that synonym-based retrieval is unsuitable for general collections.

- Topics (reviewed in Chapter 9): we studied the cluster-based retrieval model, where the topical organization of the collection is employed to restrict the set of documents that are matched to the query. The model is based on the cluster hypothesis, stating that relevant documents will tend to concentrate in few clusters. Previous studies established the model's potential and reported on gaps between this potential and experimental results, but provided very little insight on the causes for cluster-based retrieval's inability to attain its potential. Our study corroborated previous knowledge and demonstrated Precision and Recall losses as fewer clusters are associated with a query. This was the first study of cluster-based IR where alternative realizations of the model were explored (i.e. queries were associated with a different number of clusters), thus demonstrating the correlation between the number of clusters associated with queries and retrieval effectiveness. In addition, our study revealed the factors inhibiting the model's performance. We found that, to a large extent, the cluster hypothesis underlying the model holds, and that the model is limited by difficulties in realization, specifically in associating the query with the most relevant clusters. Lastly, to the best of our knowledge, our study provides the first empirical evidence for the effect of the clustering algorithm (and specifically, the number of clusters the collection is decomposed into) on retrieval effectiveness. We believe the potential of cluster-based retrieval could be attained by addressing the limitations we have exposed.

Despite significant differences in performance levels for semantic units, overall, concept-based and topic-based retrieval did not yield substantial improvements beyond the performance levels obtained for the traditional token-based retrieval model. The inability of concept-based and topic-based retrieval to provide substantial performance improvements demonstrate the difficulty in automatically extracting meaningful patterns (i.e. 'artificial semantics') from text. We conclude that artificial semantic representations are useful for enhancing retrieval effectiveness, but alone could not resolve completely the problems of accurate retrieval in large and heterogeneous collections. Hence, semantic units should be used to complement other retrieval approaches, as discussed in Chapter 18.

17.3.2 Key Findings: Combinations of Semantic Units

The major findings from Part III of the dissertation (addressing the second research question) were that semantic units from distinct categories could be combined into a coherent retrieval model, and that this combination can result in substantial performance gains. Specifically, we explored the following combinations of semantic units:

- Topic-Token combination (explored in Chapter 11): we proposed two extensions to the cluster-based model. 'Cluster-Based Weighting' suggested that once documents are assigned to a specific cluster, the indexing process be adjusted (or more precisely suggest that the token-weighting process change). 'Cluster-Based Matching' proposed that the additional information available through clustering (i.e., query-profile and profile-document similarities) be employed in the matching process. For each of these two theoretical principles we proposed a simple realization, and tested that realization empirically. Cluster-based weighting showed significant performance improvements (especially when few clusters are associated with the query), and when complemented with cluster-based matching additional performance gains were obtained. Furthermore, when the two proposed principles were employed, cluster restriction resulted in Precision gains, and performance levels with 10/100 clusters per query were 15% higher than those with no cluster restriction (i.e., the classic Vector-Space model).

- Topic-Composite combination (explored in Chapter 12): we proposed that the two-step matching process of cluster-based retrieval be based on composite concept indexes (instead of token-based indexes) for both documents and queries. Two interesting results were obtained: first, cluster-based IR with composites is significantly more effective than the traditional token-based model (with Precision gains of 60% and Recall gains of 50%); second, cluster restriction hardly affects performance of composite-based retrieval (very differently from the results observed for the traditional token-based model), and when only 5/100 clusters are associated with the query performance is similar (i.e. Precision loss of 1% and Recall loss of 2%) to that obtained with no cluster restriction.

- Topic-Synonym combination (explored in Chapter 13): we proposed that the semantic space for Latent Semantic Indexing (LSI) be generated in topically coherent clusters (referred to as 'Topic-LSI'), thus addressing two of LSI's main limitations: (a) scalability, and (b) homogeneity of the sub-collection. Topic-LSI outperformed traditional LSI (where the document corpus was arbitrarily decomposed into sub-collection) substantially, resulting in 51%-66% Precision gains and 13% Recall gains). We then proposed to extend this model and employ the topical organization to restrict the number of clusters associated with each query (i.e. cluster-based retrieval in LSI's semantic space, referred to as 'Cluster-Based LSI'), thus addressing an additional limitation of LSI – run-time efficiency. Cluster-restriction in the LSI space resulted in Precision losses (6%-19% losses with 10/200 clusters per query), very similar to the effect of cluster restriction on token-based retrieval.

- Token-Composite combination (explored in Chapter 14): we proposed that the matching process (i.e. estimating document's relevancy to a query) be based on both token and composite indexes, and tested the model to show significant improvements over the individual token-based and composite-based retrieval. We obtained best performance levels for the combined model with the similarity function:

$$S(Query, Document) = 0.33 \times S_{Token}(Query, Document) + 0.67 \times S_{Composite}(Query, Document).$$

With the above function, the combined model performed 30%-32% better than token-based retrieval and 16%-33% better than composite-based retrieval.

- Token-Synonym combination (explored in Chapter 15): we proposed that the matching process be based on both token and synonym indexes, and tested the model to show some improvements over the individual token-based and synonym-based retrieval. We obtained best performance levels for the combined model with the similarity function:

$$S(Query, Document) = 0.86 \times S_{Token}(Query, Document) + 0.14 \times S_{Composite}(Query, Document)$$

With the above function, the combined model performed similarly to token-based retrieval[83] and substantially better (i.e. 78%-105% in Precision; 39% in Recall) than synonym-based retrieval. The Token-Synonym combination was the least successful

---

[83] The highest gains for the combined model were obtained for Precision[10] – 4.5%.

of all the combinations explored in Part III, probably due to the difficulties associated with synonym concept extraction.

The studies in Part III provided an initial exploration into the area of semantic unit combination. Alternative realizations of the combinations we explored, or different types of combinations, are possible and have the potential to improve retrieval performance beyond the levels we obtained.

17.4 Contributions

This dissertation combines breadth (in studying the broad area of artificial semantics in IR) and depth (in conducting comprehensive studies of several models) and makes several contributions. First, we make a contribution by studying the field of IR from a unique perspective – focusing on artificial semantic units – and in the development of the "Semantic Unit Categorization" framework. We believe that the field of IR could benefit by adopting a conceptual modeling approach, and that our proposed framework could be used to map previous research and guide future research. A second contribution is in establishing typical performance levels for representations based on distinct semantic units. By identifying the representation's main advantages and limitations, we enable system designers to choose the semantic unit that best fits their needs. A third contribution is made through the in-depth analysis of models that are built on distinct semantic units by providing a deeper understanding of these retrieval models. For example, our analysis of Composite Concepts was the first large-scale evaluation of that model on a well-accepted benchmark, and our investigation of topic-based models provided revealed the factors inhibiting the effectiveness of cluster-based retrieval. Lastly, we make a fourth contribution in developing novel retrieval models that integrate distinct semantic units, and in testing these novel models empirically to attain performance gains. For instance, we demonstrated that by combining 'Topics' with 'Synonym'-based representations, retrieval effectiveness could be enhanced. The lack of research regarding semantic unit combination and the positive results we have obtained suggest that our proposed combined models may be the greatest theoretical contribution of this dissertation. We hope our explorations will open the door for more research on the interactions between semantic units.

When addressing such a broad question such as the automatic extraction of meaningful patterns from text, it is obvious that the analysis depth of each method is somewhat restricted. Our approach for studying the extraction techniques for each semantic unit was based on: (a) choosing one representative method, (b) identifying the critical parameters of that method and the appropriate value ranges for each parameter (through literature review), and (c) testing the performance of the method by exploring different values for the critical parameters. We believe that our approach enabled us to get a good understanding of the effectiveness of each semantic unit, and that we achieved a fine balance between breadth and depth. Based on our findings, future studies could extend our work and dig deeper into each of the methods we explored. Such future work could explore alternative values for parameters we've studied [e.g., in cluster-based IR (see Chapter 9), we've explored the effect of the number of clusters the collection is decomposed into, by testing a 100 and 200-cluster, decomposition; alternative decompositions, such as 500-cluster, may yield better performance], or by exploring different parameters [e.g., test the effect of directionality in Composite Concepts (see Chapter 7)].

This research should, in addition to being of theoretical interest [in introducing the "Semantic Unit Categorization" framework (see Chapter 3), in analyzing (See Chapter 9) and enhancing (see Chapter 11) the Cluster-Based Retrieval model, and in proposing that concepts be extracted within topically-coherent clusters (see Chapter 13)] be of substantial interest to practitioners, who can build on the ideas introduced in this work to design more effective retrieval systems. Obvious areas of application would include library systems, web search engines, and diverse knowledge management systems, all of which depend greatly on the efficiency of Text Retrieval. Further, the indexing principles detailed here can be applied to improve the performance of any computer application that helps users to access textual data. By allowing people access to more relevant information sources, organizations could better exploit their large document repositories to gain a competitive advantage.

Knowledge of the typical performance levels of semantic units and of the optimal parameter setting for each semantic unit (discussed in Part II) have direct implications for the design of retrieval systems. It is expected that IR systems designers will utilize our findings to design systems that better address their Precision and Recall requirements. For instance, semantic units that enable high Precision (e.g. composite Concepts) are appropriate for retrieval tasks where users are interested in few documents that address their needs; other types of semantic units (e.g. Synonym Concepts) enable Recall gains (usually at the cost of Precision losses) and are appropriate for retrieval tasks where the users are interested in exploring a large portion of the results lists (for instance in searching for medical information).

The innovative models combining different semantic units (proposed in Part III) should be of interest to practitioners, who could build on our proposed models in the design of retrieval systems. For example, designers interested in addressing the problem of synonymy for a large collection may find that synonym-based retrieval (e.g. LSI) are not scalable to large collections. Our proposed approach for scaling-up LSI, through topical organization of the corpus, may be of special interest to these system designers.

In the next chapter, we will conclude this dissertation with a discussion of the limitations of our research and highlight some of the possible future research directions for our work.

Chapter 18: Limitations and Future Research

Further research should be conducted to both refine implementation of the principles and models proposed in this dissertation, and to generalize the results. Future research directions for each specific study were discussed in Parts 2 and 3; below we discuss more general limitations and future research directions.

Although our research focused on the use of artificial semantic units for general-collection text retrieval, the ideas we have proposed and the findings from our empirical studies are expected to generalize to other closely related areas in the following ways.

First, our findings are not restricted to large and heterogeneous collection. Rather, they could very well apply to retrieval systems in restricted organizational settings. Automatically-extracted semantic units could be used to index documents in these organizational settings. However, in restricted organizational settings, where the document collection is rather small and homogeneous, manual techniques and domain-specific resources (e.g. ontologies) could complement the automatic techniques discussed in this dissertation.

Second, our findings could also generalize to alternative information access techniques, such as Information Filtering (Oard 1997). In Information Filtering users need are assumed to be static and the flow of documents is assumed to be dynamic (e.g. filtering an incoming stream of news articles to interested users). Despite these differences from Information Retrieval (where information need are assumed dynamic and the collection is static), both information access approaches work by matching the content of an information request to the content of a document. Hence, both IR and Information Filtering are interested in (automatically) generating meaningful representations of textual content, and the ideas and model we proposed in the context of IR could very well be applied to alternative information access approaches.

Lastly, our findings regarding the extraction of semantic units and their effectiveness could be generalized beyond information access. Other applications that are interested in semantics (and artificial semantics) might find our results relevant. For instance, the approaches we investigated for automatically extracting semantic units could be utilized in the automatic construction of semantic resources (such as taxonomies or ontologies), or alternatively in translation of text documents between languages.

The research methods we used enabled us to study the effect of semantic units in isolation, by fixing exogenous factors (i.e. retrieval models, methods and instantiations). In addition the unique benchmark we employed, which included manual query-document relevance judgements, allowed us to test several retrieval models on a heterogeneous and large text collection. However, a shortcoming of this research is that the results we obtained are restricted to the specific experimental settings. Below we expand on this limitation, and discuss future plans to strengthen and generalize our findings.

Our findings are based on tests with a single data collection using a single set of queries – the TREC collection (disks #4 and #5). Although the TREC collection is the best simulation of general collections to be found and TREC has gained the status of the de-facto standard test-bed for text retrieval, our findings should be confirmed for additional data sets. We plan to replicate our experiments on alternative large and heterogeneous text collections.

We established typical performance level for different semantic units based on representative models, as follows. We extracted *tokens* with standard procedures (i.e. removal of high and low frequency words and stemming); *composite concepts* extraction was performed with statistical proximity models; *synonym*-based retrieval with Latent Semantic Indexing; and *topic*-based retrieval with cluster-based IR. The findings from this study are restricted to the specific methods used for extracting the meaningful patterns from text. Although we've argue for our choice of methods and try to choose the most representative technique for each category of semantic units, alternative choices of methods are likely to influence results.

In order to strengthen our findings on the typical performance levels of each semantic unit, alternative models should be studied in the future. For instance, composite concept extraction could be done with asymmetric (instead of symmetric) co-occurrence sets, and synonyms extraction could be performed through token clustering (instead of factor-analytic techniques).

In an effort to isolate the effect of the 'Constructs' (i.e. artificial semantic units) in retrieval system design, we fixed the 'Model', 'Methods', and 'Instantiations'. Thus our findings are specific to the particular choices we've made, as explained below:

- Model: we employed the classic Vector-Space model (Salton et al. 1975) for all the semantic units, as well as for the interactions between semantic units. The weighting scheme we employed for calculating term's resolving power in document indexes was the de-facto standard weighting scheme Term-Frequency Inverse-Document-Frequency (TF-IDF), for all semantic units and their combinations. In order to generalize our findings, we plan to repeat our studies, with alternative retrieval models [e.g. the Probabilistic Model (Robertson & Spark-Jones 1976)] and weighting schemes [e.g. BM25 (Robertson et al. 1998)].

- Methods: for each semantic unit, we explored only a subset of the possible extraction methods. For example, for synonym-based retrieval with LSI we tested only two levels for the number of dimensions (i.e. concepts; we tested 150 and 300), and it is very likely that a different number of dimensions will yield different results. In the future we plan to explore alternative methods for extracting semantic units, in order to strengthen our conclusions.

- Instantiations (i.e. retrieval systems): the scope of our research was restricted to using the document collection as a source for extracting semantic representations, thus we did not include in our implementations features such as query refinement and expansion, user modelling, or advanced user interfaces. All these additional features are essential for designing an effective retrieval system[84], and in the future we plan to study the effect of semantic units in the presence of additional retrieval features.

In conclusion, our investigation of the effect of artificial semantic units on retrieval performance has yielded some significant results, highlighting the importance of the semantic unit at the core of document and query representations. The approach we have taken (i.e. proposing the 'Semantic Unit Categorization' framework, and comparing the performance of semantic units by fixing all exogenous factors) is novel, as prior IR

---

[84] The differences between the performance levels of state-of-the-art systems (Spark-Jones 1999) and the levels we obtained (see discussion in Chapter 10) stress the need for features that go beyond the indexing units.

research focuses on algorithms and system development. To the best of our knowledge no prior study offers such a clear picture on the effect of semantic units. In addition, we proposed novel retrieval models that integrate distinct semantic units into a coherent retrieval model, and demonstrated how these combinations could enhance retrieval performance. In addition to the academic contribution in this dissertation, our findings are of importance to practitioners interested in the design of retrieval systems. Our research is, in many ways, only preliminary, and it opens the door and invites future studies on the effect of semantic units. Above we have highlighted some of the future directions that we intend to take in order to further explore how semantic patterns could be automatically extracted from text, and in an effort to reveal design principles that are essential for addressing the problem of word ambiguity. We hope that by departing from previous traditions in IR focusing on algorithms and system development, and by investigating the impact of semantic units in isolation, we could contribute to the design of effective retrieval systems that will deliver relevant (and only relevant) information to users.

Bibliography

Adams E., A Study of Trigrams and Their Feasibility as Index Terms in a Full Text Information Retrieval Systems, Ph.D. thesis, George Washington University, 1991.

Agre P.E., Changing Places: Contexts of Awareness in Computing, *Human-Computer Interaction*, 2001.

Alavi M. and Leidner D.E., Knowledge Management and Knowledge Management Systems: Conceptual Foundations and Research issues, *MIS Quarterly*, Vol. 25, No. 1, pages 107-136, 2001.

Aslam J., Pelekhov K., and Rus D., Information Organization Algorithms, in *Proceedings of the International Conference on Advances in Infrastructure for Electronic Business, Science, and Education on the Internet (SSGRR)*, 2000.

Asnicar F.A., Di Fant M., and Tasso C., User Model-Based Information Filtering, *Fifth Conference of the Italian Association for Artificial Intelligence (AI*IA97)*, 1997

Attar R. and Fraenkel A.S., Local Feedback in Full-Text Retrieval systems, *Journal of the ACM*, 24,3, pages 397-417, 1977.

Attardi G., Di Marco S., Salvi D., and Sebastiani F., Theseus: Categorization by Context, *Proceedings of WebNet'98*, Orlando, Florida, Springer, 1998.

Baeza-Yates R. and Ribeiro-Neto B, *Modern Information Retrieval*, Addison Wesley / ACM Press, 1999.

Berthouzoz C., A Model of Context Adapted to Domain Independent Machine Translation, in P. Bouquet et al. editors, *Proceedings of Context'99*, Lecture Notes in AI 1688, pages 54-66, Springer-Verlag, 1999.

Borko H. and Bernick M.D., Automatic Document Classification, Journal of the ACM, 10, pages 1151-1162, 1963,.

Brin S. and Page L., The Anatomy of a Large-Scale Hypertextual Web Search Engine, http://decweb.ethz.ch/WWW7/1921/com1921.htm, 1998.

Brodie M.L., Mylopoulos J., and Schmidt J.W. editors, *On Conceptual Modelling: Perspectives from Artificial Intelligence, Databases, and Programming Languages*, Springer, 1984.

Brouard C. and Nie J.Y., The System RELIEFS: a New Approach to Information Filtering, in Proceedings of the 9th Text Retrieval Conference, 2000.

Brown P., Pietra D., Pietra V., and Mercer R., Word Sense disambiguation Using Statistical
Methods, in Proceeding of the Annual Meeting of the ACL, 1991, 264-270.

Brusilovski P., Methods and Techniques for Adaptive Hypermedia, *User Modelling and User
Adapted Interaction,* Vol. 6, No. 2-3, pages 87-129, 1996.

Burke M. E. and Hall H., *Navigating Business Information Sources,* Library Association, July,
1998.

Caid W.R., Dumais S.T., and Gallant S.I., Learned Vector-Space Models for Document
Retrieval, *Information Processing and Management,* 31 (3), pages 419-429, 1995.

Carmel D., Amitay E., Herscovici M., Maarek Y., Petruschka Y., and Soffer A., Juru at TREC
10 - Experiments with Index Pruning, in Proceedings of the 10th Text Retrieval
Conference, 2001.

Chakrabarti S., Dom B., Agrawal R., and Raghavan P., Scalable Feature Selection,
Classification and Signature Generation for Organizing Large Text Databases into
Hierarchical Topic Taxonomies, *VLDB Journal: Very Large Data Bases,* 7 (3), pages
163-178, 1998.

Chakrabarti S., Dom B., and Indyk P., Enhanced Hypertext Categorization using Hyperlinks,
Proceedings of the ACM SIGMOD 1998, Seattle, Washington, 1998.

Chakrabarti S., van den Berg M., and Dom B., Focused Crawling: A New Approach to Topic-
Specific Web Resource Discovery, in *Proceedings of the Eighth International World-
Wide Web Conference,* Elsevier Science, 1999.

Chalmers M., Rodden K., and Brodbeck D., The Order of Things: Activity-Centered Information
Access, *Computer Network and ISDN Systems,* Vol. 30, pages 359-367, 1998.

Charikar M., Chekuri C., Feder T., and Motwani R., Incremental Clustering and Dynamic
Information Retrieval, *Proceedings of the 29th Symposium on Theory of Computing,*
pages 626-635, 1997.

Chen C. and Cribbin T., Visualising and animating visual information foraging in context, in
Smith, Salvendy, and Koubek editors, *Proceedings of the 9th International Conference
on Human-Computer Interaction (HCI International '2001),* New Orleans, Louisiana,
USA, 2001.

Chen, H., and Dumais, S. T., Bringing order to the web: Automatically categorizing search results, in *Proceedings of CHI'00, Human Factors in Computing Systems,* Den Haag, 2000.

Chen C., *Information Visualization and Virtual Environments,* Springer-Verlag, 1999.

Chen H., Knowledge Management Systems: A Text-Mining Perspective, The University of Arizona, 2001.

Chen C., Information Visualization, *Information Visualization,* 1, pages 1-4, 2002.

Chen H., Houston A.L., Sewell R.R., and Schatz B.R., Internet browsing and searching: User evaluations of category map and concept space techniques, *Journal of the American Society for Information Science,* 49(7), pages 582--603, 1998.

Ching C., Network Organizations and Information Technology: A Special Issue of the Journal of Introduction to the Special Issue on Network Organizations, *Organizational Computing & Electronic Commerce,* Vol 7, No. 2&3, pages 79-81, 1997

Cohen W.W., and Singer Y., Context-Sensitive Learning Methods for Text Categorization, in *Proceedings of the 19th ACM International Conference on Research and Development in Information Retrieval* (SIGIR'96), ACM Press, 1996, 307-315.

Comlekoglu F.M., *Optimizing a Text Retrieval system Utilizing N-Gram Indexing*, Ph.D. thesis, George Washington University, 1990.

Croft W.B., A Model of Cluster Searching Based on Classification, *Information Systems*, 5, pages 189-195, 1980.

Croft, W. B., Boolean queries and term dependencies in probabilistic retrieval models, *Journal of the American Society for Information Science*, 37, 2, pages 71-77, 1986..

Croft, W. B., Turtle, H. R., and Lewis, D. D., The use of phrases and structured queries in information retrieval, in A. Bookstein, Y. Chiaramella, G. Salton, and V. V. Raghavan, SIGIR `91: *Proceedings of the Fourteenth Annual International ACM/SIGIR Conference on Research and Development in Information Retrieval*, ACM Press, 1991, 32-45.

Cross R., Parker A., Prusak L., and Borgatti S., Knowing What We Know, *Organizational Dynamics,* Vol 30, No. 2, 2001.

Crye W.R., Capture, Integration, and Analysis of Digital System Requirements with Conceptual Graphs, *IEEE Transactions on Knowledge and Data Engineering,* Vol. 9, No. 1, February, 1997.

Cutting D.R., Pedersen J.O., Karger D., and Tukey J.W., Scatter/Gather: A Cluster-based Approach to Browsing Large Document Collections, *Proceedings of the Fifteenth Annual International ACM SIGIR Conference on Research and Development in Information Retrieval,* pages 318-329, 1992.

Dagan I., *Multilingual Statistical Approaches for Natural Language Disambiguation*, Ph.D. thesis, Technion, Israel, 1992.

Dagan I., Marcus S., and Markovitch S., Contextual Word Similiraty and Estimation from Sparse Data, *Meeting of the Association for Computational Linguistics*, pages 164-171, 1995.

Davenport T.H. and Prusak L., *Working Knowledge: How Organizations Manage What They Know*, Harvard Business School Press, Boston, MA, 1998.

De Bra P., Brusilovski P., and Houben G.J., Adaptive Hypermedia: From systems to Framework, *ACM Computing Surveys,* Vol. 31, No. 4es, 1999.

Deerwester S., Dumais S., Furnas G., Landauer T., and Harshman R., Indexing by Latent Semantic Analysis, *Journal of the American Society of Information Science (JASIS),* 41, 6, pages 391-407, 1990.

Diekema A., Oroumchian F., Sheridan P., and Liddy E.D., TREC-7 Evaluation of Conceptual Interlingua Document Retrieval (CINDOR) in English and French, *Proceedings of the 8th Text Retrieval Conference,* NIST Special Publication, 1998.

Dillon, M., and Gray, A. S., FASIT: A fully automatic syntactically based indexing system, *Journal of the American Society for Information Science*, 34, 2, pages 99-108,1983.

Dumais S., LSI Meets TREC: A Status Report, *Proceedings of the TREC1,* 1992.

Dumais S., Latent Semantic Indexing (LSI) and TREC2, *Proceedings of TREC2,* 1993.

Dumais S., Latent Semantic Indexing (LSI): TREC3 Report, *Proceedings of TREC3,* 1994.

Eagly A.H. and Chaiken S., *The psychology of attitudes,* Harcourt Brace Jovanovich College Publishers, Fort Worth, Texas, 1993.

Fairthorne R.A., The mathematics of classification, *Towards Information Retrieval,* Butterworths, London, 1961.

Favela J., Capture and Dissemination of Specialized Knowledge in Network Organizations, *Organizational Computing & Electronic Commerce,* Vol 7, No. 2, pages 201-226, 1997.

Finkelstein L., Gabrilovich E., Matias Y., Rivlin E., Solan Z., Wolfman G., and Ruppin E., Placing Search in Context, *The 10th International World Wide Web Conference (WWW10)*, Hong Kong, May, 2001.

Gale W., Church K., and Yarowsky D., A Method for Disambiguating Word Senses in a Large Corpus, Statistical Research Report, 104, AT&T Bell Laboratories, 1992.

Gale W., Church K., and Yarowsky D., Work on Statistical Methods for Word Sense Disambiguation, in Probabilistic Approaches to Natural Language, Working Notes, AAAI Fall Symposium Series, pages 54-60, 1992.

Gallant S.I., Hecht-Nielsen R., Caid W.R., Qing K.P., Carleton J., Sudbeck D., *HNC's MatchPlus System, Proceedings of TREC1*, 1992.

Gangemi A., Guarino N., Oltramari A., Pisanelli D., and Steve G., Conceptual Analysis of Lexical Taxonomies: The Case of WordNet Top-Level, *LADSEB-CNR Internal Report*, 2001.

Gangolly J. and Wu Y., On the Automatic Classification of Accounting Concepts: Preliminary Results of the Statistical Analysis of Term-Document Frequencies, *The New Review of Applied Expert Systems and Emerging Technologies*, V. 6, pages 81-88, 2000.

Garfield, E., Use of Journal Citation Reports and Journal Performance in Measuring Short and Long Term Journal Impact, *Croatian Medical Journal*, 41: (4), pages 368-374, December, 2000.

Gartner Group, Knowledge Management Report, Summer, 1999.

Golub G.H. and van Loan C.F., *Matrix Computations*, 2nd edition, Johns Hopkins, 1993.

Gonzalo J., Verdejo F., Chugur I., and Cigarran J., Indexing with WordNet Sunsets Can Improve Text Retrieval, in Proceedings of the COLING/ACL Workshop on Using WordNet for Natural Language Processing, Montreal, Canada, 1998.

Good I.J., Speculations Concerning Information Retrieval, *Research Report PC-78*, IBM Research Centre, Yorktown Heights, New York, 1958.

Grise M. L., Information overload: Addressing the productivity paradox in face-to-face electronic meetings, *Journal of Management Information Systems*, 1999.

Hall D., Koch H., and Mangal K., An Examination of the Internet as a Research Tool: Implications for Researchers, *Proceedings of the American Society of Business and Behavioral Sciences*, Volume 7, Number 5, 2000.

Han J. and Kamber M., Chapter 9 - Mining Complex Types of Data, *Data Mining: Concepts and Techniques* , Section 9.5 : Mining the web, Morgan Kaufmann Publishers, April, 2000.

Harman D., Overview of the Third Text Retrieval Conference (TREC-3), Proceedings of the 3rd Text Retrieval Conference, NIST Special Publication, 1994.

Harter A., Hopper A., Steggles P., and Ward A., The Anatomy of a Context-Aware Application, *Mobile Computing and Networking,* pages 59-68, 1999.

Hearst M.A., Chapter 10 - User Interfaces and Visualization , in *Modern Information Retrieval,* pages 257-324, Addison Wesley / ACM Press, 1999.

Hearst M.A., Karger D.R., and Pedersen J.O. , Scatter/Gather as a Tool for the Navigation of Retrieval Results, *Proceedings of the American Association for Artificial Intelligence Conference, Fall Symposium "AI Applications in Knowledge Navigation and Retrieval",* Cambridge, MA, pages 65-71, 1995.

Henzinger M.R., Hyperlink Analysis for the Web, *IEEE Internet Computing,* pages 45-50, January-February, 2001.

Hill W., Stead L., Rosenstein M., and Furnas G., Recommending and evaluating choices in a virtual community of use , in *Proceedings of ACM CHI'95 ,* pages 194-20, 1995.

Holland J., *Adaptation in Natural and Artificial Systems,* University of Michigan Press, Ann Arbor, 1975.

Honkela T., Connectionist Analysis and Creation of Context for Natural Language Understanding and Knowledge Management, in P. Bouquet et al. editors, Proceedings of Context'99, Lecture Notes in AI 1688, Springer-Verlag, pages 479-482, 1999.

Husbands P., Simon H., and Ding C., On the Use of SVD for Text Retrieval, in M. Berry editor, *Proceedings of SIAM Computational Information Retrieval Workshop,* October, 2000.

Hyoudo, Y., Niimi, K., and Ikeda, T., Comparison between proximity operation and dependency operation in Japanese full-text retrieval, in W. B. Croft et al. editors, Proceedings of the 21st Annual International ACM SIGIR Conference on Research and Development in Information Retrieval, ACM Press, pages 341-342, 1998.

Ide E. and Salton G., Interactive Search strategies and Dynamic File Organization, The SMART Retrieval System: Experiments in Automatic Document Processing, Prentice-Hall, 1971.

Jacoby J., Speller D. E., and Kohn C. A., Brand choice behavior as a function of information load, *Journal of Marketing Research,* 11(1), pages 63–69, February, 1975.

Jain A. and Dubes R., *Algorithms for Clustering Data,* Prentice Hall, 1988.

Jardine N. and van Rijsbergen C.J., The use of hierarchical clustering in information retrieval, *Information Storage and Retrieval,* 7, pages 217-240, 1971.

Jelinek F, Mercer R. L., and Roukus S., Principles of Lexical Language Modeling for Speech Recognition, in Furui S. and Sondhi M. editors, Advances in Speech Signal Processing, Mercer Dekker Inc., pages 651-699, 1992.

Jennings A. and Higuchi H., A Personal News Service Based on a User Model Neural Network, *IEICE Transactions on Information and Systems,* 75(2), pages 198-209, March, 1992

Jones K.S., Summary Performance Comparisons TREC-2 Through TREC-7, Proceedings of the 7th Text Retrieval Conference, NIST Special Publication, 1998.

Jones K.S., Summary Performance Comparisons TREC-2 Through TREC-8, Proceedings of the 8th Text Retrieval Conference, NIST Special Publication, 1999.

Keen E.M., Some Aspects of Proximity in Text Retrieval Systems, Journal of Information Science, 18, 2, pages 89-98, 1992.

Kendall E., Malkoun M. and Jiang C., The Layaerd Agent Patterns, in *Proceedings of the Third Annual Conference on The Pattern Languages of Programs (PLoP'96),* Allerton Park, Illinois, 1996.

Khoo C., Myaeng S., and Oddy R., Using Cause-Effect Relations in Text to Improve Information Retrieval Precision, Information Processing and Management, 37, pages 119-145, 2001.

Kohonen T., *Self-Organizing Maps,* Third edition, Springer Series in Information Sciences, Vol. 30, Springer, 2001.

Koll, M. An approach to concept-based information retrieval. *ACM SIGIR Forum,* 1979.

Korkea-aho M., Context-Aware Application Survey, Helsinki University of Technology, 2000.

Kumar R., Raghavan P., Rajagopalan S., and Tomkins A., Trawling the Web for Emerging Cyber Communities, *Proceedings of the Eighth World Wide Web Conference,* Toronto, Canada, May, 1999.

Landauer T.K., Foltz P.W., and Laham D., Introduction to Latent Semantic Analysis, *Discourse Processes,* 25, pages 259-284, 1998.

Lau R., Rosenfeld R., and Roukus S., Adaptive Language Modeling Using the Maximum Entropy Principle, ARPA, 1993.

Lawrence S., Context in Web Search, *IEEE Data Engineering Bulletin,* 29 (3), pages 25-32, 2000.

Lawrence S. and Giles C.L., Accessibility of Information on the Web, *Nature,* Vol. 400, July, 1999.

Liddy, E. D., and Myaeng, S. H, DR-LINK's linguistic-conceptual approach to document detection, in K. Harman editor, The First Text REtrieval Conference (TREC-1), NIST Special Publication, National Institute of Standards and Technology, pages 500-207, 1993.

Liddy, E. D., and Myaeng, S. H, DR-LINK: A system update for TREC-2, in K. Harman editor, The Second Text REtrieval Conference (TREC-2), NIST Special Publication, National Institute of Standards and Technology, pages 500-515, 1994.

Liddy E.D., Enhanced Text Retrieval Using Natural Language Processing, *Bulletin of the American Society for Information Science,* Vol. 24, No. 4, 1998.

Liu, G. Z., Semantic vector space model: Implementation and evaluation, Journal of the American Society for Information Science, 48, 5, pages 395-417, 1997.

Lively L., *Managing Information Overload,* Amacom, 1996.

Losee R. M., Minimizing Information Overload: The Ranking of Electronic Messages, *Journal of Information Science,* 15 (3), pages 179–189, 1989.

Lu X., An Application of Case Relations to Document Retrieval, Ph.D. thesis, University of Western Ontario, 1990.

Luhn H.P., A Business Intelligence System, IBM Journal of Research and Development, 2, 4, pages 314-319, 1958.

Maarek Y., Berry D., and Kaiser G., An Information Retrieval Approach for Automatically Constructing Software Libraries, IEEE Transactions on Software Engineering, 17, 8, August, 1991.

MacQueen, J., Some methods for classification and analysis of multivariate observations. In Le Cam, L. M. and Neyman, J., editors, *Proceedings of the Fifth Berkeley Symposium on Mathematical Statistics and Probability*, volume 1, pages 281-297, Berkeley, California. University of California Press, 1967.

Malhotra N. K., Information load and consumer decision making, *Journal of Consumer Research,* 9, pages 419–430, March, 1982.

Malhotra N. K., Jain A. K., and Lagakos S. W., The information overload controversy: An alternative viewpoint, *Journal of Marketing,* 46(2), pages 27–37, Spring, 1982.

March S. and Smith G., Design and Natural Science Research on Information Technology, *Decision Support Systems,* 15, pages 251 – 266, 1995.

Maron M.E. and Kuhns J.L., On Relevance, Probabilistic Indexing and Information Retrieval, Journal of the ACM, 7, pages 216-244, 1960.

Martin P., Conventions and Notations for Knowledge Representation and Retrieval, *Proceedings of ICCS 2000, 8th International Conference on Conceptual Structures,* Darmstadt, Germany, August 14-18, 2000; Lecture Notes in AI 1867, pages 41-54, Springer-Verlag, 2000.

Martin W.J.R., Al B.P.F., and van Strenkenburg P.J.G., On the Processing of Text Corpus: from Textual Data to Lexicographical Information, in Hartman R.R.K. editor, Lexicography: Principles and Practice, Applied Language Studies Series, Academic Press, London, 1983.

Martin P. and Alplay L., Conceptual Structures and Structured Documents, *Proceedings of ICCS'96, 4th International Conference on Conceptual Structures,* Sydney, Australia, August 19-22, 1996, Lecture Notes on AI 1114, pages 145-159, Springer-Verlag, 1996.

Marwick A.D., Knowledge Management Technology, *IBM Systems* Journal, 2001.

Mauldin M.L., *Conceptual Information Retrieval: A Case Study in Adaptive Partial Parsing,* Kluwer Academic Press, September, 1991.

Mayfield J., Ontologies and Text Retrieval, *The Knowledge Engineering Review*, Vol. 17:1, pages 71-75, 2002.

McDonald D., Issues in the Representation of Real Texts: The Design of KRISP, in Iwanska L. and Shapiro S. editors, Natural Language Processing and Knowledge Representation, AAAI Press / MIT Press, pages 77-110, 2000.

Megerdoomian K., Text Mining, Corpus Building, and Testing, in *Handbook for Knowledge Engineers*, Farghaly A. editor, CSLI Publications, 2003.

Melnik S., Raghavan S., Yang B., and Garcia-Molina H., Building a Distributed Full-Text Index for the Web, World Wide Web, pages 396-406, 2001.

Miller G.A., WordNet: A Lexical Database, Communications of the ACM, 38, 11, pages 39-41, 1995,.

Myaeng, S. H., and Liddy, E. D., Information retrieval with semantic representation of texts, in Proceedings of the Second Annual Symposium on Document Analysis and Information Retrieval, pages 201-215, 1993.

Myaeng, S. H., Khoo, C., and Li, M., Linguistic processing of text for a large-scale conceptual information retrieval system, in W. M. Tepfenhart, J. P. Dick, and J. F. Sowa editors, Conceptual Structures: Current Practices: Second International Conference on Conceptual Structures, ICCS `94, Springer-Verlag, pages 69-83, 1994.

Nakov P., Getting Better Results with Latent Semantic Indexing, in *Proceedings of the Students Presentations at ESSLLI-2000,* Birmingham, UK, pages 155-156, 2000.

Neto J.L., Santos A.D., Kaestner C., and Freitas A., Document Clustering and Text Summarization, in *Proceedings, 4th Int. Conference on Practical Applications of Knowledge Discovery and Data Mining (PADD-2000),* pages 41-55, The Practical Application Company, 2000.

Nguyen H., Saba M., Santos E., and Brown S.M., Active User Interface in a Knowledge Discovery and Retrieval system, *Proceedings of the International Conference on Artificial Intelligence (ICAI2000),* Las Vegas, Nevada, June, 2000.

Nonaka I. and Takeuchi H., A Dynamic Theory of Organizational Knowledge Creation, *Organizational Science*, 5, No. 1, pages 14-37, 1994.

Nonaka I. and Takeuchi H., *The Knowledge Creating Company*, Oxford University Press, Oxford, UK, 1995.

Oard D. W., The State of the Art in Text Filtering, User Modeling and User-Adapted Interaction, 7, 3, pages 141-178, 1997.

Ouksel A. M. and Naiman C.F., Coordinating context building in heterogeneous information systems, *Journal of Intelligent Information Systems (JIIS),* 3:(2), pages 151-183, April, 1994.

Ounis I. and Pasca M., The RELIEF Retrieval system, in *Proceeding of KDEX,* Newport Beach, California, November 4, 1997.

Owen C., Design Research: Building the Knowledge Base, *Journal of the Japanese Society for the Science of Design*, 5(2), pages 36-45, 1997.

Page P., Brin S., Motwani R. and Winograd T., The PageRank Citation Ranking: Bringing Order to the Web, *Stanford Digital Library Technologies Project*, 1998.

Peat H.J. and Willett P., The Limitation of Term Co-Occurrence Data for Query Expansion in Document Retrieval Systems, Journal of the American Society for Information Science, 42, 5, pages 378-383, 1991.

Pedersen J., Internet Search Tutorial, *Proceeding of the 26th Annual International ACM SIGIR Conference*, Toronto, Canada, July, 2003.

Petty R.E. and Cacioppo J.T., *Communication and Persuasion: Central and Peripheral Routes to Attitude Change,* Springer-Verlag, New York, 1986.

Pirolli P. and Card S.K. , Information Foraging, *Psychological Review,* 106 (4), pages 643-675, 1999.

Pirolli P. and Card S.K. , Information Foraging in Information Access Environments , in *Proceedings on Human factors in computing systems conference (CHI'95),* 1995.

Polanyi M., *The Tacit Dimension*, Routledge & Kegan Paul, London, 1996.

Porter M.F., An Algorithm for Suffix Stripping, *Program,* 14(3), pages 130-137, 1980.

Rasmussen, E. *Clustering Algorithms.* In W. B. Frakes and R. Baeza-Yates (eds.) Information Retrieval Data Structures and Algorithms, Prentice Hall, N. J., 1992.

Robertson S. E. and Spark Jones K., Relevance Weighting of Search Terms, *Journal of the American Society for Information Sciences,* 27 (3), pages 129-146, 1976.

Robertson S.E,, Walker S., and Beaulieu M., Okapi at TREC-7: automatic ad hoc, filtering, VLC and interactive track, in Voorhees E.M. and Harman D.K. editors, *Proceedings of the 7th Text REtrieval Conference*, pages 253–264, Gaithersburg, MD, November 1998.

Rungsawang A., A Distributional Semantics Based Information Retrieval System , *ENST-Paris, Department of Computer Science, Paris, France,* Ph.D. thesis, 1997.

Sadler V., Working with Analogical Semantics: Disambiguation Techniques in DLT, Foris Publications, 1989.

Sahami M., Yusufali S., and Baldonado M.Q.W., SONIA: A Service for Organizing Networked Information Autonomously, in *Proceedings of the 3rd Annual Conference on Digital Libraries,* pages 200-209, 1998.

Salton G. and Lesk M.E., Computer Evaluation of Indexing and Text Processing, in Salton G. editor, *The SMART Retrieval System: Experiments in Automatic Document Processing,* pages 143-180, Prentice-Hall, 1971.

Salton G. and Lesk M.E., Computer Evaluation of Indexing and Text Processing, in Salton G. editor, The SMART Retrieval System: Experiments in Automatic Document Processing, Prentice-Hall, pages 143-180, 1971.

Salton G. and McGill M.J., *Introduction to Modern Information Retrieval,* McGraw-Hill, 1983.

Salton G., *Automatic Information Organization and Retrieval,* McGraw-Hill, 1968.

Salton G., Wong A., Yang C. S, A vector space model for automatic indexing, *Communications of the ACM,* 18 (11), pages 613-620, 1975.

Shardanand U. and Maes P., Social information filtering: algorithms for automating 'word of mouth', in *Proceedings of ACM CHI'95,* 1995.

Shaw W.M., Controlled and Un-Controlled Subject Descriptions in the CF Database: A Comparison of Optimal Cluster-Based Retrieval Results, *Information Processing & Management,* 29, pages 751-763, 1993.

Shaw W. M., Burgin R., amd Howell P., Performance Standards and Evaluations in IR Test Collections: Cluster-Based Retrieval Models, *Information Processing and Management,* 33, 1, pages 1-14, 1997.

Sheridan T.B. and Ferrell W.R., *Man-Machine Systems: Information, Control, and Decision Models of Human Performance,* MIT Press, 1974.

Simon H. A., *The Sciences of the Artificial,* Third edition, MIT Press, 1996.

Singhal A. and Pereira F., Document Expansion for Speech Retrieval, *Research and Development in Information Retrieval,* pages 34-41, 1999.

Smadja F. and McKeown K., Automatically Extracting and Representing Collocations for Language Generation, in Proceeding of the Annual Meeting of the ACL, 1990.

Smeaton, A. F., and van Rijsbergen, C. J., Experiments on incorporating syntactic processing of user queries into a document retrieval strategy, in Y. Chiaramella editor, Eleventh International Conference on Research and Development in Information Retrieval, ACM Press, pages 31-51, 1988.

Smeaton, A. F., O'Donnell, R., and Kelledy, F., Indexing structures derived from syntax in TREC-3: System description, in K. Harman editor, Overview of the Third Text REtrieval Conference (TREC-3), NIST Special Publication, National Institute of Standards and Technology, pages 500-225, 1995.

Smeaton A.F. and Quigley I., Experiments on Using Semantic Distances Between Words in Image Caption Retrieval, *SIGIR 1996,* pages 174-180, 1996.

Sowa J., Knowledge Representation: Logical, Philosophical, and Computational Foundations, Brooks/Cole, 2000.

Sowa J., Ontology, Metadata, and Semiotics, Conceptual Structures: Logical, Linguistic, and Computational Issues, Lecture Notes in AI #1867, pages 55-81, Springer-Verlag, 2000.

Sowa J., Semantic Networks, www.jfsowa.com/pubs/semnetw.htm, 2002.

Spark-Jones K., Automatic Keyword Classification for Information Retrieval, Butterworths, London, 1971.

Spark-Jones K., Summary Performance Comparisons TREC-2 Through TREC-8, Proceedings of the 8th Text Retrieval Conference, NIST Special Publication, 1999.

Stetina J., Kurohashi S. and Nagao M., General Word Sense Disambiguation Method Based on a Full Sentential Context, Usage of WordNet in Natural Language Processing, Proceedings of COLING-ACL Workshop, Montreal, Canada, July, 1998.

Stiles H.F., The Association Factor in Information Retrieval, Journal of the ACM, 8, pages 271-279, 1961.

Takeda H., Veerkamp P., Tomiyama T., and Yoshikawam H., Modeling Design Processes, *AI Magazine*, pages 37-48, Winter, 1990.

Theodorakis M. and Constantopoulos P., Context-Based Naming in Information Bases, *International Journal of Cooperative Information Systems,* 6 (32), pages 269-292, 1997.

Theodorakis M., Analyti A., Constantopoulos P., and Spyratos N., A Theory of Context in Information Bases, *Information Systems,* 27, pages 151-191, 2002.

Transley R., Bird C., Hall W., Lewis P., and Weal M., Automating the Linking of Content and Concept, *Multimedia,* pages 445-447, ACM Press, 2000.

UCLA Internet Report: Surveying the Digital Future, Year Three, http://ccp.ucla.edu/pdf/UCLA-Internet-Report-Year-Three.pdf, University of California at Los Angeles, 2002.

Van Alstyne, The State of Network Organizations: A Survey in Three Frameworks, Journal of Organizational Computing and Electronic Commerce, 7(3), 1997.

van Rijsbergen C.J. and Spark-Jones K., A test for the separation of relevant and non-relevant documents in experimental retrieval collections, *Journal of Documentation,* 29, pages 251-257, 1973.

van Rijsbergen C.J., Information Retrieval, Dept. of Computer Science, University of Glasgow, 1979.

Voorhees E., The effectiveness and efficiency of agglomerative hierarchical clustering in document retrieval, *Department of Computer Science, Cornell University,* Ph.D. thesis, 1985.

Voorhees E. and Harman D., Overview of the Seventh Text Retrieval Conference (TREC-7), Proceedings of the 7th Text Retrieval Conference, NIST Special Publication, 1998.

Voorhees E. and Harman D., Overview of the Eighth Text Retrieval Conference (TREC-8), Proceedings of the 8th Text Retrieval Conference, NIST Special Publication, 1999.

Voorhees E. M. and Harman D., Overview of the Ninth Text Retrieval Conference (TREC-9), Proceedings of the 9th Text Retrieval Conference, NIST Special Publication, 2000.

Waddington P., Dying for Information? A Report on the Effects of Information Overload in the UK and Worldwide, Reuters, 1997.

Watts Sussman S. and Siegal W.S., Informational Influence in Organizations: An Integrated Approach to Knowledge Adoption, *Information Systems Research,* 14 (1), 2003.

Wilkinson R., User Modeling for Information Retrieval on the Web, *Proceedings of the 2nd Workshop on Adaptive Systems and User Modeling on the WWW,* 1999.

Willett P., Recent Trends in Hierarchical Document Clustering: A Critical Review, *Information Processing and Management,* 24, 5, pages 577-597, 1988.

Wondergem B., van Bommel P., and van der Weide T., Nesting and Defoliation of Index Expressions for Information Retrieval, *Knowledge and Information systems,* 2, pages 33-52, Springer-Verlag, 2000.

Wurman R., *Information Anxiety,* Doubleday, New York, 1989.

Xu, J. L., Internet Search Engines: Real World IR Issues and Challenges, *Conference on Information and Knowledge Management,* Kansas City, Missouri, 1999.

Xu J. and Croft W. B., Cluster-Based Language Models for Distributed Retrieval, in *Research and Development in Information Retrieval,* pages 254-261, 1999.

Yang Y. and Chute C.G., An Example-Based Mapping Method for Text Categorization and Retrieval, ACM Transactions on Information Systems, 12, 3, pages 252-277, July, 1994.

Zack M. H., Researching Organizational Systems using Social Network Analysis, *Proceedings of the 33rd Hawai'i International Conference on System Sciences,* Maui, Hawai'i, January, 2000.

Appendix 1 – Queries Used in Experiments

Query Number: 351
Title: Falkland petroleum exploration
Description: What information is available on petroleum exploration in the South Atlantic near the Falkland Islands?

Query Number: 352
Title: British Chunnel impact
Description: What impact has the Chunnel had on the British economy and/or the life style of the British?

Query Number: 353
Title: Antarctica exploration
Description: Identify systematic explorations and scientific investigations of Antarctica, current or planned.

Query Number: 354
Title: journalist risks
Description: Identify instances where a journalist has been put at risk (e.g., killed, arrested or taken hostage) in the performance of his work.

Query Number: 355
Title: ocean remote sensing
Description: Identify documents discussing the development and application of spaceborne ocean remote sensing.

Query Number: 356
Title: postmenopausal estrogen Britain
Description: Identify documents discussing the use of estrogen by postmenopausal women in Britain.

Query Number: 357
Title: territorial waters dispute
Description: Identify documents discussing international boundary disputes relevant to the 200-mile special economic zones or 12-mile territorial waters subsequent to the passing of the "International Convention on the Law of the Sea".

Query Number: 358
Title: blood-alcohol fatalities
Description: What role does blood-alcohol level play in automobile accident fatalities?

Query Number: 359
Title: mutual fund predictors
Description: Are there reliable and consistent predictors of mutual fund performance?

Query Number: 360
Title: drug legalization benefits
Description: What are the benefits, if any, of drug legalization?

Query Number: 361
Title: clothing sweatshops
Description: Identify documents that discuss clothing sweatshops.

Query Number: 362
Title: human smuggling
Description: Identify incidents of human smuggling.

Query Number: 363
Title: transportation tunnel disasters
Description: What disasters have occurred in tunnels used for transportation?

Query Number: 364
Title: rabies
Description: Identify documents discussing cases where rabies have been confirmed and what, if anything, is being done about it.

Query Number: 365
Title: El Nino
Description: What effects have been attributed to El Nino?

Query Number: 366
Title: commercial cyanide uses
Description: What are the industrial or commercial uses of cyanide or its derivatives?

Query Number: 367
Title: piracy
Description: What modern instances have there been of old fashioned piracy, the boarding or taking control of boats?

Query Number: 368
Title: in vitro fertilization
Description: Identify documents that discuss in vitro fertilization.

Query Number: 369
Title: anorexia nervosa bulimia
Description: What are the causes and treatments of anorexia nervosa and bulimia?

Query Number: 370
Title: food/drug laws
Description: What are the laws dealing with the quality and processing of food, beverages, or drugs?

Query Number: 371
Title: health insurance holistic
Description: What is the extent of health insurance coverage of holistic or other non-traditional medicine/medical treatments (for example, acupuncture)?

Query Number: 372
Title: Native American casino
Description: Identify documents that discuss the growth of Native American casino gambling.

Query Number: 373
Title: encryption equipment export
Description: Identify documents that discuss the concerns of the United States regarding the export of encryption equipment.

Query Number: 374
Title: Nobel prize winners
Description: Identify and provide background information on Nobel prize winners.

Query Number: 375
Title: hydrogen energy
Description: What is the status of research on hydrogen as a feasible energy source?

Query Number: 376
Title: World Court
Description: What types of cases were heard by the World Court (International Court of Justice)?

Query Number: 377
Title: cigar smoking
Description: Identify documents that discuss the renewed popularity of cigar smoking.

Query Number: 378
Title: euro opposition
Description: Identify documents that discuss opposition to the introduction of the euro, the European currency.

Query Number: 379
Title: mainstreaming
Description: Identify documents that discuss mainstreaming children with physical or mental impairments.

Query Number: 380
Title: obesity medical treatment
Description: Identify documents that discuss medical treatment of obesity.

Query Number: 381
Title: alternative medicine
Description: What forms of alternative medicine are being used in the treatment of illnesses or diseases and how successful are they?

Query Number: 382
Title: hydrogen fuel automobiles
Description: Identify documents that discuss the use of hydrogen as a fuel for piston driven automobiles (safe storage a concern) or the use of hydrogen in fuel cells to generate electricity to drive the car.

Query Number: 383
Title: mental illness drugs
Description: Identify drugs used in the treatment of mental illness.

Query Number: 384
Title: space station moon
Description: Identify documents that discuss the building of a space station with the intent of colonizing the moon.

Query Number: 385
Title: hybrid fuel cars
Description: Identify documents that discuss the current status of hybrid automobile engines, (i.e., cars fueled by something other than gasoline only).

Query Number: 386
Title: teaching disabled children
Description: What methods are currently utilized or anticipated in the teaching of disabled children?

Query Number: 387
Title: radioactive waste
Description: Identify documents that discuss effective and safe ways to permanently handle long-lived radioactive wastes.

Query Number: 388
Title: organic soil enhancement
Description: Identify documents that discuss the use of organic fertilizers (composted sludge, ash, vegetable waste, microorganisms, etc.) as soil enhancers.

Query Number: 389
Title: illegal technology transfer
Description: What specific entities have been accused of illegal technology transfer such as: selling their products, formulas, etc. directly or indirectly to foreign entities for other than peaceful purposes?

Query Number: 390
Title: orphan drugs
Description: Find documents that discuss issues associated with so-called "orphan drugs", that is, drugs that treat diseases affecting relatively few people.

Query Number: 391
Title: R&D drug prices
Description: Identify documents that discuss the impact of the cost of research and development (R&D) on the price of drugs.

Query Number: 392
Title: robotics
Description: What are the applications of robotics in the world today?

Query Number: 393
Title: mercy killing
Description: Identify documents that discuss mercy killings.

Query Number: 394
Title: home schooling
Description: Identify documents that discuss the education of children at home (home schooling).

Query Number: 395
Title: tourism
Description: Provide examples of successful attempts to attract tourism as a means to improve a local economy.

Query Number: 396
Title: sick building syndrome
Description: Identify documents that discuss sick building syndrome or building-related illnesses.

Query Number: 397
Title: automobile recalls
Description: Identify documents that discuss the reasons for automobile recalls.

Query Number: 398
Title: dismantling Europe's arsenal
Description: Identify documents that discuss the European Conventional Arms Cut as it relates to the dismantling of Europe's arsenal.

Query Number: 399
Title: oceanographic vessels
Description: Identify documents that discuss the activities or equipment of oceanographic vessels.

Query Number: 400
Title: Amazon rain forest
Description: What measures are being taken by local South American authorities to preserve the Amazon tropical rain forest?

Query Number: 401
Title: foreign minorities, Germany
Description: What language and cultural differences impede the integration of foreign minorities in Germany?

Query Number: 402
Title: behavioral genetics
Description: What is happening in the field of behavioral genetics, the study of the relative influence of genetic and environmental factors on an individual's behaviour or personality?

Query Number: 403
Title: osteoporosis
Description: Find information on the effects of the dietary intakes of potassium, magnesium and fruits and vegetables as determinants of bone mineral density in elderly men and women thus preventing osteoporosis (bone decay).

Query Number: 404
Title: Ireland, peace talks
Description: How often were the peace talks in Ireland delayed or disrupted as a result of acts of violence?

Query Number: 405
Title: cosmic events
Description: What unexpected or unexplained cosmic events or celestial phenomena, such as radiation and supernova outbursts or new comets, have been detected?

Query Number: 406
Title: Parkinson's disease
Description: What is being done to treat the symptoms of Parkinson's disease and keep the patient functional as long as possible?

Query Number: 407
Title: poaching, wildlife preserves
Description: What is the impact of poaching on the world's various wildlife preserves?

Query Number: 408
Title: tropical storms
Description: What tropical storms (hurricanes and typhoons) have caused significant property damage and loss of life?

Query Number: 409
Title: legal, Pan Am, 103
Description: What legal actions have resulted from the destruction of Pan Am Flight 103 over Lockerbie, Scotland, on December 21, 1988?

Query Number: 410
Title: Schengen agreement
Description: Who is involved in the Schengen agreement to eliminate border controls in Western Europe and what do they hope to accomplish?

Query Number: 411
Title: salvaging, shipwreck, treasure
Description: Find information on shipwreck salvaging: the recovery or attempted recovery of treasure from sunken ships.
Query Number: 412
Title: airport security
Description: What security measures are in effect or are proposed to go into effect in airports?

Query Number: 413
Title: steel production
Description: What are new methods of producing steel?

Query Number: 414
Title: Cuba, sugar, exports
Description: How much sugar does Cuba export and which countries import it?

Query Number: 415
Title: drugs, Golden Triangle
Description: What is known about drug trafficking in the "Golden Triangle", the area where Burma, Thailand and Laos meet?

Query Number: 416
Title: Three Gorges Project
Description: What is the status of The Three Gorges Project?

Query Number: 417
Title: creativity
Description: Find ways of measuring creativity.

Query Number: 418
Title: quilts, income
Description: In what ways have quilts been used to generate income?

Query Number: 419
Title: recycle, automobile tires
Description: What new uses have been developed for old automobile tires as a means of tire recycling?

Query Number: 420
Title: carbon monoxide poisoning
Description: How widespread is carbon monoxide poisoning on a global scale?

Query Number: 421
Title: industrial waste disposal
Description: How is the disposal of industrial waste being accomplished by industrial management throughout the world?

Query Number: 422
Title: art, stolen, forged
Description: What incidents have there been of stolen or forged art?

Query Number: 423
Title: Milosevic, Mirjana Markovic
Description: Find references to Milosevic's wife, Mirjana Markovic.

Query Number: 424
Title: suicides
Description: Give examples of alleged suicides that aroused suspicion of the death actually being murder.

Query Number: 425
Title: counterfeiting money
Description: What counterfeiting of money is being done in modern times?

Query Number: 426
Title: law enforcement, dogs
Description: Provide information on the use of dogs worldwide for law enforcement purposes.

Query Number: 427
Title: UV damage, eyes
Description: Find documents that discuss the damage ultraviolet (UV) light from the sun can do to eyes.

Query Number: 428
Title: declining birth rates
Description: Do any countries other than the U.S. and China have a declining birth rate?

Query Number: 429
Title: Legionnaires' disease
Description: Identify outbreaks of Legionnaires' disease.

Query Number: 430
Title: killer bee attacks
Description: Identify instances of attacks on humans by Africanized (killer) bees.

Query Number: 431
Title: robotic technology
Description: What are the latest developments in robotic technology?

Query Number: 432
Title: profiling, motorists, police
Description: Do police departments use "profiling" to stop motorists?

Query Number: 433
Title: Greek, philosophy, stoicism
Description: Is there contemporary interest in the Greek philosophy of stoicism?

Query Number: 434
Title: Estonia, economy
Description: What is the state of the economy of Estonia?

Query Number: 435
Title: curbing population growth
Description: What measures have been taken worldwide and what countries have been effective in curbing population growth?

Query Number: 436
Title: railway accidents
Description: What are the causes of railway accidents throughout the world?

Query Number: 437
Title: deregulation, gas, electric
Description: What has been the experience of residential utility customers following deregulation of gas and electric?

Query Number: 438
Title: tourism, increase
Description: What countries are experiencing an increase in tourism?

Query Number: 439
Title: inventions, scientific discoveries
Description: What new inventions or scientific discoveries have been made?

Query Number: 440
Title: child labor
Description: What steps are being taken by governments or corporations to eliminate abuse of child labor?

Query Number: 441
Title: Lyme disease
Description: How do you prevent and treat Lyme disease?

Query Number: 442
Title: heroic acts
Description: Find accounts of selfless heroic acts by individuals or small groups for the benefit of others or a cause.

Query Number: 443
Title: U.S., investment, Africa
Description: What is the extent of U.S. (government and private) investment in sub-Saharan Africa?

Query Number: 444
Title: supercritical fluids
Description: What are the potential uses for supercritical fluids as an environmental protection measure?

Query Number: 445
Title: women clergy
Description: What other countries besides the United States are considering or have approved women as clergy persons?

Query Number: 446
Title: tourists, violence
Description: Where are tourists likely to be subjected to acts of violence causing bodily harm or death?

Query Number: 447
Title: Stirling engine
Description: What new developments and applications are there for the Stirling engine?

Query Number: 448
Title: ship losses
Description: Identify instances in which weather was a main or contributing factor in the loss of a ship at sea.

Query Number: 449
Title: antibiotics ineffectiveness
Description: What has caused the current ineffectiveness of antibiotics against infections and what is the prognosis for new drugs?

Query Number: 450
Title: King Hussein, peace
Description: How significant a figure over the years was the late Jordanian King Hussein in furthering peace in the Middle East?

Appendix 2 – Queries Used for Testing Composite Concepts; Case #1 – After Pruning Concept List with *Strict* Lower Cut-Off Threshold

The list of TREC topics (i.e., queries) that include at least one concept and were employed for the tests is presented bellow.

351, 352, 353, 354, 355, 356, 357, 358, 359, 360, 361, 363, 364, 365, 367, 368, 370, 371, 372, 373, 374, 375, 376, 377, 378, 379, 380, 381, 382, 383, 384, 385, 386, 387, 388, 389, 390, 391, 394, 395, 396, 398, 399, 400, 401, 402, 403, 404, 405, 406, 407, 408, 409, 410, 411, 412, 413, 414, 415, 416, 418, 420, 421, 422, 424, 426, 427, 428, 429, 430, 431, 432, 434, 435, 436, 437, 440, 441, 442, 443, 444, 445, 446, 447, 448, 449, 450.

The queries that had no concepts and were excluded from the experiment are:
362, 366, 369, 392, 393, 397, 417, 419, 423, 425, 433, 438, 439.

For the details of these queries, please see Appendix 1.

Appendix 3 – Queries Used for Testing Composite Concepts
Case #2 – After Pruning Concept List with *Lenient* Lower Cut-Off Threshold

The list of TREC topics (i.e., queries) that include at least one concept and were employed for the tests is presented bellow.

351, 352, 353, 354, 355, 356, 357, 358, 359, 360, 363, 364, 366, 367, 368, 370, 371, 372, 373, 374, 375, 376, 377, 378, 379, 380, 381, 382, 383, 384, 385, 386, 387, 388, 389, 390, 391, 392, 394, 395, 396, 398, 399, 400, 401, 402, 403, 404, 406, 407, 408, 409, 410, 411, 412, 413, 414, 415, 416, 418, 419, 420, 421, 422, 424, 425, 426, 427, 428, 429, 430, 431, 432, 433, 434, 435, 436, 437, 438, 439, 440, 441, 442, 443, 444, 445, 446, 447, 448, 449, 450.

The queries that had no concepts and were excluded from the experiment are: 361, 362, 365, 369, 393, 397, 405, 417, 423.

For the details of these queries, please see Appendix 1.

Appendix 4 – Example of a Document

Document #: FBIS-A00012

Document text:

"Hanoi Reports Success in Fight Against Malaria

9 March 1994

A 26 February VNA report on a conference on the anti-malarial effort in Vietnam's northern provinces suggests that Hanoi has made considerable progress in overcoming what the media two years ago had indicated was a serious malaria problem. According to VNA, all three targets of Vietnam's anti-malaria program for 1993 were met as the death rate dropped by 30 percent, the number of malaria sufferers fell by nearly 20 percent, and the number of malaria epidemics decreased by 84 percent compared to 1992. VNA reported particular progress in combatting malaria in Vietnam's central highlands--which the report said was "one of the worst affected areas " --noting that the death rate in that region had fallen by "50 percent."

Despite the progress, VNA noted that Hanoi is planning to intensify its efforts in combatting malaria in 1994. According to VNA, the government will allot 60 billion dong for the 1994 anti-malaria campaign--an increase of 10 billion dong over 1993--in hopes of reducing the mortality rate by 30 percent and the number of malaria outbreaks by 20 percent in comparison to 1993.

(AUTHOR: HEBBEL. QUESTIONS AND/OR COMMENTS, PLEASE CALL, CHIEF, ASIA DIVISION ANALYSIS TEAM, (703) 733-6534.)

EAG/BIETZ/ta 07/2101z mar "

www.ingramcontent.com/pod-product-compliance
Lightning Source LLC
LaVergne TN
LVHW022305060326
832902LV00020B/3291